# THE WELSH ALMANAC

Terry Breverton

Wales Books
Glyndŵr Publishing
2002

ISBN 1-903529-107

*For Those Who Care*

Published in 2002 by Wales Books (Glyndŵr Publishing),
Porth Glyndŵr, Sain Tathan, Bro Morgannwg CF62 4LW
www.walesbooks.com

ISBN 1 903529 107

Printed and bound in Wales by
J&P Davison, 3 James Place,
Trefforest, Pontypridd

Terry Breverton studied in the universities of Manchester, Birmingham and Lancaster, has had a career in international management consultancy, and has been a board level director of multinational companies. Upon returning to live in Wales, and take up a post in academia, he founded Wales Books (Glyndŵr Publishing), to counter-balance existing material upon Wales, and to promote Welsh heritage and culture to the Welsh people and potential tourists. The purposes of Wales Books are two-fold: to link Welsh societies across the globe; and to encourage further research and publications upon 'forgotten' Welshmen such as Dr Richard Price and Owain Llawgoch. It is hoped that such work will also rehabilitate Iolo Morganwg in the eyes of academics and force them to reassess history from original sources, rather than from the opinion of their teachers' teachers.

Breverton has in the past published research papers upon multinational tax avoidance, children's books and is the author of the acclaimed 'An A-Z of Wales and the Welsh', 'The Secret Vale of Glamorgan', 'The Book of Welsh Saints', '100 Great Welsh Men' and '100 Great Welsh Women'. He has also published a volume of poetry, 'The Path to Inexperience'. This present volume will be followed by 'The Book of Welsh Pirates and Buccaneers' and 'The Glamorgan Seascape Walks'. Wales Books (Glyndŵr Publishing) receives no support from any funding bodies, and its publications have been priced to break even and to cover the costs of publishing more books upon Wales. Forthcoming publications are detailed in the back of this book. We welcome submissions of manuscripts, by which method we will be publishing a rational reassessment of Prince Madoc, a life of the great warrior Owain Llawgoch and Glamorganshire Castles (Volume I of Castles of Wales) in 2002.

# PREFACE TO THE WELSH ALMANAC

*'Progress, far from consisting in change, depends on retentiveness….. Those who cannot remember the past are condemned to fulfil it.'* George Santayana 1905

The rationale for this publication is two-fold. On the surface it is for Welsh people to build up and remember their loved ones' birthdays, anniversaries, important dates and events against days of the year. There is also an A-Z section annexed, so that addresses, telephone numbers, email addresses and the like can be entered. Thus we can keep our personal and social records in one easy-to-find book, rather than delve among scraps of paper, fading memories, or boot up the computer. On the other hand, it is to let us know about famous Welsh people and events upon each of these days. For each day, there is also a quotation, usually from a Welsh source, often tying in with the people and events of the day. The author hopes that readers will be enthused to find out more about Wales and the Welsh from the entries in this book. Many important dates in our history do not exist any longer, as records were destroyed during the taking of land, and it is hoped that this publication will allow more information to surface about the heroes, heroines and events that shaped the nation.

The genesis of the book was the work of the author for 'The Book of Welsh Saints'. Wales has over 900 saints from the Dark Ages of the rest of Europe, and apart from David and Dwynwen (the Welsh Valentine) they are universally neglected. We have records of our saints' days, only because their feasts were kept until the 18th and 19th centuries in the places still named after them. Their llannau were sparks of Christianity and learning in a pagan world, but the Welsh contribution to the survival of Christianity has never been properly addressed. The book was a call for their churches to once more become centres for social life, for fairs and feasts to be held on their days, for economic and cultural regeneration. Thus, each day begins with the Welsh Saints' Days. No other country has such a heritage from these times, yet our saints are forgotten. The author was in Cadoc House at Barry Grammar School for Boys. The other houses were of the notable local saints Dyfan, Illtud and Baruc, but we knew nothing of them, and were taught nothing about them. Welsh history began in 1066 - i.e. it was Saxon and Norman - German and French - history, not British history. History is written by conquerors, and over the decades and centuries becomes separated from truth.

For any errors and omissions, the author is at fault, and would welcome any information from readers in this respect. However, there is not one penny of taxpayers' money involved in this publication, and any critics should remember that their self-anointed task is far easier than that of construction.

Yr Gwir yn Erbyn Y Byd

# THE WELSH ALMANAC

## JANUARY - IONAWR
### Genver (Breton); Genvar (Cornish)

## January 1

*FEAST DAYS OF SAINTS* GWYNHOEDL 6th century at Llangwnadl, Llannor; MACHRAETH 6th century at Llanfachraith; MAELRHYS 6th century at Llanfaelrhys; MEDWYN 1st century at Michaelstone-y-Fedw; TYFRYDOG 6th century at Llandyfrydog; and HENWYN (see January 6). *DYDD CALAN, NEW YEAR'S DAY.* In 1136, a force led by Hywel ap Meredudd of Breconshire defeated the Normans in the Battle Of Gower on Carn Goch Common; In 1632, Katherine Philips, 'the Matchless Orinda' was born; Birth of the poet Goronwy Owen at Llanfair-mathafarn-eithaf, Anglesey in 1723; 'Seren Gomer', the first Welsh-language newspaper, started in Swansea in 1814; In 1844, 12 miners died at Dinas Middle Colliery, Rhondda; Birth in Llanelli, Breconshire in 1845 of Bishop Francis John, who revitalised St David's College, Lampeter; Death in 1845 of the soldier Sir William Nott at Carmarthen; Birth of the psychoanalyst Ernest Jones at Gowerton in 1879 (see February 11); In 1902, the Riot Act was read at Bethesda, as soldiers were brought in during the 3-year slate-workers' lock-out; Birth in 1903 at Merthyr of Horace Evans, 1st Baron Evans of Merthyr Tydfil, physician to Queen Mary, George VI and Queen Elizabeth (see October 26); Billy Meredith's first game for Manchester United, 1907; In 1907, the first touring team from South Africa was beaten by Cardiff 17-0; 1910 saw the first rugby match between France and Wales, Wales winning 49-14 at Swansea; In 1935, the Welsh Football Union changed its name to the Welsh Rugby Union; In 1945, 'The Fed' (the South Wales Miners' Federation) was subsumed into the new national Union of Mineworkers; The 1st Queens Dragoon Guards was formed in 1959, 'The Cavalry Regiment of Wales', from the merger of the King's Dragoon Guards and the Queens Bays, 2nd Dragoon Guards; In 1998, Petula Sally Olwen Clark was awarded the CBE

*'....Not like the surly, dark month*
*That rebukes every one for loving;*
*That makes sad rain for a short day,*
*And wind to plunder woods;*
*And weakness, the fragility of fear,*
*And a long cloak and hailstone rain,*
*And provokes tidal flow and cold,*
*And in streams grey deluges,*
*And a full roar in rivers,*
*And makes the day angry and wrathful,*

*And the sky heavy and widely cold*
*With its colour veiling the moon.'*

Extract from 'May and January' by Dafydd ap Gwilym (c.1320-1380) trans. R.M. Loomis

*On this day...*

...............................................................................................................................................

...............................................................................................................................................

...............................................................................................................................................

# January 2

*FEAST DAY OF SAINT* BODFAN 7th century (also June 2) at Abergwyngeryn. In 1854, the railway reached Haverfordwest; John Viriamu Jones, Principal of the University of Wales at Cardiff, was born in Swansea; Dr Martha Carey Thomas, educator and feminist, was born in 1857; Death in 1929 of David James of Swansea, who with his brother Evan formed the most brilliant pair of rugby half-backs of their time, and innovated half-back tactics; Madoline Thomas, the actress, was born Madoline Mary Price at Abergavenny in 1890 (see December 30); Arthur Joseph Gould, the great rugby player, died in Newport in 1919, aged 54 (see October 10); In 1941, 165 people died in Cardiff during German air-raids, with 427 seriously injured. (23 had already died in 1940, and another 110 were to be killed up to 1944)

*"Three things it is best to avoid: a strange dog, a flood, and a man who thinks he is wise". –* Welsh proberb.

*On this day...*

...............................................................................................................................................

...............................................................................................................................................

...............................................................................................................................................

# January 3

*FEAST DAYS OF SAINTS* GWENNOG 6th century (her fair was held on January 14 at Llanwenog and TEWDRIC (see April 1); Holy Day of Morriss Williams, priest and poet 1874; MIDWINTER (Old Style). Death of the Mormon missionary Daniel Jones in 1861 at Salt Lake City; Death in 1874 of Morris Williams (see August 20); Birth at Cardiff in 1882 of John Lewis Williams, rugby wing for Cardiff, Wales and the British Lions (see July 12); Reginald Alfred John Truscott-Jones was born in Neath in 1908, and went on to become the Oscar-winning film star Ray Milland (see March 10); Death in 1919 of General James Hills-Johnes (see August 20); Llandaf Cathedral and the Arms Park were severely damaged by German bombing in 1941.

*'Between 1890 and 1911 ... the majority of the population ceased to speak Welsh. As a result of losing their language, people lost the connection with their own past. And this was not only a matter of losing connection with the religious past. It meant also losing a sense of national identity. For those who knew Welsh, religious services and Sunday schools and concerts and publications were a link between them and their national and Christian past. The Christian churches were increasingly forced to bear the responsibility for safeguarding the national tradition and culture.... Complicity with the state of affairs which considered Welsh a holy language, the language of poets, writers and prophets, and English the language of all else was a fatal path for the churches'* - R. Tudur Jones, 'Ffydd ac Argyfwng Cenedl'

*On this day...*

.................................................................................................................................
.................................................................................................................................
.................................................................................................................................

# January 4
In 1847, the Point of Ayr lifeboat capsized off Rhyl, the crew of 13 drowning; Augustus John, society painter and bohemian, born in Tenby in 1878; Birth in 1940 Professor Professor Brian Josephson in Cardiff, joint-winner of the 1973 Nobel Prize for Physics; Death at Bethesda in 1956 of the noted poet Robert Williams Parry (see March 6); Death in 1964 of Arthur Wade-Evans (see August 31); Death in 1970 of the writer David John Williams

*'Welsh is of this soil, this island, the senior language of the men of Britain; and Welsh is beautiful.'* - 'The O'Donnell Lecture', J.R. Tolkien (1892-1973)

*On this day...*

.................................................................................................................................
.................................................................................................................................
.................................................................................................................................

# January 5
FEAST DAYS OF SAINTS CYNWYL 6th century (also January 8, April 30 and November 21) at Cynwyl Elfed, Penrhos, Bangor-is Coed (Cynwyl Gaio and Aberporth Fairs were other days) and EDWARD (see October 13); CHRISTMAS EVE (Old Style). Birth of John Fisher, Welsh scholar and historian, near Llandebie in 1862 (see May 9); In 1989 Jonathan Davies of Llanelli and Wales joined Widnes Rugby league team for a world record fee

*'Speaking of the blowing of the Holy Thorn and the kneeling and the weeping of the oxen*

*on old Christmas Eve (tonight) Priscilla said "I have known old James Meredith 40 years and I have never known him far from the truth, and I said to him one day, "James, tell me the truth, did you ever see the oxen kneel on old Christmas Eve at the Weston?" And he said, "No, I never saw them kneel at the Weston, but when I was at Hinton at Staunton-on-Wye I saw them. I was watching them on old Christmas Eve and at 12 o'clock the oxen that were standing knelt down upon their knees and those that were lying rose up on their knees and there they stayed kneeling and moaning, the tears running down their faces." ' - from the Diary of the Rev. Francis Kilvert, this day in 1878*

**On this day...**

...........................................................................................................................

...........................................................................................................................

...........................................................................................................................

# January 6

FEAST DAYS OF SAINTS EDERN 7th century (also December 2) at Bodedern, Edern; ABBOT HENWYN (also January 1) at St Hywyn's at Aberdaron; MERIN (April 4 in Brittany) at St Merin's, Llanferin, Bodferin, Lanmerin; YLCHED at Llanulched; LLAWDDOG (see 15); JUTHWARA (see December 23); and EUGRAD (see June 8); *EPIPHANY (GWYLL YSTYLL, the STAR FESTIVAL, was unique to the Celtic Church, and also known as SEREN WYL in the Welsh Prayer Book)*; OLD CHRISTMAS DAY at St Ffagans, now only at the Gwaun Valley near Fishguard; JESUS was born according to the Eastern Orthodox Church; TWELFTH NIGHT; In Brittany, from this day, the days begin to lengthen by the span of a cockerel's stride. Evan Davies (Myfyr Morganwg), bard, born near Pencoed, Glamorgan in 1801 (see Febriary 23); Birth in 1827 (or 1828) of Evan William Evans near Swansea, mathematician and first professor of mathematics at Cornell University (see May 22); Death in 1891 of the famous surgeon Hugh Owen Thomas (see August 23); Idris Davies, the great poet, was born in Rhymney in 1905 (see April 6); In 1934 the novelist Dorothy Edwards committed suicide, aged just 31; Barry John, 'the King', perhaps the greatest fly-half in the history of rugby, was born in Cefneithin in 1945

*'Make us, O Lord, a people fit for poetry,*
*And grant us clear voices to praise all noble achievement.*
*Make our guardians wiser than their fathers before them*
*Who sought the name below the easy jingle*
*And starved the poet without a name.*
*Give us fresh eyes to see Thy earth anew,*
*To see the animal and the grass and the water*
*As the first man saw them in the dawn.*
*Grant us, O Lord, Thy benediction*
*When we are restless and groping in the shadows,*
*And lead us to the shining mountains.*

*Make us worthy of the golden chorus*
*That the sons of God have always yearned to sing.*
*Make us, O Lord, a people fit for poetry.'* - Idris Davies, 'Psalm', c.1952

**On this day...**

....................................................................................................................................

....................................................................................................................................

....................................................................................................................................

## January 7

*FEAST DAYS OF SAINTS* BRANNOC 6th century at Braunton; CELYNIN, CEITHO, GWYN, GWYNORO and GWYNO 7th century - at Llanpumsaint - Gwyl Pumsaint was a huge fair held upon this day to celebrate these quintuplets; CYWYLLOG 6th century at Llangywyllog; and GWRDDELW 6th century at Capel Gartheli, Caerleon; *CHRISTMAS DAY in RUSSIA*; in Wales and Cornwall, the Christmas 'greenery' was taken down, but not burnt, for this would be unlucky; In 1566, the foundations of the Royal Exchange (later the Stock Exchange), the idea of Richard Clough of Bachygraig, were laid down; Birth in 1863 at Wrexham of James Trainer 'the prince of goalkeepers', who played for Bolton, Preston and Wales; In 1893, Wales won their first rugby international against England, at Cardiff's Arms Park; Meeting of Saunders Lewis, W. Ambrose Bebb and G.J. Williams in Penarth in 1924 to establish a 'new Welsh movement'

*'I went to the little farmhouse of Dolfach on the hill to see the Holy Thorn there in blossom. The tree (a graft from the old Holy Thorn at Tibberton now cut down) bloomed on old Christmas Eve and there were 15 people watching round the tree to see it blow at midnight. I found old John Perry sitting at tea by the cheerful firelight in the chimney corner. His kind daughter gave me a bit of a spray of the Holy Thorn which was gathered from the tree at midnight, old Chrismas Eve. She set great store by the spray and always gathered and kept a bit each year. The blossoms were not fully out and the leaves were scarcely unfolded but the daughter of the house assured me that the little white bud clusters would soon come out into full blow if put in soft water.'* Rev. Francis Kilvert's Diary, this day in 1878

**On this day...**

....................................................................................................................................

....................................................................................................................................

....................................................................................................................................

## January 8

*FEAST DAY OF CYNWYL* (see January 5) at Cynwyl Gaio; DYDD GWYL GEILIAU (The Festival of the Sheepfolds); Alfred Wallace was born in Usk in 1823, the real founder of the theory of evolution; A collision in the Dee in 1839 between the 'Pennsylvania' and the 'Lockwood', carrying Welsh emigrants to the

USA, caused 68 deaths; At Edinburgh in 1883, Scotland beat Wales in the first rugby international between the two nations; Death in 1884 of the missionary Thomas Morgan Thomas (see March 13); Shirley Bassey, international diva, born in Bute Street, Cardiff in 1937; Death in 1970 of Leonard Twiston Davies (see May 16)

*'Dydd Gwyl Geiliau, at y bara haidd a'r bacsau' (Plough Monday, resume ordinary food and working clothing)* - Monmouthshire saying

*On this day...*

..........................................................................................................................................

..........................................................................................................................................

..........................................................................................................................................

# January 9

Death in 1833 of Admiral Sir Thomas Foley of Llawhaden (born 1757), who helped relieve Gibraltar in 1770, fought near Toulon in 1793, led the British line at the Battle of the Nile, and was with Nelson at Trafalgar in 1815; In 1886, the Severn Tunnel officially opened; Haydn Tanner, rugby star, was born in Swansea in 1917; Death in 1917 at Merthyr of John Mathias Berry (see May 2); D.J. Williams, Lewis Valentine and Saunders Lewis* were convicted at the Old Bailey in 1937, for setting fire to building materials at the RAF Bombing School at Penyberth - a Welsh-speaking jury had previously failed to convict them at Caernarfon; The Miners' Strike began in 1972

*'I wish I were there, and I certainly wish I were forty years younger. I should be prepared to risk a protest which would be a defiance. If I were Saunders Lewis I would not surrender at the Old Bailey: I would insist on them arresting me, and I am not sure that I would not make it difficult for them to do that... It makes my blood boil.'* - letter from the 73 year-old David Lloyd George to his daughter Megan

*On this day...*

..........................................................................................................................................

..........................................................................................................................................

..........................................................................................................................................

# January 10

FEAST DAY OF TATHAN (New Style, see Dec. 30); Holy Day of Bishop William Laud (1645). The great rugby player, Maurice Turnbull of Cardiff, became the first Glamorgan cricketer to play for England, at Christchurch, New Zealand in 1930; 23 people died on Moel Siabod, Snowdonia, when a Dakota crashed into the mountain in 1952; Death of the scholar and Nationalist G.J. Williams in 1963 (see July 19); Carwyn James of Llanelli and Wales, successful British Lions coach but neglected by the WRU, died in 1983 in Amsterdam

'*Some of the more obstinate Criminals are punished by Suspension, but not by the Neck, as here in England, but by the Writsts, Thumb-roped together with a String of Hay, and so fastened to a Peg; well! This is but the beginning... The Sting will follow: The offending Taffy thus dangling in the Air, the Beadle approaches with a stick imp'd with a Teather at one End, and tickles his Testicles; these softer Titillations engender some vibrations of the Body, and nimble Friskings, which are shrewdly chastised by a Cat-of-Nine-Tails. For several Crimes they have various punishments. That grand enormity of Breaking-wind is chastised there as it is in England, that is, the Hand of Magistracy doth usually inflict a pretty lusty Cobbling, that is, for every Report of Loss of an Hair, though some that have been very much addicted to that Infirmity, and therefore have been guilty of a Stink, have endured the Cruelty of tormenting Fairies, that is, have been pinched into Manners, and a better Smell.*' - 'A Collection of Welsh Travels and Memoirs of Wales', John Torbuck, 1738

*On this day...*

..........................................................................................................................

..........................................................................................................................

..........................................................................................................................

## January 11

FEAST DAY OF SAINT LLUWCHAIARN (see January 12); Holy Day of the poet-priests RHYS PRICHARD (1644), WILLIAM WILLIAMS* (1791) and ISAAC WILLIAMS (1875); William Williams (Pantycelyn), Wales' finest poet, died in 1791, and is buried at Llanfair-ar-y-bryn; Birth in 1818 at Llanarth of Daniel Silvan Evans, translator, editor, cleric and lexicographer (see April 13); Birth near Llanaelhaearn in 1827 of John William Jones, editor from 1852 of the Welsh-American paper Y Drych (see October 8); In 1872, 11 miners died at Oakwood No. 1 Colliery, Maesteg; Death in 1902 of James James, composer of 'Hen Wlad fy Nhadau'; Sir Pryce Pryce-Jones, the pioneer of mail-order, died in Newtown in 1920 (see October 16); A debt-ridden Ronald Lewis, aged 52, committed suicide in 1982 (see December 11); George Ewart Evans, oral historian, died in 1988

*\*'Guide me, O thou great Jehovah,*
*Pilgrim through this barren land;*
*I am weak but Thou art mighty,*
*Hold me with thy powerful hand.*
*Bread of Heaven, Bread of Heaven,*
*Feed me till I want no more.*' - William Williams (Pantycelyn) 1722-1791

*On this day...*

..........................................................................................................................

..........................................................................................................................

..........................................................................................................................

## January 12

*FEAST DAY OF SAINT LLWCHAIARN* 6th - 7th century (also 11) at Llanllwchaiarn, Llanmerewig, Llanychaiarn; HEN GALAN - The *'Old New Year's Day'* is still celebrated in the Gwaun Valley with a *'noson lawen'*. At Llandysul Church there is a Hen Galan service with *'pwnc'* chanting, a local style of singing. This was the traditional time for Welsh fire festivals and for the Mari Llwyd and Calennig customs, until the date change in 1752. Glyndŵr signed a ratification of the French-drafted treaty of alliance in 1406, at Aberystwyth Castle; Sir Harford Jones (who later took the surname of Brydges), diplomat and author, was born at Presteign in 1764 (see March 17); In Newport in 1884, Wales beat Scotland in the first home international between the nations; In 1967, Coxwain Richard Evans of Moelfre became the first man to be twice awarded the Royal National Lifeboat Institute's Gold Medal for Gallantry; Evan Eynon Evans of Nelson, actor-playwright, died aged 84 in Trelewis in 1989

From Edgar W. Parry's edited version of *'Tour of Wales and its Churches'* by the Rev. John Parker (1878-1860): *'The church at Llanmerewig is dedicated to St Llwchaiarn to whom two churches in Cardiganshire are dedicated as well as the neighbouring church of Llanllwchaiarn near Newtown. It is beautifully situated on the ridge of a hill overlooking the Severn Valley and within a circular cemetery. It has been suggested that these circular cemeteries have been influenced by the early Celtic churches. It is quite likely that the Druids after their conversion to Christianity acted as priests of the new faith, and in such cases it was not unnatural that they would continue to officiate in their ancient Druidical Circles. Other examples within Montgomeryshire are to be found at Llanerfyl and Llangadfan and at Diserth in Radnorshire. Another widely held view was that they were made circular so that there would be no corners for the Devil to hide in!'*

**On this day...**

.....................................................................................................................................

.....................................................................................................................................

.....................................................................................................................................

## January 13

*FEAST DAY OF SAINTS* ANE (ANGAWD) 6th century at Llanelian; ERBIN 5th - 6th century (also May 29) at St Ervan, Erbistock; LLAWDDOG (LLEUDDAD) 6th century (also January 15, 20. August 10, 19, 20) - Ynys Enlli's patron saint, celebrated also at Cenarth, Cilgerran, Penboyr, Llanllawddog; SAERAN 6th century at Llanynys, Efenechtyd; KENTIGERN (see 14); And FAUSTUS (see 16). Sometime in January 1563, Elizabeth I was rumoured to have borne a child at Plas Uchaf near Llangollen; Birth in 1810 near Llangyfelach of John Dillwyn-Llywelyn F.R.S., botanist and photographic pioneer (see August 24); Birth in 1870 of John Conway Rees of Llandovery, who introduced the four three-quarter rugby tactic. He played for Oxford University, Cardiff, London Welsh, Barbarians, Llanelli and Wales, and spent his last 30 years teaching in India (see August 30); 63 colliers died in an explosion at Dinas, Rhondda, in 1879; Birth in 1887 of Ellis Humphrey Evans (Hedd Wyn) near Trawsfynydd, the posthumous winner of Birkenhead's 1917 National Eisteddfod (see July 31, September 6); Death in 1946 of the harpist Tom Bryant, buried at Efailisaf (see July 22)

*'Here are the three thick indispensables: liver and kidney and heart; and this is why they are so called. It is certain that whenever a disease attacks one of these three, there is no escape and death comes quickly ... The three thin indispensables are: the membrane of the brain, the small intestine and the bladder; for they are indispensable for the same reason as the others.'* - from the writings of the Doctors of Myddfai, early 13th century

**On this day...**

...................................................................................................................

...................................................................................................................

...................................................................................................................

# January 14
*FEAST DAY OF SAINTS* KENTIGERN (MUNGO) d.612 (also January 13) at Llanelwy/St Asaf, Glasgow; EILIAN 6th century (also January 13) at Llanelian; GWENNOG (see 3); and FFINNAN (see September 14). The Brecon and Abergavenni Canal was completed in 1805; In 1846, 35 miners died at Risca Colliery in Gwent; The tenor Mostyn Thomas was born in Blaina in 1896; Death of the great orthopaedic surgeon Sir Robert Jones KBE, CB near Llanfechain in 1933 (see June 28); TWW (Television Wales and the West), the precursor of Harlech and HTV, began transmitting television programmes from Cardiff in 1958

*'When you rise in the morning, walk a little, then stretch out your limbs, bending your head and your neck; that will strengthen the body, and bending the head will make the spirit rise from the stomach to the head, and from the head, and when you sleep, it slips back to the body again. In summer, take a bath in cold water; that will keep the heat in the head and thence cause an appetite. Afterwards, put on fair clothing, because man's mind rejoices in fair things, and the heart will be cheered.'* - from the writings of the Doctors of Myddfai, early 13th century

**On this day...**

...................................................................................................................

...................................................................................................................

...................................................................................................................

## January 15

FEAST DAYS OF SAINTS LLAWDDOG (see 13) at Llanllawddog, Cenarth, Penboir, Cilgerran; SAWYL 6th century? at Llansawyl; ILAR 6th century (also 13 and 14) at Llanilar, St Hilary; and MWROG (see 24). The first recorded strike at the Pembrokeshire slate quarries began in 1879; In 1895, Lady Charlotte Guest, translator of the Mabinogion, died; David Ivor Davies (Ivor Novello), film star and musical playwright, was born in Cardiff in 1893; The first radio sports commentary in Britain was the rugby match between England and Wales at Twickenham in 1927; Death in 1929 of Sir William Boyd Dawkins (see December 26); Death in 1951 of the Welsh Cob breeder Thomas Rees near Llangeitho (see January 31); Death in 1963 of Morgan Phillips, General-Secretary of the Labour Party from 1944-1962 (see June 18)

'Near by flows a noble salmon river called the Teifi. It is better stocked with the finest salmon than any other stream in Wales. Near Cilgerran, at a spot called Cenarth Mawr, on the topmost point of a rock where Saint Llawdog hollowed out with his own hands, is a flourishing fishing-station. The waters of the Teifi run ceaselessly over this rock, falling with a mighty roar into the abyss below. Now it is from these depths that the salmon ascend into the concave rock above, which is a remarkable leap, about as far as the height of the tallest spear. This may seem hard to believe, but it is the nature of the fish to perform such feats. This particular species has developed the habit of leaping into the air.' - Giraldus Cambrensis, 'Journey Through Wales' 1188

*On this day...*

..............................................................................................

..............................................................................................

..............................................................................................

## January 16

FEAST DAYS OF SAINTS FAUSTUS 5th century (also 13, and September 28) at Riez, St Faustus; and MWROG (see 24); Following the 1536 Act of Union, this day saw the first Westminster Parliament with elected Welsh MP's in 1542; In 1741 Hester Lynch Piozzi was born, Hester Salusbury, at Bachygraig; In 1840, the Newport Chartist leaders Frost, Williams and Jones were sentenced to be hung, drawn and quartered for treason, but later the sentence was commuted to transportation for life; In 1884, 10 miners died in a shaft accident at Garth Colliery, Llynfi Valley; In 1896, a packed meeting of the South Wales Liberals in Newport, led by a Bristolian, effectively ended David Lloyd George's hopes for Cymru Fydd and Welsh independence;* The first party reached the Magnetic South Pole, led by Sir Edgeworth David of St Ffagan's, in 1909

*'Is the mass of the Welsh nation willing to be dominated by a coalition of English capitalists who have come to Wales, not to benefit the people, but to make their fortune?' - David Lloyd George, in 'Y Faner' 1896

## January 17

*FEAST DAY OF SAINTS* CYNFELIN (6th century) at Llangynfelin, Trallwng (Welshpool); and BERWYN (see February 2). In 1781 General Daniel Morgan defeated the English and Hanoverian army under Banaster Tarleton at the Battle of Cowpens in the American War of Independence; David Lloyd George, Prime Minister, world statesman, and according to Hitler 'the man who won the First World War', born in 1863; Augusta Waddington, Lady Llanover, died in 1896; In 1941, 58 people were killed in German air-raids in Swansea

*'Tri peth ni wna les nes curo ei ben - cyn, polyn tid a thaeog' - 'Three things that are useless unless hit on the head - a chisel, a tethering bost and a boor.'*

*On this day...*

## January 18

*FEAST DAY OF SAINTS* CYNIN 5th century (also January 7 and November 24) at Llangynin and TYGWY 6th century (also January 13) at Llandygwy. Edward I took Dolwyddelan Castle in 1283, forcing Dafydd ap Gruffudd to flee to the hills; Henry VII married Elizabeth of York in 1486, uniting the Houses of Lancaster and York and ending the Wars of the Roses; Henry Morgan, the world's most successful buccaneer, took Panama City in 1671; Birth at Swansea in 1809 of the noted conchologist, John Gwyn Jeffreys FRS (see January 24); In 1879, England beat Wales 2:1 at Kennington Oval in the first football international between the teams; Petty Officer Edgar Evans of Rhossili reached the South Pole with Captain Scott in 1912; Death in 1962 of Aneurin Iolo Williams (see June 18)

*'To extract a tooth without pain: Take some newts, by some called lizards, and those nasty beetles which are found in ferns during summer, calcine them in an iron pot, and make a powder thereof. Wet the forefinger of the right hand, insert it in the powder, and apply it to the tooth frequently, refraining from spitting off, when the tooth will fall away without pain. It is proven.' - Meddygon Myddfai*

*On this day...*

# January 19

FEAST DAY OF SAINT BERWYN (see February 2). Eleanor de Montfort, wife of Llywelyn ap Gruffudd, died in 1282 after giving birth the the ill-fated Gwenllian; Henry VIII founded Christ College, Brecon in 1541; Death in 1601 of Henry Herbert, 2nd Earl of Pembroke (of the second creation), and 'the eye of all Wales'; In 1915, Anna Harriette Leonowens, tutor to the King of Siam's children, died in Canada; The first day of 7 weeks of blizzards and sub-zero temperatures across Britain in 1947

*'Tri chwerthin ffwl - am ben y da, am ben y drwg ac am ben nas gwyr pa beth' - 'Three things the fool laughs at - what is good, what is bad, and what he does not understand.'*

*On this day...*

..................................................................................................................

..................................................................................................................

..................................................................................................................


# January 20

FEAST DAY OF SAINT BERWYN (see February 2) in the Berwyn Hills. In 1288, Rhys ap Maredudd's last stronghold, at Newcastle Emlyn, was taken by Edward I (see June 8 and September 5); The Great Flood along the Wentloog Levels and the South Wales coast in 1607* - probably 2000 people drowned; Birth near Neath in 1782 of Sir William Nott, hero of the First Afghan War (see January 1); In 1969, Nicholas Allen Jones (known as Nicky Wire because of his tall, lean body) of the Manic Street Preachers was born in Blackwood

*'Flood, n. A superior degree of dampness. Specifically, a great storm described by Berosus and Moses, when, according to the latter's rain-gauge, there was a precipitation of moisture to the depth of one-eighth of a mile in 24 hours for 40 days. The former did not measure, apparently, for he simply explains (in pretty good Greek) that it rained cats and dogs. The learned author of the cuneiform inscriptions from the Mesopotamian mounds draws a number of carpet-tacks on a brick to signify that it was "quite a smart shower considering the season".'* - Ambrose Gwinnett Bierce, A Devil's Dictionary, 1911

*On this day...*

..................................................................................................................

..................................................................................................................

..................................................................................................................

## January 21

FEAST DAY OF SAINTS LLAWDDOG (see 15); and GWYNIN (see January 31); In Celtic lore, the sun rose in the constellation of Aquarius, heralding the ceremony of Imbolc. Death in 1808 of the hated slate magnate Richard Pennant (Lord Penrhyn), who built Penrhyn Castle while his workers starved; Helen Hamilton Gardener (Alice Chenoweth Day), the writer, reformer, feminist was born in 1853; In 1905, 11 miners died at Elba Colliery, Gowerton; Wales won at Twickenham for the first time in 1933; Lewis Jones, novelist and miners' leader, died in Cardiff in 1939; Wales' lowest temperature of -10 degrees fahrenheit, - 23.3 degrees centigrade was recorded in Rhayader in 1940

*'There are three things excellent among worldly affairs:*
*hating folly, loving virtue, and*
*endeavouring constantly to learn'* - from the Welsh Triads of Virtues

*On this day...*

..................................................................................................................................................

..................................................................................................................................................

..................................................................................................................................................

## January 22

FEAST DAY OF SAINT TIMOTHY - Eastern Feast of TIMOTHY 1st century (see 26). Sir Thomas Myddleton, Parliamentary commander, died in 1667; David Lewelyn Wark Griffith* (D.W. Griffith), film pioneer, born in 1875; In 1879, 600 men from the South Wales Borderers were killed by Zulus at Isandhlwana, the regiment winning two Victoria Crosses; Birth in 1894 of Charles Langbridge Morgan (Menander), novelist and playwright (see February 6); David Edward Hughes of Corwen, polymath, inventor, musician, radio wave pioneer, died in 1900 (see May 16); Birth at Bangor in 1912 of Henry Owen Parry (Harry Parry), clarinettist and 'Britain's Jazz King' (see October 11); Ryan Davies, the great Welsh comedian, was born in Glanaman, Carmarthenshire, in 1937 (see April 22)

*\*'D.W. Griffith seemed almost inhuman: he was of Welsh extraction, and the Welsh are a very peculiar breed - poetic, unpredictable, remote and fiercely independent.'* - Anita Loos

*On this day...*

..................................................................................................................................................

..................................................................................................................................................

..................................................................................................................................................

## January 23

*FEAST DAY OF SAINT* ELLI (see August 12). In 1674 the buccaneer Henry Morgan was made deputy-governor of Jamaica (see August 26); Howell Harris, the 'Father of Methodism in Wales' born in 1714 at Trefeca; In 1879, the day after Isandhlwana, at the Battle of Rorke's Drift, the Victoria Cross was won by 11 members of the South Wales Borderers, a record for a single engagement; Dr Willaim Price, druid and pioneer of cremation, died in 1893; In 1968, Howard Winstone of Merthyr Tudful won boxing's World Featherweight Title; In 1970 Sir Ifan ab Owen Edwards, the founder of Urdd Gobaith Cymru, died in Aberystwyth (see July 25); Britain's 'best' UFO sighting over Cadair Bronwen, near Llandrillo, in 1974; The Welsh National Opera gave its first performance in 1976 at Cardiff's Sherman Theatre

*'From his childhood onward this boy (the future Edward VIII) will be surrounded by sycophants and flatterers by the score – (Cries of 'Oh, oh!') – and will be taught to believe himself as of a superior creation. (Cries of 'Oh, oh!') A line will be drawn between him and the people whom he is to be called upon some day to reign over. In due course, following the precedent which has already been set, he will be sent on a tour round the world, and probably rumours of a morganatic alliance will follow – (Loud cries of 'Oh, oh!' and 'Order!') – and the end of it all will be that the country will be called upon to pay the bill. (Cries of Divide!)'* - Keir Hardie, MP for Merthyr

**On this day...**

..................................................................................................................................

..................................................................................................................................

..................................................................................................................................

## January 24

*FEAST DAY OF SAINTS* CADOCUS d.490 at Beneventum?; MWROG (also January 6, 15, 16) at Llanfwrog; Western Feast of TIMOTHY 1st century (see 26); LLAWDDOG (see 15) at Cenarth; and CYNOG (see October 9); St Paul's Pitcher Day in Cornwall, the day before his great fair in Bodmin. Radnor Castle was relieved by an English relief column, from its siege by Glyndŵr's men in 1404; Thomas Gee, Calvinistic Methodist minister, journalist, politician and founder of Baner Goch (now Y Faner) was born in Denbigh in 1815 (see September 28); Death in 1885 of the lawyer and concholgist John Gwyn Jeffreys (see January 18); Death in 1897 of Sarah Edith Wynne (see March 11); David Lloyd George received the Freedom of Cardiff in 1908*

**'500 men, ordinary men, chosen accidentally from among the unemployed'* - David Lloyd George, referring to the House of Lords in 1909

**On this day...**

..................................................................................................................................

..................................................................................................................................

..................................................................................................................................

# January 25

FEAST DAY OF SAINT DWYNWEN at Llanddwynwen, Porthddwynwen. DYDD SANTES DWYNWEN - On Dwynwen's day, love tokens were traditionally exchanged, sometimes in the form of love spoons from the male, and in Wales this is replacing Valentine's Day; CONVERSION OF ST PAUL (also June 25, 29, 30) Henry Tudor, Earl of Richmond, born at Pembroke Castle in 1457, who went on to defeat Richard II at Bosworth Field* and begin the greatest dynasty of British kings and queens; In 1891, Gwen Ffrangcon Davies, an actress for eight decades, was born in 1891; In 1932, 11 miners died at Glamorgan Collliery, Llwynypia; First radio broadcast of 'Under Milk Wood' in 1954; Tŷ Hafan, Wales' first children's hospice, was opened at Sully in 1999, thanks to a huge fund-raising effort by the people of Wales and no help from state resources nor the National Lottery

*Bacon recorded of the Battle of Bosworth 'To the Welsh people, his victory was theirs; they had thereby regained their freedom'. This feeling was echoed by the Venetian Ambassador: 'For the Welsh, it can now be said that they have won back their old independence, for Henry VII is a Welshman, a fortunate and wise Welshman.' The historian G.M. Trevelyan said: 'Here, indeed, was one of fortune's freaks: on a bare Leicestershire upland a few thousand men in close conflict foot to foot... sufficed to set upon the throne of England the greatest of all her royal lines, that should guide her through a century of change down new and larger streams of destiny.'

*On this day...*

..................................................................................................................................................

..................................................................................................................................................

..................................................................................................................................................

# January 26

FEAST DAY OF SAINT TIMOTHEUS 1st century (since 1969, with TITUS) at Ephesus, Rome. Birth in 1841 of Ellias Pierce near Dolwyddelan, author and bookseller (see July 31); In 1914, the boxer Percy Jones of Porthcawl won the World Flyweight Title in London (see December 24 and 25); Death in 1967 of the missionary Mary Myfanwy Wood (see September 16); In 1969, nine Free Wales Army members were arrested; Death of Archdruid Cynan, Sir Albert Evans-Jones, in 1970 (see April 14); Death of Lord Harlech in 1985; Death of the novelist and critic Raymond Williams in 1988

Laws passed by the French-speaking Parliament in London in 1402, to stem support for the Glyndŵr war, included: 'No Welshman is permitted to purchase any land in England. He is not allowed to hold any corporate office, nor to bear arms within any city, borough or market town. No Welshman can hold important public office in Wales. All castles and walled towns to be garrisoned by Englishmen. No Welshman, unless he is a bishop or a temporal lord, can possess a castle or defend his home. No Englishman can be convicted at the law-suit of any Welshman. No provisions or arms are to be received in

*Wales without special permission from the king or his council. An Englishman married to a Welsh woman loses his right to hold any public office in Wales and the Marches. A Welshman marrying an English woman is subjected to severe penalties; and all Englishmen marrying Welsh women are disenfranchised in the boroughs. No Welshman is to have the charge of any castle, fortress, or place of defence even though he might be the owner of it, nor to fulfil the offices of Lieutenant, Justice, Chancellor, Treasurer, Chamberlain, Sheriff, Steward, Coroner or any office of trust, not withstanding any patent or licence to the contrary. No Englishman can marry with any one of the family of Owain Glyndŵr. Also it is ordained and established that no Englishman married to any Welsh in friendship or alliance with Owain Glyndŵr, traitor to our lord the king, or to another Welshwoman since the revellion of the said Owain, or who in time to come shall make himself to be married to any Welsh woman, shall be put in any office in Wales or the said March.' No Welsh child is to be brought up as a scholar, nor permitted to be apprenticed to any trade in any town in the kingdom.'* Laws were also passed against bards travelling through the countryside, and against any assemblies of Welshmen even to gather the harvest

**On this day...**

..................................................................................................................................

..................................................................................................................................

..................................................................................................................................

# January 27

FEAST DAY OF SAINT SILYN 6th century (also September 1) at Capel Sant Silin. In 1529 Elis Gruffydd (The Soldier of Calais) of Llanasa, translator and chronicler, enlisted with the Calais garrison; The great harpist David Davies was born at Gelligaer in 1817; Death in Rome in 1866 of the sculptor John Gibson, aged 75 (see June 19); In 1883, a great gale wrecked the 'James Grey' on Tusker Rock, with 25 drowning; the Agnes Jack at Port Eynon, with 18 drowned; and 4 members of the Mumbles Lifeboat also perished; In 1884, 14 miners died at the Naval Steam Colliery, Penygraig; On this Election Day in 1906, for the first time no Conservative MP's were elected in Wales; 'The Try' in 1973 at Cardiff for the Barbarians against the unbeaten New Zealanders - Phil Bennet to JPR to Pullin (England) to John Dawes to Tommy David to Derek Quinnell to Gareth Edwards, who intercepted Quinnell's pass to John Bevan. The final score was 23-11, in the days when rugby was amateur, understandable and entertaining; In 1992, two days after her 101st birthday, the classical actress Gwen Frangcon Davies died

*'Cat, n. A soft indestructible automaton provided by nature to be kicked when things go wrong in the domestic circle'* - Ambrose Gwinnett Bierce, 'The Devil's Dictionary' 1911

**On this day...**

..................................................................................................................................

..................................................................................................................................

..................................................................................................................................

## January 28

FEAST DAY OF SAINT GILDAS the WISE c.498-c.570 (also January 29) at 15 sites in Brittany, plus Ireland, Flat Holm, Wick (Llanildas), Rhuys in Morbihan - Gildas was the first British historian, writing 'De Excidio Britanniae' (c.540) describing the pagan attacks on his country. Llywelyn Bren appears before the King at Parliament in Lincoln in 1316, to argue for restitution of his rights in Glamorgan; 'The Cambrian', the first English-language newspaper in Wales, was first published in Swansea in 1804; John Rowlands, a.k.a. Sir Henry Morton Stanley, born in 1841; Sir Tannatt William Edgworth David, geologist and polar explorer, was born in St Ffagan's in 1858 (see August 28); In 1896 an explosion at Tylorstown Colliery killed 57 miners; Henry Blackwell (born Northop, Flintshire, August 2, 1851), publisher and cultural activist in America, died in New York in 1928

*'Wealth comes, and wealth it goes away,*
*Wealth serves for nothing.*
*Wealth passes like the yellow pears:*
*Love endures for ever.*
*More is worth a handful of love*
*Than an oven full of gold and silver.'* - concluding lines from an 18th century Breton love song

*On this day...*

..................................................................................................................................

..................................................................................................................................

..................................................................................................................................

## January 29

FEAST DAY OF SAINT GILDAS (see 28) Catherine Alice Evans, the bacteriologist who discovered the cause of Brucellosis, was born in 1881; Birth in 1909 of George Thomas, later Viscount Tonypandy, a professional 'Welsh' politician who should be remembered for his successful recommendation to Cabinet that the charitable donations for the families of Aberfan be used to remove the slag tips, rather than using NCB or Government money. The hagiographic accounts of the life of this man, and his sainted treatment by the media and crachach are a sad indictment upon the knowledge that is filtered down to us.

*'If a man vomits excessively, let him immerse his testicles in vinegar. It will cure him'* - from the 'Meddygon Myddai' the 13th century writings of the Physicians of Myddfai

*On this day...*

..................................................................................................................................

..................................................................................................................................

..................................................................................................................................

## January 30

*FEAST DAY OF SAINTS* MAELOG (see November 13) and TYBIE 5th century (also December 26) at Llandybie*; Glyndŵr raids Ruthin in 1402, the estate of his arch-enemy de Grey ; Charles I executed at Whitehall. Two of the 'regicides' were Welsh - John Jones MP for Meirionydd and Thomas Wogan MP for Cardigan. John Jones of Fonmon conveniently missed signing the death warrant; In 1826, the Menai Suspension Bridge opened; The death of 'Gentleman' Jim Driscoll in Cardiff in 1925, which led to the greatest funeral march Wales has ever seen; Death in Australia in 1965 of the poet Harri Jones (see December 21); Christian Bale, film star, born in Haverfordwest in 1974

*\*'Dances were held on Banc y Naw Garreg and in another place called Pan-teg. The dance was to begin on St John's Day and to continue, if the weather were favourable, for nine days. There were one or two harpists, and the assembly, both males and females, used to dance. They used to set a birch tree in the earth and decorate its branches with wreaths of flowers. The prettiest wreaths were placed on the highest branches. This custom was kept until 1725.' - The Rev. Gomer Robers writing in 1863 about Capel Hendre, Llandybie.*

*On this day...*

....................

## January 31

*FEAST DAY OF SAINTS* AIDAN (MAEDOC) d.626 at Lawhaden, Nolton, Haroldston West, Solfach, St Bride's Bay; EWRYD 5th century at Bodewryd; GWYNIN 7th century (also 21, and December 31 at Llandygwynin, Dwygyfylchi; TYSSUL 6th century (February 11 New Style, also February 3, November 11) at Llandysul, Llanfynydd, St Ives, Vihan, Lan-Zul; and MELANGELL (see May 28). The missionary Thomas Bevan (born Neuadd-lwyd, Ceredigion, 1796) died in 1819 in Madagascar; Birth in 1862 at Capel Cynon of Thomas Rees, responsible for the survival of the Welsh Cob (see Jaunary 15); In 1893, Dr William Price was cremated at Caerlan Field, Llantrisant, an event for which he had sold tickets; Birth in 1882 of Gwendoline Elizabeth Davies, art collector and benefactress (see July 3); 1948 saw the first Barbarians match, when Australia was beaten at the Arms Park

*'At chapel, pier or out at sea*
*Sweet Christ the fisher comfort me.*
Prayer in St Leonard's Chapel at St Ives

*Suffice for me my daily bread,*
*Some fishes and a dry, safe bed.*

*On this day...*

....................

# FEBRUARY - CHWEFROR
## C'houevrer (Breton), Huevral (Cornish)

## February 1

FEAST DAY OF SAINTS ELLDEYRN 5th century at Capel Llanilltern; FFRAID c450-c525 (also March 24) at Diserth, St Brides, Llansantffraid; INA 5th century at Llanina; SELYF 5th - 6th century (also June 25) at Lansalos, St Levan; and SEIRIOL (see 15): THE CELTIC FEAST OF IMBOLC Also known as Ogronius, 'The Time of Ice'; The start of the lambing season for the Celts. In 1806, Jane Willams (Ysgafell) was born; In 1858, George Eliot's 'Adam Bede' was published;* Sidney Gilchrist Thomas, creator of the modern steel industry, dies in 1885; Cardiff's Coal Exchange, the site of the first million pound deal in the world, opened in 1886; Langston Hughes, poet, born in Missouri in 1902; RAF Penrhos opened in 1937 on the Llŷn Peninsula, for which Welsh protesters had been imprisoned; The Lake Vrynwy pipeline was damaged by an explosion in 1967; David John White (David Jason), with a Welsh mother, was born in 1940; Terence Graham Parry (Terry) Jones, author-comedian-director, of Monty Python fame, was born in Colwyn Bay in 1942; Richey Edwards of The Manic Street Preachers vanished from the London Embassy Hotel in 1995 (see December 22, February 16)

*'I've never any pity for conceited people, because I think they carry their comfort about with them'. 'The happiest women, like the happiest men, have no history.' Mary Ann Evans (George Elliot) 'The Mill on the Floss' 1860

*On this day...*

..........................................................................................................................
..........................................................................................................................
..........................................................................................................................

## February 2

FEAST DAY OF SAINT BERWYN (GERWYN, BRANWALADR, BRELADE) 5th-6th century (Also January 17, 20, February 9, May 16, June 6, July 5) at St Brelade, Milton, St Broladre; NICHOLAS OWEN d.1606 was hung, drawn and quartered in the Tower of London; CANDLEMAS - The Catholic Feast of the Purification of the Blessed Virgin Mary, now called The Presentation of Our Lord. 1141 - Cadwaladr ap Gruffudd ap Cynan captures King Stephen at Lincoln in 1141 (see February 29); In 1461, Owain Tudor, father of Jasper Tudor, Earl of Pembroke, and grandfather of Henry VII, was captured at the Battle of Mortimer's Cross*, a bloody engagement between two Welsh armies fighting for the Yorkists and Lancastrians. He was later executed; Nell Gwyn, the mother of the First Duke of St Albans, was born in 1650; Birth of Richard Morris ar

Llanfihangel Tre'r Beirdd, Anglesey, in 1703, the founder of the Cymmrodorion Society; The Football Association of Wales was formed in Wrexham in 1876; RAF Brawdy opened in Pembrokeshire in 1944; Bertrand Russell, the 20th century's most important liberal thinker, died in 1970 at Penrhyndeudraeth

*'This pedestal is erected to perpetuate the memory of an obstinate bloody and decisive battle fought near this spot in the Civil Wars between the ambitious Houses of York and Lancaster on the 2nd Day of February 1461 between the forces of Edward Mortimer, Earl of March (afterwards Edward IV), on the side of York and those of Henry VI on the side of Lancaster. The King's troops were commanded by Jasper, Earl of Pembroke. Edward commanded his own in person and was victorious. The slaughter was great on both sides. Four thousand being left dead on the Field and many Welsh persons of the first distinction were taken prisoners among whom was Owen Tudor (great-grandfather of Henry VIII and a descendant of the illustrious Cadwallader), who was afterwards beheaded at Hereford. This was the Battle which fixed Edward IV on the Throne of England, who was proclaimed king in London on the 5th of March following.' - Monument at Mortimer's Cross, erected in 1799

'Wednesday, February Day, Candlemas Eve: Sarah Witney came to my rooms this evening for an old pair of trousers I had promised her. She had told me that Mrs Jones, the jockey's wife at the corner, had a fortnight ago left some linen drying out on the churchyard hedge all night having forgotten to take it in. By morning Mrs Jones declared two pairs of drawers and a "shimmy" had been stolen, and her suspicions fell on some of the neighbours. She and her husband consulted the ordeal of the key and Bible (turning the key in the Bible). The key said "Bella Whitney". Then Jones the jockey went to the churchyard and got some clay which he made into a ball. Into the ball he put a live toad. The clay ball was either boiled or put into the fire and during the process of boiling or baking, the toad was expected to scratch the name of the thief upon a piece of paper put into the clay ball along with him. Some other horrible charm was used to find the thief, the figure of a person being pricked out on a piece of clay. It is almost incredible.'
From Francis Kilvert's Diary on this day in 1871

**On this day...**

2

# February 3
FEAST DAY OF SAINTS IA 6th - 7th century (also October 22, 27) at St Ives, Venton Ia, Plouye; MEIRION 6th century (also 4) at Llanfeirion, Cricieth; TYSSUL (see January 31) and SEIRIOL (see 15). Chester surrendered to besieging Parliamentarian forces in 1646; Richard 'Beau' Nash of Swansea,

Master of Ceremonies, died at Bath in 1761 (see October 18); Birth in 1812, at Pen-y-Bont Fawr, Montgomeryshire, of Robert Ellis (Cynddelw), minister, orator and man of literature (see August 19); Over 100,000 people watch Jim Driscoll's 2-mile long funeral cortege in 1925; In 1935, 60,000 people marched in the Rhondda, 50,000 in the Cynon Valley and 20,000 in Pontypool, protesting against changes to unemployed benefits; Death in 1965 of the courageous surgeon Hugh Morriston Davies (see August 10)

*'Woman, n. An animal usually living in the vicinity of Man, and having a rudimentary susceptibility to domestication. It is credited by many of the elder zoologists with a certain vestigial docility acquired in a former state of seclusion, but naturalists of the postusananthony period, having no knowledge of the seclusion, deny the virtue and declare that such as creation's dawn beheld, it roareth now. The species is the most widely distributed of all beasts of prey, infesting all habitable parts of the globe, from Greenland's spicy mountains to India's moral strand. The popular name (wolfman) is incorrect, for the creature is of the cat kind. The woman is lithe and graceful in its movements, especially the American variety (Felis pugnans) is omnivorous and can be taught not to talk.'* - Ambrose Gwinnett Bierce, 'The Devil's Dictionary' 1911

**On this day...**

.................................................................................................................................

.................................................................................................................................

.................................................................................................................................

# February 4

*FEAST DAY OF SAINTS* BISHOP ELDAD (ALDATE) d.577 - Churches in Gloucester and Oxford. Martyred at the battle of Dyrham near Bath; MEIRION (see 3) and DILWAR. In 1257, Carmarthen received its charter as a borough; Death of Richard Davies (*'Tafolog'*) of Mallwyd, poet and critic in 1904; Death of the philosopher Sir Henry Jones in 1922 (see November 30); A new world landspeed record was set at Pendine sands by Sir Malcolm Campbell in 'Bluebird' in 1927, of 175mph; In 1935, female marchers wrecked the Unemployed Assistance Board offices in Merthyr, and there were violent incidents at Blaenau and Abertyleri. 250,000 people across Wales were involved in civil disobedience; In 1970, 14 members of the Welsh Language Society were imprisoned for 3 months; In 1976, the film actor Roger Livesey died (see June 25); The war-correspondent who was the first to land in Normandy, the broadcaster and writer Wynford Vaughan Thomas, died at Fishguard in 1987 (see August 15)

*'At 7pm the farmers came to dine at the Vicarage. I had ten guests, Haywood, Evans, Stokes, Preece, Price, Parry, Bates, James Griffiths, James and Tom Davies. The dinner was very nice. White soup, roast beef, boiled chickens and ham, curried rabbit, stewed woodpigeons, beef-steak pie, potatoes and stewed celery, plum pudding, custard, plum tart, mince pies, apricot jam tart.'*

*On this day...*

.....................................................................................................................................................

.....................................................................................................................................................

.....................................................................................................................................................

# February 5

*FEAST DAY OF SAINT DWYNWEN* (New Style, see January 25). 'Black Bart' Roberts, the most successful pirate in history, was killed in action by the Royal Navy in 1722; Death in 1860 at Coedriglan Mansion of John Montgomery Traherne (see October 5); Sir David Brunt, eminent meteorologist and chemical warfare researcher, died in 1965 (see June 17); Michael Sheen, actor, born in Newport in 1969

'While serving as a corporal with the Monmouthshire Regiment in April 1945, Ted Chapman won one of the last Victoria Crosses to be awarded in the European theatre in the Second World War. Although the end of the war in Europe was only a month away, there was still fierce fighting to be done as the Allies pushed deep into Germany after piercing the Siegfried Line. Chapman performed the spectacular deeds which led to his decoration as the 3rd Monmouths came up against fanatical last-ditch resistance in Westphalia. This was in the difficult terrain of the Teutoberger Wald, an area made famous in miltary history through the destruction there of three Roman legions by the Germanic Cherusci tribe more than 1900 years before. Edward Thomas Chapman was born the son of a Welsh coalminer, John Chapman, and his wife Rachel in 1920, in Pontlottyn, in the Rhymney Valley. He was educated at Fochrhiw School until the age of 14 when he left to go down the pit in the Ogilvy Colliery. There he worked until 1940, when he enlisted with the Monmouthshire Regiment and was posted to the 2nd Battalion. He first saw action in June 1944, when his battalion landed in Normandy as part of the 160th Brigade in the 53rd Welsh Division. He was a corporal commanding a section throughout the fighting in the beachhead and wounded in the breakout at Falaise in August. When he came out of hospital five weeks later he was posted to the 3rd battalion and saw action with it in the fighting in the Low Countries in the autumn of 1944, and in the crossing of the Rhine and the advance into Germany in 1945. He won his VC during the advance on Osnabrick after the crossing of the Dortmund-Ems Canal.

On April 2, 1945, the 3rd Monmouths began what were to develop into repeated - and costly - attacks on the thickly wooded ridge of the Teutoberger Wald. This symbolic forest was being held by a fanatically dedicated force of German officer cadets and their instructors from the Officer School in Hanover, who were making their last stand. Chapman was leading his section in his company's advance along a narrow track through the woods when a machinegun opened fire on them at short range, inflicting heavy casualties and causing considerable confusion. Chapman seized his section's Bren gun and advanced alone, firing from the hip. He mowed down his opponents at point-

*blank range and forced them to retire in disorder. At this point his company was ordered to retire but the order did not reach Chapman and his section was left isolated in its advanced position. The Germans closed in and delivered a number of bayonet charges under cover of intense machinegun fire. Chapman again rose with his Bren gun to meet the assaults and on each occasion halted the attackers with his fire.*

*He was soon running out of ammunition, so shouting to the survivors of his section for more bandoliers, he dropped into a fold in the ground, rolled on to his back and covered those bringing up the ammunition by firing the Bren over his shoulder. The Germans made every attempt to eliminate him with grenades, but with his magazine reloaded he closed with them and once more drove them off. During the company's withdrawal, his company commander had been severely wounded and was lying in the open a short distance from Chapman's postion. Still under heavy fire, Chapman reached him and carried him back to comparative safety, but as he did so the officer was hit again, the round wounding Chapman in the thigh as well. But when he reached cover, he found that his company commander was dead. He himself refused to be evacuated until the position was finally secured ... Ted Chapman VC, BEM, born in Pontlottyn, January 13, 1920. He died on February 3, 2002.'* - Lines from Obituary in The Times, this day in 2002

**On this day...**

........................................................................................................................................

........................................................................................................................................

........................................................................................................................................

## February 6

FEAST DAYS OF SAINTS MEL d.488 at Ardagh; and RIOC 6th century (also August 1) at Lough Ree, St Rock's, Kilkenny. The death of Hywel Gwynedd, Glyndŵr's main warrior in the north-east of Wales, defending his stockade on Halkyn Mountain in night-fighting; In 1890, 176 men and children were killed at the Llanerch Colliery, near Pontypool; 1929 saw a riot involving 700 people at Cwmfelinfach, because of the employment of 'scabs' at Nine Mile Point Colliery; Death in 1958 of Charles Morgan (Menander); Death in Monte Carlo in 1968 of Viscount Kemsley (see May 7)

*'When I consider the dimensions of this once magnificent Abbey (Cwm Hir) as compared with those of our cathedrals all of which they rival or exceed, I am struck with astonishment that such an immense pile, and of such costly workmanship, should have been erected in a spot which is remote from all the influence created by similar works of art. In the heart of Radnorshire, the wildest of all Welsh counties, in a neighbourhood where the roads must always have been difficult for travellers, in this lonely though beautiful retreat, arose one of the purest and richest models of sacred architecture that could be found in the kingdom.'* - entry on this day in 1828 on the Rev. John Parker's 'Tour of Wales and its Churches'

## 6

## February 7

*FEAST DAY OF SAINTS* AUGULUS d.305; ILLTUD d.c. 537 (also November 6, 7) Caldey Island, Llanilltud Fawr, Llantrithyd, Llanhamlach, Ilston, Lantwit-juxta-Neath, Llanhilleth, Lantwood, Lanhari, Llantwit Fardre, Brittany; and MOSES, a British Apostle to the Saracens. In 1301 the French-speaking Prince Edward was named as the first English Prince of Wales; In 1601 the Earl of Essex, his right-hand man Gelli Meurig and Welsh followers and allies rebelled against Elizabeth I in London; The opera singer Stuart Burrows was born at Cilfynydd, near Pontypridd, in 1933; Gerald Davies, of Cardiff, Wales and the British Lions, was born at Llansaint, Cydweli in 1945; In 1948, 10 players from Cardiff rugby club, including all the seven backs, play for Wales against Scotland, still a record in international rugby; Snowdonia was designated as a National Park in 1951*

*'Snowdon or Eryri is no single hill, but a mountainous region, the loftiest part of which, called Y Wyddfa, nearly 4000 feet above the level of the sea, is generally considered to be the highest point of Southern Britain. The name Snowdon was bestowed upon this region by the early English on account of its snowy appearance in winter; Eryri by the Britons, because in the old time it abounded with eagles, Eryri in the ancient British language signifying an eyrie or breeding-place of eagles. Snowdon is interesting on various accounts. It is interesting for its picuresque beauty. Perhaps in the whole world there is no region more picturesquely beautiful than Snowdon, a region of mountains, lakes, cataracts and groves, in which Nature shows herself in her most grand and beautiful forms' - George Borrow, 'Wild Wales', 1826*

## 7

## February 8

*FEAST DAY OF SAINT KEW (CIWA)* 5th century at Llangiwa, Kew. Christening in 1719 of William Edwards in Eglwysilan, the architect of the world-famous Pontypridd Bridge, which succeeded on his fifth attempt to build it (see August 7): Death of Sydenham Teak Edwards in Chelsea in 1819 (see August 5); The harpist Osian Ellis was born at Ffynnongroew, Clwyd in 1928; Rachel Thomas, actress, died in Cardiff in 1995; Meredith Edwards of Rhoslanerchrugog, actor and pacifist, died in 1999, aged 81

*'Oes gafr eto?*
*Oes heb ei godro?*
*Ar y creigiau geirwon mae'r hen afr yn crwydro.*
*Gafr wen, wen, wen,*
*Ie finwen, finwen, finwen*
*Foel gynffon wen, foel gynffon wen*
*Ystlys wen a chynffon*
*Wen, en, wen'*

'Cyfri'r Geifr', Counting the Goats, has always been a popular children's song, which becomes quicker and quicker, and usually ends in mistakes and laughter. Other colours are added as the song becomes longer. The lines mean: 'Is there another goat? Is there, not milked? On the rugged rocks the old goat is wandering. A white goat, yes, white lip, bald white tail, white flank and a tail, white, white, white'.

**On this day...**

.............................................................................................................................

.............................................................................................................................

.............................................................................................................................

# February 9

*FEAST DAY OF SAINTS* EINION 6th century (also February 10 and 11, August 5) at Llanengyn, Ynys Enlli, Penmon; and TEILO d.566 or 580 (also November 26) at Llandeilo, Penally, Llantilio Crosseny, Marloes, Brechfa, Merthyr Mawr, Trefgarn, Penally, Manorbier, Lanion, Talgarth, Llowes. In 1655, Henry Morgan the buccaneer was indentured to a Bristol cutler, to sail for Barbados (see August 26); Birth in 1943, in Cwm, Ebbw Vale of Ryland Davies the world-famous opera singer; In 1996, Wales national newspaper, The Western Mail, was sold to a Chester company

*'Land of my mothers, how shall my brothers praise you?*
*With timbrels or rattles or tins?*
*With fire.*
*How shall we praise you on the banks of the rhymneying waters,*
*On the smoky shores and the glittering shores of Glamorgan,*
*On wet mornings in the bare fields behind the Newport docks,*
*On fine evenings when lovers walk by Bedwellty Church,*
*When the cuckoo calls to miners coming home to Rhymney Bridge,*
*When the wild rose defies the Industrial Revolution*
*And when the dear old drunken lady sings of Jesus and a little shilling.'*
- first verse of 'Land of My Mothers', by Idris Davies

# February 10

*FEAST DAY OF SAINT* FFAGAN d.c. 193 (also August 8 and May 24, 26) at St Ffagans, Llanmaes; John Jones (Tegid) was born at Bala in 1792, and transcribed The Red Book of Hergest for Lady Charlotte Guest; The first barge (carrying iron) arrived in Cardiff on the newly-completed Glamorganshire Canal from Merthyr Tudful in 1794; Birth in 1826 of Edward Williams, ironmaster of Middlesborough, and grandson of Iolo Morganwg (see June 9); This date was the first 'dry' Sunday in 1882, after the passing of the Sunday Closing Act; Rachel Thomas, the actress, was born Rachel Roberts in Alltwen, Swansea Valley, in 1905 (see February 11); A pylon at Trywerin Reservoir was damaged by an explosion in 1963; Grace Williams, composer, died in Barri in 1977

| | |
|---|---|
| Ac erbyn hyn nid oes yno ond coed, | And by this time there are only trees, |
| A'u gwreiddiau haerllug yn sugno'r hen bridd: | Their impudent roots sucking the old earth; |
| Coed lle y bu cymdogaeth, | Trees where once was neighbourhood, |
| Fforest lle bu ffermydd, | A forest where once were farms |
| Bratiaith Saeson y De lle bu barddoni a diwinydda, | The lingo of the English-speakers of the South where once was poetry and divinity |
| Cyfarth cadnoid lle bu cri plant ac wyn | The barking of foxes where once was the cry of children and lambs, |
| | |
| Ac yn y tywyllwch yn ei chanol hi | And in the darkness in the middle of it |
| Y mae ffau'r Minotawros Seisnig; | The lair of the English Minotaur; |
| Ac ar golfenni, fel ar groesau, | And on the branches, as though on crosses, |
| Ysgerbydau beirdd, blaenoriaid, | Skeletons of poets, deacons, ministers and |
| gweinidogion ac athrawon Ysgol Sul | Sunday School teachers |
| Yn gwynnu yn yr haul, | Bleaching in the sun, |
| Ac yn cael eu golchi gan y glaw a'u sychu gan y gwynt. | Washed by the rain and dried by the wind. |

Gwenallt's response to the Forestry Commission's destruction of his homelands in 'Rhydcymerau', 1977

# February 11

*FEAST DAY OF SAINTS* CYNOG (see October 9); SEIRIOL (see 15); and TYSSUL (see January 31). Geoffrey of Monmouth (born c.1090), author of Historium Regum Britanniae, was ordained a priest at Westminster in 1152; Arthur Blayney, the last of the Blayneys of Gregynog, was born in 1716 (see October 1); Mary Quant, of Welsh parentage, was born in 1934; The psychoanalyst Ernest Jones, the friend and biographer of Freud, died in 1958 (see January 1); Rachel Thomas died in Cardiff in 1995, aged 90 (see February 10)

Because of moronic legislation to help anglers, the 2000-year craft of coracle-fishing is finally dying out in Wales. In Hornel's 'British Coracles', 1938, we read *'new boats are made each year, woven of withies on a frame of hazel rods cut in the Autumn after the leaves have fallen, and allowed to season over winter, and the whole covered with an ox-hide. Such boats are light and easy to manoeuvre'.* Even the epic 7th century 'Gododin' mentions 'ef lledi bysc yng corwc' (he would kill a fish in his coracle) and Giraldus Cambrensis in 1188 gives us a vivid description of coracle fishing. The author strongly recommends a 1999 booklet available - 'The Coracle' by J. Geraint Jenkins, available at the National Coracle Centre at Cenarth.

*On this day...*

..................................................................................................................................

..................................................................................................................................

..................................................................................................................................

# February 12

*FEAST DAY OF SAINT* FFILI 6th century at Rhosilli, Lamphil, Kervili, Caerffili; traditional beginning of salmon-netting in inland waters of Wales. David ab Owen ap Deio, Bishop of St Asaf, died in 1512; Death in 1589 of Blanche Parry, confidante of Queen Elizabeth; Megan Watts Hughes, singer and duettist with Jennie Lind, born at Dowlais in 1842 (see October 29); The great miners' leader, John L. Lewis, was born in Iowa in 1880; Dr William Price was cleared in Cardiff in 1884, of illegally cremating his son, Iesu Grist (Jesus Christ Price); Birth in 1848 of Beriah Gwynfe Evans, journalist and dramatist, at Nantyglo (see November 4); BBC Radio began broadcasting from Cardiff in 1923

*'Maredudd always had a round of roebuck*
*And venison, steaming hot.*
*For supper, the spit was never without an ox;*
*And there's stag broth any night you will..*
*For me, on that mountain brow, there was plenty of wine,*
*And plenty of dishes of stag numbles.'* Lines from a poem to the lord of Penamnen, Dolwyddelan, by Lewys Môn (c.1480-1527). (Numbles, or umbles, were offal such as lung, spleen and gut cooked in broth and sometimes wine, of which our

present dish of liver and onions is a relic. 'Umble pie' was thus a dish for the lower classes).

...........................................................................................................................

...........................................................................................................................

...........................................................................................................................

# February 13

FEAST DAY OF SAINT DYFYNOG 7th century at Llanrhaiadr, Ddyfynog. After the most bitterly cold winter in remembrance, Harlech Castle finally surrendered around this time in 1409. Edmund Mortimer had been killed and amont the starving survivors captured were Glyndŵr's wife Marged, two of her daughters and four grandchildren. All were dead in London within a few years; Saunders Lewis's 'fate of the language' lecture 'Tynged yr Iaith' on BBC Radio in 1962, which led to the founding of the Welsh Language Society; Death in 1947 of 'Pastor Dan' (see May 5); Death in 1962 of the politician Hugh Dalton (see August 26)

'*Shrove Tuesday, 13 February, 1872. Dined at the vicarage at 5.30 and at 7 drove with the Venables and Crichton to the Rifle Volunteer Concert in the National Schoolroom at Hay. We had tickets for the first row, and in the third row I immediately espied Daisy and Charlotte. I had the good fortune to get a chat with Daisy before the seats were filled up, and she was so nice and I was so happy. She told me there had been two balls and I told her how disappointed I was not to meet her at the Crichtons' Ball. She said she had enjoyed her balls very much, and I said I heard that the ladies who "came out" at the Hereford Hunt Ball (of whom she was one) had all looked very pretty and been very much admired. She smiled and blushed and looked pleased. I told her how well I remembered the last time I saw her nearly 3 months ago. "It's a long time since you have been over to Llan Thomas. I suppose you have been very busy. If you come over you will find some of us at home. We don't usually go out till half past three." "I am afraid", I said, "that you have all forgotten me." "Oh, no," she said. I was so happy talking to her. I had been hoping and thinking all day that I might meet her at the concert this evening. But now the seats began to fill. Fanny Bevan her great and inseparable friend sat on one side of her and her father on the other. I sat in the row before them. Henry sang. Oh Daisy.*' - from the Rev. Francis Kilvert's Diary

...........................................................................................................................

...........................................................................................................................

...........................................................................................................................

# February 14

FEAST DAY OF SAINT VALENTINE, NECTAN 6th century (also May 18 and June 17) at Hartland, Launceston, St Nectan's, Wells; and MEUGAN (see September 24) at Exeter, Lan-Neizant, Poundstock. In 1345 on Valentine's Day, Henry de Shaldeforde was killed near Caernarfon, and the English burgesses in Wales were in a state of panic because of rising discontent; Birth in 1745 of David Davis (Davis Castellhywel), minster, poet, schoolmaster and friend of Richard Price and Iolo Morganwg; In 1844, 40 miners were lost in flooding in Lanshipping Colliery, Pembrokeshire; Birth in 1881 of William John Gruffydd near Bethel, Caernarfon, scholar, poet, critic and editor (see September 29); Birth in Blaina in 1891 of William John Parry Jones, the famous tenor who survived the sinking of the Lusitania (see December 26); Jimmy Wilde won the world flyweight championship in 1916; Murray the Hump arranged Chicago's St Valentine's Day Massacre in 1929

*'Septuagesima Sunday, St Valentine's Eve: Preached at Clyro in the morning. Very few people in church, the weather fearful, violent deadly E. wind and the hardest frost we have had yet. Went to Bettws in the afternoon wrapped in two waistcoats, two coats, a muffler and a mackintosh, and was not at all too warm. Heard the Chapel bell pealing strongly for the second time since I have been here and when I got to the Chapel my beard moustaches and whiskers were so stiff with ice that I could hardly open my mouth and my beard was frozen on to my mackintosh. There was a large christening party from Llwyn Gwilym. The baby was baptised in ice which was broken and swimming about in the font.'*
From Francis Kilvert's Diary, 1870

*On this day...*

.................................................................................................................................

.................................................................................................................................

.................................................................................................................................

# February 15

FEAST DAY OF SAINTS ABBOT SEIRIOL 6th century (also February 1, 3 and 11) at Penmon, Puffin Island (Ynys Seiriol), Clorach; and MABYN (see November 18). In 1405 Lady Despenser was captured at Cheltenham with the two nephews of Edmund Mortimer, the heirs to the English throne - they were on their way to join their uncle and Glyndŵr at Harlech; Birth in 1803 of Owen Jones, architect, ornamental designer and superintendent of the Great Exhibition of 1851 (see April 19); Birth at Bontnewydd of Sir William Henry Preece FRS, electrical engineer and scientific pioneer (see November 6); Death of the Nonconformist Walter Coffin, son of a Bridgend tanner, who became a colliery pioneer and MP for Cardiff, in 1867 at Llandaff Court; Death in 1964 of Sir Guildhaume Myrddin-Evans (see December 17); Rhodri Morgan was elected First

Secretary of the British Assembly in Cardiff in 2000, after Alun Michael's resignation

*'The force that through the green fuse drives the flower*
*Drives my green age; that blasts the roots of trees*
*Is my destroyer.*
*And I am dumb to tell the crooked rose*
*My youth is bent by the same wintry fever.'* - Dylan Thomas, first verse of 'The Force That Through the Green Fuse Drives the Flower', 1953

*On this day...*

.................................................................................................................................

.................................................................................................................................

.................................................................................................................................

## February 16

FEAST DAY OF SAINT LEONORE 6th century (also July 1,3 and October 13) at Aleth, Limoges. Death in 1847 at Merthyr of Taliesin Williams (see July 9); Thomas Edward Ellis, Liberal MP for Merioneth and chief Liberal whip, was born near Bala in 1859 (see April 5); Birth of the weaver and folk-singer Philip Tanner at Llangennith in 1862, probably the last of the Welsh 'wedding bidders' (see February 19); Mai Jones, the composer and radio producer, was born in Newport in 1899 (see May 7); Sir Geraint Evans, opera singer, was born in Cilfynydd in 1922; In 1943, 34 people died in Swansea during German air-raids; the poet John Tripp died in Cardiff in 1986; Richey Edwards' car found abandoned at the Severn Bridge service-station (see February 1)

*'Cambria is called Wales nowadays, that having become its usual name, although it is a foreign word and not really correct. It is two hundred miles long and about one hundred miles wide. It takes some eight days to travel the whole length, from the mouth of the river Gwygir in Anglesey to Portskewett in Gwent. In breadth it stretches from Porthmawr, that is the Great Port, near St David's, to Rhyd-Helyg, the Welsh for Willow Ford, called Walford in English. Because of its high mountains, deep valleys and extensive forests, not to mention its rivers and marshes, it is not easy to access. The Britons who were left alive took refuge in these parts when the Saxons first occupied the islands and they have never been completely subdued since, either by the English or the Normans. Those who retreated to the southern corner of the island could not continue their resistance, for their territory has no natural protection. It is called Cornwall, after their leader Corineus. There was a third group of Britons left unconquered, and these occupied Brittany, in Southern Gaul. They were moved there by the tyrant Maximus (Macsen Wledig), long before the fall of Britain. Their young soldiers supported Maximus in many hard battles, and in gratitude the imperial authorities gave them these lands which stick out from Gaul.'* - Giraldus Cambrensis, 'The Description of Wales, 1193-1194

16

....................................................................................................................................

....................................................................................................................................

....................................................................................................................................

## February 17

FEAST DAY OF SAINT CURIG (see June 16); In 1536, Henry VIII's Act of Union between England and Wales; Death in 1863 at Clynnog of the poet Ebenezer Thomas (Eben Fardd); In 1903 Dr Joseph Parry, writer of 'Myfanwy'* died aged 61 in Penarth (see May 21); Edgar Evans died with Captain Scott returning from the South Pole in 1912; The actor Clifford Evans was born in 1912 at Senghenydd; In 1951 there was a world record attendance for a club rugby match at Cardiff Arms Park (48,500), when Newport beat Cardiff

*'All names in this quiet valley*
*speak of war -*
*Rhyd y Meirch, ford of war-horses:*
*Rhiw Felen, blood-coloured hill;*
*Maes Galanas, field of slaughter.*
*A small wind strokes, rain washes.*
*Are names all that remain?'*
    *Lines from 'Rhyd y Meirch', by Ruth Bidgood, from 'Selected Poems' (Seren Books)*

17

....................................................................................................................................

....................................................................................................................................

....................................................................................................................................

## February 18

FEAST DAY OF SAINT AUGULUS (New Style, see 7); In 1504 Prince Henry Tudor (Henry VIII) was created Prince of Wales, on the death of his brother Arthur; Mary Tudor born in 1516; The Battle of the Heath in the Civil War in 1646, saw Cardiff and its castle being taken by the Parliamentarians; Birth in 1796 near Machynlleth of Hugh Williams, solicitor and Chartist and Rebecca Rioter supporter (see October 19); Thomas Artemus Jones, historian, journalist and judge, born at Denbigh in 1871 (see October 15); In 1887, an explosion at Ynyshir's National Pit killed 39 colliers; The actor Mervyn Johns (the father of Glenys) was born in Pembroke in 1899 (see September 6)

*The Welsh people are light and agile. They are fierce rather than strong, and totally*
*dedicated to the practice of arms. Not only the leaders but the entire nation are trained*
*in war. Sound the trumpet for battle and the farmer will rush from his plough to pick up*
*his weapons as quickly as the courtier from the court. One cannot say here, as*

*elsewhere, "the farmer's toil is one long round."* - Giraldus Cambrensis, 'The Description of Wales', 1193/1194

**On this day...**

..................................................................................................................................................

..................................................................................................................................................

..................................................................................................................................................

## February 19

Holy Day of Thomas Burgess, Bishop and Teacher (1837). In 1862, 47 miners died at Gethin Colliery, Merthyr Tydfil; In 1881, Wales lost the first rugby international with England, at Blackheath; Clement Davies, the leader of the Liberal Party, was born in Llanfyllin in 1884 (see March 23); In 1906, Grace Williams the composer was born in Barry; On this and the following two days in 1941, 240 people were killed in Swansea during German air-raids; Cardiff's last electric tram ran in 1950; Death of the folk-singer Philip Tanner in 1950, at Penmaen, in Gower (see February 16)

*(The Welsh) plough the soil once in March and April for oats, a second time in summer, and then they turn it a third time when the grain is being threshed. In this way the entire population lives almost entirely on oats and the produce of their herds, milk, cheese and butter. They eat plenty of meat, but little bread. They pay no attention to commerce, shipping or industry, and their only preoccupation is military training. They are passionately devoted to their freedom and to the defence of their country: they will take up their weapons and willingly sacrifice their lives. They esteem it a disgrace to die in bed, but an honour to be killed in battle. They agree with the words of the poet "Turn peace away, For honour perishes with peace."* - Giraldus Cambrensis, 'The Description of Wales', 1193/1194

**On this day...**

..................................................................................................................................................

..................................................................................................................................................

..................................................................................................................................................

## February 20

*FEAST DAY OF SAINTS* EINION and TEILO (New Style, see 9) - Teilo's fairs were held at Llandaf and Llandeilo Fawr. Death in 1071 in Normandy of William FitzOsbern, who built castles on the Welsh borders at Wigmore, Clifford, Ewyas Harold, Monmouth, Chepstow, conquered Gwent and the Mercians, and fought Maredudd ab Owain of Deheubarth and Cadwgan ap Meurig of Morgannwg; The Welsh emigrant ship 'Governor Fenner' sank off Holyhead in 1841, with 122 people drowning; Birth in 1878 at Goginan, Ceredigion, of Humphrey Owen Jones, the chemist and mountaineer, who was elected FRS aged just 24 (see August 15); Richard Tecwyn Williams, eminent biochemist and toxicologist, was born in Abertillery in 1909 (see December 19);

*'Leave to Robert Browning*
*Beggars, fleas and vines;*
*Leave to squeamish Ruskin*
*Popish Appenines,*
*Dirty stones of Venice*
*And his gas-lamps seven;*
*We've got the stones of Snowdon*
*And the lamps of heaven.'* - Charles Kingsley, 1856

**On this day...**

.......................................................................................................................
.......................................................................................................................
.......................................................................................................................

## February 21

FEAST DAY OF SAINT CWRDA at Jordanston. Possible death date in 1286 of Gruffudd ap Gwenwynwyn, leader of the plot to assassinate Llywelyn II in 1274, whose son Owen took the surname de la Pole; 1693, Theophilus Evans*, cleric, historian and man of letters, was christened at Llandygwydd Church, Ceredigion (see September 11); In 1804, the world's first steam locomotive, built by Richard Trevithick, carried passengers for 21 miles between Penydarren and Abercynon, 21 years before Stevenson's 'Rocket'; Sir William Goscombe John, the great sculptor, was born in Cardiff in 1860 (see December 15); Dr Mary Edwards Walker, the only woman to win the Congressional Medal of Honour, died in 1919; Last day of the 3-day bombing blitz in Sansea in 1941, which killed 240 people; Alan Sidney Rickman, actor, was born in 1946 - his mother was from Trefforest; James Dean Bradfield of the Manic Street Preachers was born in Blackwood in 1969; Charlotte Church, singer, born in 1986 in Cardiff

*'*It is an onerous, sad, and vexing task to relate the misfortunes of the Cymry; their difficulties and their worldly troubles in every age and every land that they inhabited from that time when the language was compounded in the Tower of Babel. For is it not a sad and sorrowful thing to relate how ungrateful they were to God, how ready to fall into the temptations of the world, the flesh and the devil, how inclined to rebel against him, all of which being responsible for their afflictions and lack of success.'* - Theophilus Evans

**On this day...**

.......................................................................................................................
.......................................................................................................................
.......................................................................................................................

## February 22

FEAST DAY OF SAINT CANOC (New Style, see 11). In 1403, the town of Hope is burnt by Glyndŵr's men, just a few miles outside the English base of Chester; Bleddyn Williams, the great Cardiff, Wales and Lions centre was born in Taffs Well in 1933 - all five of his brothers also played for Cardiff

'Three antagonists of goodness:
Pride, Passion And Covetousness.' - from the Welsh Triads of Virtues

*On this day...*

.............................................................................................................

.............................................................................................................

.............................................................................................................

## February 23

FEAST DAY OF SAINTS FFINIAN d.549 (also December 12) at        Clonard; MILBURG 7th century at Llanfilo in Radnor, Wenlock; MINVER 6th century (also February 24, November 23, 24) at Minwear, Tredesick, St Minver; SHROVETIDE, in Welsh YNYD*. In 1716 Winifred Herbert, Lady Nithsdale, rescued her husband from the Tower of London on the eve of his execution; Richard Price, philosopher and Wales' greatest thinker, born at Tynton near Llangeinor in 1723; In 1794, the last invasion of British soil finally landed at Llanwnda; John Quincy Adams, Welsh-American President, (The Diplomat President) died in 1848; Death in Cardiff of Evan Jones (see September 5) in 1852; In 1866 Jefferson Davis married Varina Banks Howell; In 1963 the Welsh Language Society blocked Trefechan Bridge, Aberystwyth, in their campaign for bilingual road signs; Death of the archdruid Myfyr Morganwg at Pontypridd in 1888 (see January 6)

*'It is still customary on certain estates to make annual payments to the landlord called YNYD, or GIEIR YNYD, usually consisting of one hen and twenty eggs. In one case brought before the Commission the payment was of two fat geese and forty eggs' - 1895 Welsh Land Commission Minutes

*On this day...*

.............................................................................................................

.............................................................................................................

.............................................................................................................

## February 24

FEAST DAYS OF SAINTS CADOG c450-510 (also September 25) at Cadoxton, Llancarfan, Llangattock, Pendeulwyn, Llanmaes, Portheinon, Trefethin, Ile de Cado, Ploucadeuc; and MINVER (see 23); *Nickanan Night* in

Cornwall, where people threw water, rubbed soot on one another and took doors and gates, before the soberness of Lent. In 1152, Geoffrey of Monmouth (c.1090-1155) was consecrated Bishop of Lambeth, just 13 days after being ordained as a priest (see February 11); In 1405 Owain Glyndŵr, Edmund Mortimer and Earl Percy of Northumberland sign the Tripartite Indenture, dividing Henry IV's kingdom and securing the nationhood of Wales; In 1416 Owain Glyndŵr's son Maredudd was sent to offer Owain a pardon, after 16 years of war with England - the rest of his family were all dead. The pardon was offered in 1417 to Maredudd alone, but he refused it until 1421(see April 8); Thomas Bowdler died in Swansea in 1797; The Chartist John Frost was given a free pardon in 1857; 37 miners were killed at Pentre, Rhondda in 1871; In 1880 the Resurgam sank near Llandudno - it was the world's first mechanically-powered submarine; Death in 1983 of the playwright Thomas Lanier (Tennessee) Williams (see March 26)

*'Mae'r goludog yn ymfrasau ar ddagrau y tlodion'* - *'The wealthy get fat on the tears of the poor'* - Welsh proverb

**On this day...**

...........................................................................................................................
...........................................................................................................................
...........................................................................................................................

## February 25
*FEAST DAY OF SAINTS* CIANAN 6th century at P l o u g u e r n e a u ; a n d NECTAN (New Style see 11). The sudden death of Daydd ap Llywelyn, Prince of Wales, at his palace of Aber in 1246, wrecked the peaceful succession of Gwynedd to the Princedom of Wales; Fulk Fitz Warin V married Margaret ferch Gruffydd ap Gwenwynwyn in 1277, and was disputing with Llywelyn the Great for land in Montgomery; General Tate surrendered the French forces at Fishguard in 1794; Birth in 1855 of Mary Davies, singer and founder of the Welsh Folk Song Society (see June 22); In 1895, Henry Austin Bruce Pryce died. Home Secretary from 1873 to 1875, he was the first Baron Aberdare, and the first Chancellor of the University College of South Wales and Monmouthshire (see April 16); Dennis O'Neill, opera singer, born in Pontarddulais in 1948; Mike Peters, singer/songwiter of 'The Alarm' born in Prestatyn in 1959; S.O. Davies, the miner's leader and Independent Labour MP, died in Merthyr in 1972

*'Usual is wind from the east;*
*Usual for a portly man to be pompous;*
*Usual a blackbird amongst thorns;*
*Usual after great violence a great lamentation;*
*Usual for ravens to get flesh in a wood;*
*Usual is wind from the north;*
*Usual for maid to be sweet;*
*Usual is a handsome man from Gwynedd;*
*Usual for a prince to provide a feast;*
*Usual is despondency after drinking.'*
- from the 12th century Welsh poem, 'Usual is Wind from the South'

.....................................................................................................

.....................................................................................................

.....................................................................................................

# February 26

FEAST DAY OF SAINT TYFAELOG (also March 1) at Llandyfaelog. In 1490, Henry VII invested Prince Arthur as Prince of Wales; The transported Chartist leader William Jones died in Tasmania in 1873; The Welsh Guards regiment was formed in 1915, part of the Guards Division; In 1942 Richard Llewellyn's 'How Green Was My Valley' won the Oscar as the best film

*'It must always be the desire of a government to render its dominions, as far as possible, homogeneous. Sooner or later the difference of language between Wales and England will probably be effaced, an event which is socially and politically desirable.'* - 'On the Study of Celtic Literature', Matthew Arnold (1822-1888)

*On this day...*

.....................................................................................................

.....................................................................................................

.....................................................................................................

# February 27

FEAST DAY OF SAINT AILBE (see Sept 12); Holy Day of George Herbert*, priest (1633); Death in 1666 of the alchemist and poet Thomas Vaughan, twin brother of Henry (see April 23); The great painter James Dickson Innes was born at Llanelli in 1887 (see August 27); Norman Biggs (born Cardiff, November 3, 1870), was killed by a poisoned arrow in Nigeria in 1908. He secured Wales' first Triple Crown in Scotland in 1893; In 1932 Richard Morgan ('Dickie') Owen, the great Swansea and Wales scrum-half, committed suicide in the Nag's Head, Landore, Swansea; 5 Welshmen were killed fighting against Franco in the Battle of Jarama in 1937

*\*'O what a cunning guest*
*Is this same grief! Within my heart I made*
*Closets; and in them many a chest;*
*And, like a master in my trade,*
*In those chests, boxes; in each box, a till:*
*Yet grief knows all, and enters when he will.'* - first verse of 'Confession', by George Herbert

*On this day...*

.....................................................................................................

.....................................................................................................

.....................................................................................................

## February 28

FEAST DAY OF SAINT LLIBIO 6th century at Llanllibio; CANDLEMAS QUARTERDAY in Scotland; the day when Cwn Annwn (the Hounds of Annwn) take to the skies, in Celtic tradition. Birth in 1851 at Nant-y-Glo of Thomas Witton Davies (d.1923), Baptist Minister and Semitic cholar, who held doctorates at Leipzig, Jena, Geneva and Durham Universities; In 1866 Amy Elizabeth Dillwyn, novelist and industrialist, was launched into London society; The writer Glyn Jones was born in Merthyr in 1905; Stanley Baker, film-star, born in Ferndale in 1928;

On this day in 1998, Victor Spinetti introduced Bridgend's Peter Karrie as '*a revolutionary Che Guevara, a tortured Judas in "Jesus Christ Superstar" and a towering Valjean in "Les Miserables"....to the world he is the Phantom of the Opera*' when compering a St David's Day broadcast cabaret, 'Wales in the West End'

*On this day...*

.................................................................................................................................

.................................................................................................................................

.................................................................................................................................

## February 29

LEAP DAY, BACHELOR'S DAY when women could propose to men in some areas, the men paying a forfeit if they refused to wed. Traditionally the luckiest day of any year. The Old Style Calendar was introduced on this day in AD45 by Julius Caesar, the Julian Calendar. The year was of 365 days, with an extra day every 4th year. It was reformed in 1582 by Pope Gregory XIII to the New Style calendar, which was not adopted in Wales until the 18th century. 1172 - death of Cadwaladr ap Gruffudd ap Cynan, buried next to his brother Owain Gwynedd in Bangor Cathedral (see February 2); Pembrokeshire Coast National Park was designated in 1952

'*To oblige a Man to confess what he has done wrong. Take a frog alive from the water. Extract its tongue and put him back in the water. Lay this same tongue on the heart of the sleeping man, and he will confess his deeds in his sleep.*' - Meddygon Myddfai, 13th century

*On this day...*

.................................................................................................................................

.................................................................................................................................

.................................................................................................................................

# MARCH - MAWRTH
## Meurs (Breton), Merth (Cornish)

## March 1

FEAST DAY OF SAINTS DAVID*, DEWI SANT - traditionally died in 589, aged over 100 (July 1 in Brittany) at St David's, Glascwm**, Llanddewi Brefi, Brechfa, Raglan, Kilpeck, Little Dewchurch, Much Dewchurch, Whitchurch, Llanychaer, Bridell, Llanddewi, Hubberston, Abergwili, Meidrim, West Country; LLONIO 6th century (also March 17) at Llandinam; SANNAN d.544 (also June 13, April 29, March 6, 8, December 17) at Llansannan, Bedwellty; CYFELACH d. 927 at Llangyfelach; and TYFEILIOG (see February 26); the traditional flowering day of the leek. In 1244, Gruffudd ap Llywelyn ap Iorwerth broke his neck, trying to escape from the Tower of London, the signal for a new rising by Dafydd ap Llywelyn; In 1827 St David's College, Lampeter, opened; In 1927, 52 miners died at Marine Colliery, Cwm, Ebbw Vale; In 1938, 51 miners died in an explosion at Marine Colliery, Ebbw Vale; David Broome, world show-jumping champion born in 1940 in Cardiff; Cardiff's Chapter Arts Centre, a model for community arts across the world, opened in Canton in 1972; In 1979, the people of Wales voted almost 4:1 against a Welsh Assembly. Most true Welshmen saw it as an extra powerless level of bureaucracy. Neil Kinnock campaigned against it because *'the promotion of "regional" alliances was a blow to the unity of the British working class'* and *'it would make it difficult for Welsh MP's to be in the mainstream of British political life'* (quotes from John Davies, 'A History of Wales'); The Dylan Thomas memorial at Poet's Corner, Westmister Abbey was dedicated in 1982; Death of the wonderful boxer Tommy Farr in 1986 (see March 12 and August 30)

*'*St David who was of royal extraction, and uncle to King Arthur, died, aged 146 years, on March 1st, still celebrated by the Welsh, perchance to perpetuate the memory of his abstinence, whose contented mind made many a favourite meal on such roots of the earth' -* 'The Episcopal Almanac', 1677

**'*In the church at Glascwm, in Elfael, there is a handbell which has most miraculous powers. It is supposed to have belonged to Sant David and is called a "bangu". In an attempt to liberate him, a certain woman took this handbell to her husband, who was chained up in the castle of Rhaiadr Gwy, in Gwrthrynion, which castle Rhys ap Gruffydd had built in our time. The keepers of the castle not only refused to set the man free, but they even seized the bell. That same night God took vengeance on them, for the whole town was burned down, except the wall on which the handbell hung.' -* Giraldus Cambrensis, 1188

*On this day...*

.........................................................................................................

.........................................................................................................

.........................................................................................................

## March 2

*FEAST DAY OF SAINTS* BISHOP CHAD 7th century at Lichfield; GWRTHL 6th century at Maesllanwrthl, Llanwrthl; JAOUA at Dauolas, Brasparts, Leon; and GWYNIO (see May 2). Henry VII gave the lordship of Glamorgan to his uncle, Jasper Tudor, in 1486, and Jasper renovated Cardiff Castle; William Parry of Northop executed in 1585 for allegedly plotting against Elizabeth; Copper was discovered on Parys Mountain in 1768, and it quickly became the greatest copper mine in the world; Michael Daniel Jones, founder of Patagonia*, born in 1822; In 1871, the rugby star W.J. (Billy) Bancroft was born in Swansea; In 1872, 19 miners died at Victoria Colliery, Ebbw Vale; John Peter Rhys (JPR) Williams, who revolutionised rugby full-back play, born in Cardiff in 1949; Champion golfer Ian Woosnam born in 1958

*'... a free farmer could tread his own land and enjoy on his own hearth, the song and harp and true Welsh fellowship... There will be chapel, school and parliament and the old language will be the medium of worship, of trade, of science, of education and of government. A strong and self-reliant nation will grow into a Welsh homeland.' -* Michael D. Jones proposing the establishment of Patagonia, the colony where women were allowed to vote before any other society in the world, and the first to give the franchise to anyone over the age of 18

**On this day...**

.................................................................................................................................

.................................................................................................................................

.................................................................................................................................

## March 3

*FEAST DAY OF SAINTS* NON 5th – 6th century (also March 2 and 5, June 15 and 25, July 3) at St Non's, Llannon, Dirinon, Altarnon and many others; GWENOLE 6th century (also April 28, June 20) at Landevennec, Gunwalloe, Locunole, Landewednack, Wonastow, Ganarew; GWYNNO 6th century at St Gwynno's at Vaynor, Llanpumsaint; LILY GWAS DEWI 5th - 6th century; and JAOUA at Brasparts, Leon, Daoulas, St Jaoua. Death in 1633 of the poet and cleric George Herbert; In 1770 the first Welsh-language magazine, 'Trysorfa Gwybodaeth' was published in Carmarthen; In 1861, 13 miners died at Blaengwawr Colliery, Aberdare; The actor-writer Arthur Llywelin Jones (Arthur Machen) was born in 1863 at Caerleon (see December 15); Edward Thomas*, poet, born in Lambeth of Tredegar parents in 1878; Birth at Rhostryfan in 1894 of the physicist and inventor William Ewart Williams (see April 29); J.G. Parry Thomas died in 'Babs' at Pendine Sands in 1927, trying to regain the world landspeed record; Death in 1932 of the physicist and educationist Ernest Griffiths (see June 15); In 1941, 51 people were killed in Cardiff and Penarth in German air-raids

*'The past is the only dead thing that smells sweet'* - Edward Thomas 1878-1917

*On this day...*

..................................................................................................................................

..................................................................................................................................

..................................................................................................................................

## March 4

FEAST DAY OF SAINT GISTLIANUS (GWESTLAN) 5th century at Hen Fynyw (also 2). In 1188, Giraldus Cambrensis began his 600-mile journey through Wales at New Radnor, campaigning for Welsh nobles to join the Crusade; Birth of Dr William Price* at Rudry, 1800 - the free-thinker, Chartist, herbalist, vegetarian, nudist, nationalist innovator of cremation; David Rice Aitchison, the Welsh-American senator for Missouri, served as President of the USA for just one day in 1849; First edition in 1857 of 'Baner Cymru'; Birth in 1906 of Dr Thomas Ellis Jones-Davies, who played as a centre for Llanelli, London Welsh and Wales (see August 25); Michael Barrett (Shakin' Stevens) born in Ely, Cardiff in 1948

*'You the coalowners... think that you can suck the life-blood out of the colliers for ever. You have grown fat and prosperous; you own the big houses; you wear the finest clothes; your children are healthy and happy; yet you do not work... Take heed, you men whose bodies are bloated by the life-blood of the poor, take heed before it is too late.'* - Dr William Price in 1880

*On this day...*

..................................................................................................................................

..................................................................................................................................

..................................................................................................................................

## March 5

FEAST DAY OF SAINTS CARON 7th century? Tregaron Fair was held on the 15th-17th March; and PIRAN d.480 (also November 18) Perranporth, Cardiff Castle. Madog ap Llywelyn was defeated at Maes Madog, outside Caereinion in 1295, ending the great rebellion which took Gwynedd and affected the rest of Wales; The Britannia Bridge across the Menai Straits opened in 1850; Frederick Hall Thomas, Freddie Welsh, world champion boxer, born in Pontypridd in 1886; Paulo Radmilovich born in Cardiff in 1886, and went on to win Olympic Gold swimming medals in 1908, 1912 and (after the Great War) 1920; David Watkins, Newport and Wales rugby union star, who had a glittering rugby league career, was born in Blaina in 1942; Alun Lewis, poet, died while serving with the South Wales Borderers in 1944 (see July 1); In 1985 colliers at the doomed Maerdy

Colliery were the last in Britain to return to work, after almost a year of strike - the pit closed a year later; In 1991, the last Cruise Missile left Greenham Common

*'The ancient history of Wales is a calendar of usurpations, depredations and murders.'* - 'A Gentleman's Tour Through Wales', Henry Penruddocke Wyndham, 1797

*On this day...*

## March 6

*FEAST DAY OF SAINTS* MILBURG (New Style see February 23); and SANNAN (see 1) in Brittany. Samuel Roberts (SR), the reformer and publisher, was born in Llanbrynmair in 1800 (see September 24); William Lewis and Lewis Johnson were killed at the Alamo in 1836; Birth at Tal-y-Sarn, Caernarfon in 1884 of Robert Williams Parry, poet and master of cynghanedd (see January 4); Ivor Novello (David Davies) died in 1951; An explosion sabotaged the Clywedog dam in 1966; The National Coal Strike began in 1984; The English critic A.N. Wilson sneered in 'The Evening Standard' in 1993 that *'the Welsh have never made any significant contribution to any branch of knowledge, culture or entertainment'*.

*'Man, n. An animal so lost in rapturous contemplation of what he thinks he is as to overlook what he indubitably should be. His chief occupation is extermination of other animals and his own species, which, however, multiplies with such insistent rapidity as to infest the whole habitable earth and Canada.'* - Ambrose Gwinnett Bierce, The Devil's Dictionary, 1911

*On this day...*

## March 7

*FEAST DAY OF SAINTS* DIER d.664 (also March 8) at Bodfari; ENODOC (see July 13); CYNGAR (see November 7) at the Llangefni Wake. Birth in 1670 or 1671 near Harlech of Ellis Wynne, cleric and author of 'Gweledigaethu y Bardd' (The Visions of the Sleeping Bard - see July 13); Birth in Swansea in 1890 of Arthur Tudor Edwards, pioneer of thoracic sugery and the first surgeon in Britain to remove a lung (see August 25); Death in 1949 of T. Gwynn Jones at Aberystwyth (see October 10); The 1966 Clywedog explosion of the previous day was attributed to the Free Wales Army; Death in 1967 of the philanthropist Sir David James, buried at Strata Florida (see May 13)

'*On March 7th, the day lengthens by the span of an ox-stride*' - Breton proverb

*On this day...*

........................................................................................................................................

........................................................................................................................................

........................................................................................................................................

# March 8

*FEAST DAY OF SAINTS* RHIAN 5th - 6th century at Llanrhian, DIER (see 7), SANNAN (see 1). In 1406, a letter from Charles VI promised Glyndŵr assistance if he would support the French Pope at Avignon; The 24th Regiment of Foot was formed in 1689, which later became the South Wales Borderers; Death in 1882 of Wiliam Bulkeley Hughes MP (see July 26); In 1877, 17 miners died at Worcester Pit, Swansea; The novelist Eric Linklater was born in Penarth in 1899

'*There is a statute of Henry VIII (27 Hen. 8, c.26) which absolutely requires that legal proceedings in Wales be conducted in English, legal proceedings had been in English for 300 years, and, moreover, the Welsh language is dying out ... probably the best thing that can happen to Wales is that the Welsh language should follow the Cornish into the limbo of dead languages.*' - The Lord Chancellor, in 1871, responding to a request from Osborne Morgan, MP, QC, for a Welsh-speaking judge in Wales, before appointing an English monoglot

*On this day...*

........................................................................................................................................

........................................................................................................................................

........................................................................................................................................

# March 9

*FEAST DAY OF SAINT* KING CONSTANTINE 6th century (also March 11, 13) at    St Merryn, Dunsford, Illogan. In the first census in 1801, the population of Wales was 587,245; Lady Charlotte Guest finished translating The Mabinogion in 1843; David Davies' workmen struck the Rhondda's richest seam of coal at Cwmparc in 1870, just as his company had run out of money to pay their wages; '*The Comedian's Comedian*', Tommy Cooper, was born in Caerffili in 1922; John Cale of 'The Velvet Underground', musician, was born in Garnant, Amman Valley in 1942; Terry Nation died in Los Angeles in 1997, aged 46 (see August 8)

*'The Welch are said to be so remarkably fond of cheese, that in cases of difficulty their midwives apply a piece of toasted cheese to the janua vitae to attract and entice the young Taffy, who on smelling it makes the most vigorous efforts to come forth'* - Francis Grose, 'A Classical Dictionary of the Vulgar Tongue' 1800

*On this day...*

...........................................................................................................................
...........................................................................................................................
...........................................................................................................................

## March 10

*FEAST DAY OF SAINT* AILBE (New Style see September 16). In 1295, 500 of Madog ap Llywelyn's army were slaughtered in their sleep by Edward I's men, at Maes Madog, Caereinion; In 1414, Glyndŵr's forces at Bala surrendered to the English; Iolo Morganwg (Edward Williams), saviour of Welsh culture, born at Pennon near Llancarfan in 1747 (see December 18); In 1846, William Williams urged the government for an inquiry into the state of education in Wales, leading to the *'Treason of the Blue Books'* in April 1847; In 1858, Mary Anne Edmunds died in Ruthin (see April 25); Birth in 1867 at Llansadwrn of Llewelyn William Williams, lawyer, author and MP who opposed the Boer War and the Great War (see April 22); 86 miners killed in Morfa Colliery, Taibach, Port Talbot in 1890; 33 miners killed at Cambrian No. 1 Pit, the Rhondda in 1905 (see May 17); Terry Holmes, scrum-half for Cardiff, Wales and the British Lions, born in 1957; Jimmy Wilde of Tylorstown, *'the greatest pound-for-pound fighter in the world'*, died in 1969 at Whitchurch Hospital (see May 12); Ray Milland of Neath died in California in 1986, aged 78 (see January 3)

*'Every day the (Welsh) Not, under its own weight as it were, would find its way from every corner of the school, to my neck. This is a comfort to me even today; I never tried to get rid of the Not by passing it on to someone else ... Damnable system, I am grateful when I remember that there is the hope that I shall see the time when I can dance on your grave. It was not the school-mistress's fault, but the system's ... I spoke one language, and the school-mistress another - and I learnt nothing. But for the Welsh Sunday School, I should be illiterate today.'* - Sir O. M. Edwards, 'Clych Atgof'.

*On this day...*

...........................................................................................................................
...........................................................................................................................
...........................................................................................................................

# March 11

FEAST DAY OF SAINTS LLIBIO (New Style see February 28); CONSTANTINE (see 9) in Scotland; and DYFRIG (see May 29) at Whitchurch near Monmouth. Rhys Gethin, victor of Pilleth, is defeated leading Glyndŵr's forces at Grosmont in 1405; Sir Richard Clough, husband of Catrin o'r Berain, died at Hamburg in 1570; The 41st Regiment of Foot, later the Welch Regiment, was formed in 1719; Birth in 1842 at Holywell of Sarah Edith Wynne (*Eos Cymru*), vocalist (see January 24); Death in 1864 of Richard Roberts, '*one of the greatest mechanical inventors of the 19th century*' (see April 22); The painter Thomas Brigstocke died in 1881 (see April 17); Birth in 1895 of Albert Edward Jenkins at Llanelli, one of Wales' greatest centre-threequarters (see October 7); Alcwyn Caryni Evans died at Carmarthen in 1902 (see May 14); Viscount Tredegar died in 1913 (see April 28); The composer Walford Davies died in 1941; 67 German prisoners-of-war escaped from Island Farm Camp, Bridgend in 1945

'*We state what appears to us to be an incontrovertible fact, that for English children no form of knowledge can take precedence of a knowledge of English, no form of literature can take precedence of English literature, and that the two are so inextricably connected as to form the only basis for a national education.*' - 1921 Government Report on 'The Teaching of English in England.'

*On this day...*

...............................................................................................................................

...............................................................................................................................

...............................................................................................................................

# March 12

FEAST DAY OF SAINT PEULIN 6th century (also October 10, November 22) at Pol de Leon, a founder Saint of Brittany - also at Llanddeusant, Ploudalmezau, Lamballe, and Llangors. SAINT DAVID'S DAY, OLD STYLE; The traditional flowering day of the daffodil. Llywelyn Bren was forced from besieging Caerffili Castle by two Norman armies in 1316; In 1853, 10 miners died at Risca Vale Colliery, Gwent; Death in 1860 of Evan Jones, '*the last of the Usk japanners*'; The Welsh Football (Rugby) Union was founded in Neath in 1881; Tommy Farr '*The Tonypandy Terror*', born in 1914, who was narrowly defeated by Joe Louis for the World Heavyweight Boxing Championship in 1937 (see March 1 and August 30); In 1950, the world's greatest air disaster at that time occurred at Llandow airport in the Vale of Glamorgan. An Avro Tudor V airplaine, returning from the Ireland-Wales rugby international, crashed, killing its crew of 5, and 75 out of 78 passengers; The Parliament for Wales Campaign was launched at Caernarfon in 1951; Gelignite found in Elan Valley water pipeline at Crossgates, Llandrindod wells, in 1967; The rugby legend Willie Llewellyn died in Pontyclun in 1973

On this day in 1188, Giraldus Cambrensis passed through Caerleon and wrote: '*We went through Caerleon, passing far away on our left Monmouth Castle and the great Forest of Dean, which is across the Wye, but still on this side of the Severn, and which supplies Gloucester with venison and iron ore. We spent the night in Newport. We had to cross the river Usk three times. Caerleon is the modern name for the City of the Legions. In Welsh "caer" means a city or encampment. The legions sent to this island by the Romans had the habit of wintering in this spot, and so it came to be called the City of the Legions. Caerleon is of unquestioned antiquity. It was constructed with great care by the Romans, the walls being built of brick. You can still see many vestiges of its one-time splendour. There are immense palaces, which, with the gilded gables of their roofs, once rivalled the magnificence of ancient Rome. They were set up in the first place by some of the most eminent men of the Roman state, and they were therefore embellished with every architectural conceit. There is a lofty tower, and besides it remarkable hot baths, the remains of temples and an amphitheatre. All this is enclosed within impressive walls, parts of which still remain standing. Wherever you look, both within and without the circuit of these walls, you can see constructions dug deep into the earth, conduits for water, underground passages and air-vents. Most remarkable of all to my mind are the stoves, which once transmitted heat through narrow pipes inserted in the side-walls and which are built with extraordinary skill.'*

On this day...

..................................................................................................

..................................................................................................

..................................................................................................

## March 13

FEAST DAY OF SAINTS TEWDWR 6th century (also October 14/15) at Darowain; and CONSTANTINE (see 9). Sir Gelly Meyrick of Lamphey was executed after the Earl of Leicester's unsuccessful revolt in 1601; Harlech Castle surrendered to Parliamentarians in 1647, the last castle except Raglan in England and Wales to hold out for Charles I; Burial in 1704 of Thomas Sebastian Price of Llanfyllin, popish recusant and antiquary; Birth at Llanharan in 1828 of Thomas Morgan Thomas, missionary to Matabele-land (see January 8); In 1889, 20 miners died at Brynally Colliery, Pentre Broughton, Clwyd; 'Two-Ton' Tessie O'Shea, entertainer, born in Riverside, Cardiff in 1914; Vernon Hartshorn of Pont-y-Waun, Labour politician and Cabinet member, died in 1931 at Maesteg; Death in 1963 of Margaret Davies (see December 14)

*'Three things must be united*
*Before good can come of them:*
*Thinking well, speaking well, and acting well'* - from the Welsh Triads of Virtues

On this day...

..................................................................................................

..................................................................................................

..................................................................................................

**March 14**

FEAST DAY OF SAINTS BISHOP CYNOG d. 606 at Llangynog; and CARON (see 5). Death of Sir Huw Wheldon in 1986 of lung cancer, aged 69. His memorial service was in Westminster Abbey, and David Attenborough called him 'the best Director-General the BBC never had' (see May 7)

*'A mine spreads out its vast machinery.*
*Here engines, with their vast huts and smoky stacks,*
*Cranks, wheels and rods, boilers and hissing steam,*
*Press'd up the water from the depths below.*
*Here fire-whims ran till almost out of breath,*
*And chains cried sharply, strain'd with fiery force.*
*Here blacksmiths hammer'd by the sooty forge,*
*And there a crusher crashed the copper ore.*
*Here girls were cobbing under roofs of straw,*
*And there were giggers at the oaken hutch.*
*Here a man-engine glided up and down,*
*A blessing and a boon to mining men:*
*And near the spot where, many years before,*
*Turn'd round and round the rude old water-wheel,*
*A huge fire-stamp was working evermore,*
*And slimy boys were swarming at the trunks.*
*The noisy lander by the trap-door bawled*
*With pincers in his hand; and troops of maids*
*With heavy hammers brake the mineral stones.*
*The cart-man cried, and shook his broken whip;*
*And on the steps of the account-house stood*
*The active agent, with his eye on all.'*
- lines from 'The Mine' by John Harris (1820-1884)

*On this day...*

.....................................................................................................................................
.....................................................................................................................................
.....................................................................................................................................

**March 15**

FEAST DAY OF SAINTS ARWYSTL HEN (ARISTOBULUS) d.99 at Glastonbury or Ynys Enlli (also 17); and TEWDWR (see October 15). Alternative date in 1405 of the Battle of Pwll Melyn (see May 5); In 1920, Billy Meredith was the oldest man to play in an international match - he was 45 years and 8 months and inspired Wales to beat England 2:1; Tonypandy's Tommy Farr won the British and Empire Heavyweight titles in London in 1937

*'Crown Buckley Brown Ale - The regal name Crown sat oddly on the shoulders of a brewery once devoted entirely to supplying working men's clubs. The Crown Brewery,*

of Pontyclun, South Wales, merged in 1989 with Buckley's, not far away in the tinplate town of Llanelli. Buckley's, once run by a minister of the Wesleyan Church, was later acquired by Brains. The name Crown survives in this brown ale, in the traditional dark, sweetish, low-alcohol style rather than the paler, stronger, drier type found in the northeast of England. Crown Buckley Brown Ale is nutty, toasty, and jammy, with a delicate touch of balancing hop dryness.' - Michael Jackson, 'Great Beer Guide'

*On this day...*

.....................................................................................................................................

.....................................................................................................................................

.....................................................................................................................................

## March 16

FEAST DAY OF SAINT CARON (see 5) at Glastonbury or Ynys Enlli. Graduation in Oxford in 1593 of Dr John Davies of Mallwyd, one of the greatest Welsh scholars (see May 15); In 1689, the 23rd Regiment of Foot was founded, later the Royal Welch Fusiliers, and now part of the Royal Regiment of Wales; Birth in 1759 at Llanmaes of Sir John Nichol, MP and King's Advocate (see August 26); Birth near Trefeglwys, Montgomeryshire in 1827 of Benjamin Piercy, famous civil engineer, friend of Garibaldi, who built railways and bridges across Wales, Sardinia, Italy and France (see March 24); Birth in 1906 at Cardiff of Maurice Turnbull, rugby player and the first Welsh cricketer to gain an English cricket cap

'To place, the kind of present a proud man would never want, a halter on the head of the King of France. To be a barber in the style of Erbin's son with lance and sword, the heavy tools of battle: to shave with his hand and strength, heads and beards as they come and swiftly set flowing their blood over their feet. A sad business for some.' - excerpt from Iolo Goch's eulogy to Hywel ap Gruffydd (Syr Hwyl y Fywall, Sir Hywel of the Battle-Axe, d.c.1381, a hero at Crecy in 1346)

*On this day...*

.....................................................................................................................................

.....................................................................................................................................

.....................................................................................................................................

## March 17

FEAST DAY OF SAINT JOSEPH OF ARIMATHEA 1st century at Glastonbury, Llanilid (also July 31, March 17, 27); PADRIG (PATRICK) c. 390-461 at Banwen, Armagh; PEULIN AP PAWL HEN 6th century at Llanbeulan (also November 1, 2); LLONIO (see 1); and PADRIG ab ALFRYD 6th century at Llanbadrig. Death in 1570 of William Herbert, 1st Earl of Pembroke (of the second creation); Sir Harford Jones (Brydges), PC and first ambassador to Persia, died in 1847 (see January 12); Lady Llanover died in 1896; Bobby Jones, the world's greatest amateur golfer, was born in 1902; Brenda Chamberlain, poet-painter, born in Bangor in 1912; Sir William Davies, journalist and editor, died in 1935 (see October 7); Wales won rugby's 'quadruple Triple Crown', by beating England in 1979, having also won it in 1976, 1977 and 1978

*'I love her foreshore and her mountains, her castle near the woods and her cultivated land, her water meadows, her valleys and her fountains, her white seagulls and gracious women ... I love her armed men, their trained stallions, her woodland, her heroes and their homes. I love the small clover on her pastures where I was honoured with a certain joy. I love all her special places to which my valour entitles me, all the wide wasteland and the wealth that hides there.'* - the poet-prince Hywel ap Owain Gwynedd, killed in 1170 at Pentraeth in Anglesey, battling against his half-brothers for Owain's kingdom. Another brother was Madoc who allegedly discovered America.

**On this day...**

....................................................................................................................................

....................................................................................................................................

....................................................................................................................................

# March 18

*FEAST DAY OF SAINT FINAN* 6th century at Llanffinan. In 1791 the emigrant ship 'Betty and Mary' sank in the Dee estuary, drowning 46 passengers; Wales won the British Football Championship for the first time in 1907; Death of Cardiff's great benefactor, the second Marquis of Bute, in 1848 at Cardiff Castle (until given to Cardiff Council by the Butes in 1947, the castle possibly had the longest recorded unbroken habitation of any building in the British Isles)

*'The name Wales does not come from that of a leader called Walo, or from a queen called Gwendolyn, as we are wrongly told in Geoffrey of Monmouth's fabulous "History", for you will find neither of these among the Welsh who ever lived. It is derived from one of the barbarous words brought in by the Saxons when they seized the kingdom of Britain. In their language the Saxons apply the adjective "vealh" to anything foreign, and, since the Welsh were certainly a people foreign to them, that is what the Saxons called them. To this day our country continues to be called Wales and our people Welsh, but these are barbarous terms.'* - 'The Description of Wales', Giraldus Cambrensis (1145-1223)

**On this day...**

....................................................................................................................................

....................................................................................................................................

....................................................................................................................................

## March 19

*FEAST DAY OF SAINTS JOSEPH 1st century; and CYNBRYD 5th century at Llandulas.* Edward I's Statute of Wales, signed at Rhuddlan, dismantled much Welsh Law and penalised the Welsh people in 1284; Death in 1804 of Philip Yorke of Erddig Hall, Welsh antiquary; In 1934 a monument was raised at Merthyr to commemorate the centenary of Richard Trevithick's death; In 1804 the world's first locomotive had run from Merthyr; In the 100th Grand National in 1937, the Welsh jockey Evan Williams of Cowbridge won on the Welsh-owned and trained 'Royal Mail'; In 1983, Colin Jones of Gorseinon drew in the World Welterweight Title boxing match in Reno, Nevada

*'One thing I am sure of. Some kind of human society, though God knows what kind, will no doubt go on occupying these two Western peninsulas of Britain, but that people, who are my people and no mean people, who have for a millennium and a half lived in them as a Welsh people, are now nothing but a naked people under an acid rain.'* - concluding lines in 'When Was Wales' by Gwyn Alf Williams, 1985

*On this day...*

................................................................................................................

................................................................................................................

................................................................................................................

## March 20

*FEAST DAY OF SAINT RHIAN (see 8).* Llywelyn Bren surrendered at Ystrafellte to the Normans, on condition that his followers were spared in 1317; On this day in 1284, Llywelyn II's kingdom of Gwynedd was divided into the counties of Anglesey, Caernarfon and Merioneth, with English sheriffs appointed to control them; In 1852, the palaeographer John Gwenogvryn Evans was born at Llanybyther (see March 25); Death of William Burges in 1881, the architect responsible for the restoration of Cardiff Castle and Castell Coch for the 3rd Marquis of Bute; Wyn Davies of Newcastle Football Club and Wales was born in Caernarfon in 1942

In St Marys' Church Conwy the Rev. John Parker noted the memorial of Nicholas Hookes: *'Here lyeth Ye Body of Nicks. Hookes of Conway Gent. Who was Ye 41st child of his Father WM. Hookes Esq., by Alice his Wife, and Ye Father of 27 children, who dyed Ye 20th Day of March 1637.'*

*On this day...*

................................................................................................................

................................................................................................................

................................................................................................................

# March 21

FEAST DAY OF SAINT ENDA (see 31); ALBAN EILER DAY - in the Celtic calendar, when the days begin to become longer than the nights. Llywelyn II's final War began on Palm Sunday in 1282, with an attack by his brother Dafydd on Hawarden Castle; David Griffiths, missionary, died in Machynlleth in 1863 (see December 20); Birth at Llandaf in 1713 of Francis Lewis, signatory of the American Declaration of Independence (see December 31); The North Wales Quarrymen's Union was formed in 1874; Lady Llanover was born in 1802; Gus Risman, the Welsh rugby union and league star, was born in Cardiff in 1911 - his son Bev went on to represent England at both codes; Michael Heseltine, the Conservative who overthrew Thatcher, was born in Swansea in 1933; Timothy Dalton, actor, was born in Colwyn Bay in 1946; Death of the blind harpist David Roberts near Llanaber in 1956

*'Despite the rapid decline in the percentage of monoglot Welsh speakers and the more gradual decline in the percentage of those able to speak the language, the actual number of Welsh speakers continued to increase. There were 930,000 of them in 1901 and more than a million in 1911; if the Cambrophones living outside Wales are taken into account, it is likely that as many as 1,100,000 people spoke Welsh in 1911 - the language's highest point, so far, in terms of numbers.'* - John Davies - 'A History of Wales' (the essential purchase for all Welsh people)

**On this day...**

..................................................................................................................................

..................................................................................................................................

..................................................................................................................................

# March 22

FEAST DAY OF SAINTS ELFODD d. 809 at Bangor; TIMOTHEUS (see 24); NICHOLAS OWEN. War broke out between Llywelyn II and England in 1282; A French army sailed from Brest to land in Wales and support Owain Glyndŵr in 1405; Birth in 1582 of John Williams, Archbishop of York and Civil War activist (see March 25); Thomas Charles Edwards of Bala died in 1900 (see September 22); The novelist Leslie Thomas was born in Newport in 1931; Flight Lieutenant Bryan Evans of Cyncoed was summarily executed in 1944 after the 'Great Escape' from Stalag Luft 3; John Toshack, Liverpool and Wales football player and Spanish manager, born in Cardiff in 1949; Hugh 'Binkie' Beaumont, impresario, died in 1973 (see March 27)

*'We started drinking at seven*
*And went out for a breather at ten,*
*And all the stars in Heaven*
*Said, Go back and drink again.'* - lines from Harri Webb's 'Big Night' 1963

**On this day...**

..................................................................................................................................

..................................................................................................................................

..................................................................................................................................

# March 23

FEAST DAY OF SAINT GWINEAR 6th century at St Gwinear's, St Guignar; The Liberal leader Clement Davies died in 1962 and is buried at Meifod (see February 19); 'Binkie' Beaumont found dead in bed (see March 22, 27)

*'The people of the Dominion of Wales have and do daily use a speech nothing like nor consonant to the natural mother tongue used within this realm... No person or persons that use the Welsh speech or language shall have or enjoy any manor, office or fees within the realm of England, Wales or other of the king's dominions upon pain of forfeiting the same offices or fees unless he or they use and exercise the speech or language of the English.'* - The Act of Union, 1536

*On this day...*

..................................................................................................................................

..................................................................................................................................

..................................................................................................................................

# March 24

FEAST DAY OF SAINTS TIMOTHEUS d.140 (also 22, August 22) - martyred in Rome, the grandson of Caradog; FFRAID (see February 1); and NYFAIN (see August 15). Llywelyn's War in 1282 advanced to Ceredigion; The red dragon on the royal arms was replaced by a unicorn, on the accession of James VI of Scotland as James I of England, on this day in 1603; Death at Marchwiel of the great engineer Benjamin Piercy in 1888 (see March 16); Death in 1939 of the great Gwyn Nicholls, the Cardiff and Wales rugby centre; In 1968 an Aer Lingus Viscount crashed into the sea at Strumble Head, killing 61 passengers and crew; Maudie Edwards died aged 84, in 1991 (see October 16)

*'The Welsh are given neither to gluttony nor to drunkenness. They spend little on food or clothes. Their sole interest in life consists of caring for their horses and keeping their weapons in good order, their sole preoccupation the defence of their fatherland and the seizing of booty. From morning to evening they eat nothing, devoting their whole energy to what business they have in hand and their whole day to their affairs, leaving everything else to chance. In the evening they eat a modest meal. If food is short or if they have none at all, they wait patiently for the next evening. Neither hunger nor cold can deter them. The spend the dark and stormy nights in observing the movement of their enemies.'* - Giraldus Cambrensis, 'The Description of Wales', 1193/1194

*On this day...*

..................................................................................................................................

..................................................................................................................................

..................................................................................................................................

# March 25

ANNUNCIATION - The Feast of the Annunciation; OUR LADY QUARTERDAY (also December 8 Conception and August 15 Assumption) - Old Lady Day was April 6 when new agricultural appointments were taken up. In 1188 Giraldus Cambrensis and Archbishop Baldwin stayed at Cruker Castle*, near Old Radnor, on their journey through Wales; Death in 1650 of Archbishop John Williams, near Llandygai (see March 22); In the Celtic Christian calendar, the earliest date for Easter. In 1807 the Swansea-Mumbles Railway, the world's first fare-paying passenger railway, opened; Death in 1855 of the actuary Griffith Davies (see December 5); In 1876, Wales played its first international football match, losing to Scotland in Glasgow; Jane Williams (Ysgafell) died in 1915; Dorothy Squires, singer, was born in Pontyberem in 1915; In 1930, John Gwenogvryn Evans died, aged 78, and was buried in a rock-grave near his house at Llanbedrog (see March 20); 1936 saw the largest mass trial ever held in Britain, with 53 men and 3 women imprisoned for rioting during the Bedlinog mining dispute in October 1935

*Giraldus wrote when in Cruker: 'At this point I must tell you what happened, in the reign of Henry I, King of the English, to the castellan of Radnor Castle, in the territory of Builth, which is not far away, being adjacent to his own lands, which he himself had conquered. He had gone into the church of St Afan, called Llanafan in Welsh, and there he had spent the night with his dogs, which was a foolish and irreverent thing to do. He got up at first light, as hunters are wont to do, but he found that all his dogs had gone mad and that he himself was blind. He had lost his sight completely and he had to grope his way out with his hand. From that day onwards he passed all his days in tedium and darkness. Then he conceived the happy idea of having himself led all the way to Jerusalem, for he did not wish his spiritual light to be extinguished as his eyes had been. Surrounded by a group of his friends, he had himself armed and, sitting on a strong warhorse, he was conducted by his men to where the war was being fought. He charged forward in the front line, but was immediately struck down by a blow from a sword and so ended his life with honour.'

On this day...

..................................................................................................................
..................................................................................................................
..................................................................................................................
..................................................................................................................

# March 26

FEAST DAY OF SAINTS GOVAN (see June 20); and TIMOTHY (see 24). Llywelyn's War in 1282 spread to Ystrad Tywi; In 1823, the 'Alert' sank off the Skerries, Anglesey, with over 100 drowning; Thomas (Tennessee) Williams, playwright, born in 1911, with ancestors from Llangallen; In 1920 the great jockey Jack Anthony of Cydweli won his 3rd Grand National on Troytown, having won in 1915 on Ally Sloper and in 1911 on Glenside; The Grand Pavilion, Victoria Pier, in Colwyn Bay, was destroyed by fire in 1922; Death of the great statesman David Lloyd George at Llanystumdwy in 1945; In 1984, all of the pits in Wales went on strike, following Arthur Scargill's call to stop pit closures, although only 10 of the 28 South Wales pits voted in favour. When dispassionate historians look at the illegalities and procedures employed by the state and police towards miners in the following few months, including the tampering of the film footage at Orgrave, they will wonder at the nature of democracy in 20th century Britain. Only 6% of South Wales miners returned to work before the strike was called off, with not one strike-breaker in Maerdy Colliery (see March 5)

*'Easter forced itself on men's notice as a visible sign of dischord, since the sudden transition from the gloom of Holy Week to the rejoicings of the Day of Resurrection was an event in the Christian year to catch the attention of the most careless, and to see one Christian still keeping to the Lenten Fast while another at his side was in the midst of Easter revels brought out in the clearest fashion how far they were from dwelling as brethren in unison together. In this way it came about that as the result of one rule, the Celtic Easter often anticipated the Roman by a week, while occasionally, through the operation of another, it would fall no less than four weeks later. Among the Celts (Welsh) 25th March was the earliest possible Easter Day, 21st April the latest, while at Rome the range of oscillation was from 22nd March to 25th April. As a result of these conflicting calculations, it was the exception for the two Easters to coincide'* - Sir John Lloyd, 'A History of Wales' 1911

**On this day...**

........................................................................

........................................................................

........................................................................

# March 27

FEAST DAY OF SAINTS GWYNLLIW 5th-6th century (also March 28, 29) at St Woolos Cathedral; TYFAI 6th century, Wales' only child saint, at Llandyfeisant, Penally, Lamphey, Foy, Lampha (also October 6); JOSEPH of ARIMATHEA (see 17); Hugh (Binkie) Beaumont, theatrical impresario, was born Hughes Griffiths Morgan in 1908 (see March 22); Death in 1932 of Frederick Charles Richards in 1932 (see December 1); Dick Richardson of Newport won the European Heavyweight boxing title, in Dortmund in 1960

*'(The Welsh) use light weapons which do not impede their quick movements, small leather corselets, handfuls of arrows, long spears and round shields. They wear helmets and sometimes iron greaves. Their leaders ride into battle on swift mettlesome horses which are bred locally. Most of the common people prefer to fight on foot, in view of the marshy, uneven terrain. The horsemen often dismount, as circumstance or occasion demand, ready to flee or to attack. They go barefoot or else wear boots of untanned*

*leather roughly sewn together. By marching through the deep recesses of the woods and climbing mountain peaks in times of peace, the young men train themselves to keep on the move both day and night. In peace they dream of war and prepare themselves for war by practising with their spears and their arrows.'* - Giraldus Cambrensis, 'The Description of Wales', 1193/1194

**On this day...**

..................................................................................................................................

..................................................................................................................................

..................................................................................................................................

## March 28
*FEAST DAY OF SAINT GWYNLLIW* (see 27); TRADITIONAL DATE OF THE BIRTH OF JESUS also April 18 and May 29. James Duke of Monmouth, the son of Lucy Walter of Roch Castle, Pembroke, was empowered to use the Royal Arms in 1663; Daniel Evans of Llanfihangel Ystrad, Ceredigion (Daniel Ddu o Geredigion, born 1792), cleric and poet, committed suicide in 1846, and is buried in Pencarreg; Neil Kinnock, Labour Party leader, was born in Tredegar in 1942; Alex Templeton of Cardiff, jazz pianist, died in Connecticut in 1963

*'The span of the Cross is wider by far*
*than their Puritanism and Socialism,*
*and there is a place for Karl Marx's fist in His Church;*
*farm and furnace live together in His estate,*
*the humanism of the coal-mine, the godliness of the country,*
*Tawe and Tywi, Canaan and Wales, earth and heaven.'*
- lines transalted from Gwenallt's 'Sir Forgannwg a Sir Gaerfyddin' (Glamorgan and Carmarthenshire)

**On this day...**

..................................................................................................................................

..................................................................................................................................

..................................................................................................................................

## March 29
*FEAST DAY OF SAINT GWLADYS* 5th-6th century (with her husband Gwynlliw) at Pencannau, Capel Gwladys. Date of the famous Pennal Letter* of Owain Glyndŵr to Pope Benedict XIII at Avignon in 1406; Christening in 1752 of Edward Jones (*Bardd y Brenin*) at Llandderfel, harpist and antiquary (see April 18); Death in 1834 of the eccentric and sportsman John Mytton of Dinas Mawddwy, in the King's Bench Debtors' Prison; On this day in 1851, there were 976,490 attendances in places of worship in Wales, out of a population of

1,163,139, indicating that 'everyone capable of attending a place of worship had done so' - John Davies; R.S. Thomas, one of Wales' greatest poets, born in Cardiff in 1913; In 1915 the liner Falaba was torpedoed off the Pembroke coast, with 104 people dying; In 1924, Billy Meredith of Manchester City played in a Cup semi-final, aged 49 years and 8 months; Death in 1932 of the folk-lorist Jonathan Ceredig Davies (see May 22)

*The Pennal letter laid down four conditions for Glyndŵr's support of Charles VI's French papacy at Avignon: That the Welsh Church sould be independent of Canterbury, with St David's as its Archbishopric, with control over 5 dioceses in England including Cornwall; That only Welsh-speaking Welshmen should be appointed to Church duties in Wales; That the Welsh Church should take possession of all church property in Wales, so that no revenues should be taken to England; and that Wales should have two universities, one in the North and one in the South, so that Welshmen need not go to English universities. Finally the false 'Henry of Lancaster' (Henry IV) who had deposed and murdered Richard II, should be excommunicated

*On this day...*

........................................................................................................

........................................................................................................

........................................................................................................

# March 30
FEAST DAY OF SAINT ROBERT FERRAR d. 1555 - executed at Carmarthen; Rawlins White was executed in Cardiff for heresy in 1555; Holy Day of John Keble, priest and teacher (1886). Death in 1822 of the poet and man of letters David Thomas of Waun-fawr (*Dafydd Ddu Eryri*); Rolf Harris, entertainer-artist, born in Australia to Cromwell and Agnes Harris of Cardiff in 1930; In 1957 Dai Dower of Abercynon lost the World Flyweight Championship in Buenos Aires; In 1980, over 50 people were arrested in night-time raids upon suspicion of arson of holiday homes - none were charged

'Three things are becoming for a man:
Knowledge, good deeds, and
Gentleness' - from the Welsh Triads of Virtues

*On this day...*

........................................................................................................

........................................................................................................

........................................................................................................

# March 31

FEAST DAY OF SAINT ENDA d.530 (also 21) at Aranmore. Birth in 1834 of Thomas Rees Morgan at Penydarren, mechanical engineer, inventor and founder of the Morgan Engineering Company in America (see September 6); In 1920, the Church in Wales was disestablished; Sir Henry Walford Davies died in 1941 (see September 6); The miners' leader, Dai Francis, died in Cardiff in 1981; Cardiff Bay Development Corporation was wound up in 2000, after 13 years of development of old docks land

'A street of miserable cottages one of which is the inn comprises the city of St David's. I had so little notion of it being the bishopric that I inquired in the street how far it was to St David's... The whole church is in a very dirty and slovenly condition, part of it is not paved, and the graves are raised within it, in the same manner as in common churches. There is something simple and pleasing in the idea of strewing flowers and evergreen over the grave of a departed friend, which is the universal custom in these parts. But when we saw the faded plants rotting on new raised earth within the walls of the church it became offensive and disgusting.' - Henry Penruddock Wyndham, 1774

*On this day...*

..................................................................................................................

..................................................................................................................

..................................................................................................................

# APRIL - EBRILL
### Ebrel or Imbrel (Breton), Ebral (Cornish)

EASTER- of all the festivals in Wales at Easter, Mabsant Tudful at Merthyr
Tudful was probably the greatest

## April 1

*FEAST DAY OF SAINTS* TEGFAN 6th century (Easter Monday) at
Llandegfan; and KING TEWDRIG d.470 (also January 3) at Mathern, Llandow,
Bedwas, Merthyr Tudful. Conwy Castle was taken in 1401, by Glyndŵr's allies,
the Tudors of Anglesey, and then besieged by 500 men under Hotspur; Birth of
Edmund Jones, *'The Old Prophet'*, Calvinist preacher, in Aberystruth, Gwent in
1702; Birth of Robert Davies, philanthropist, at Llangefni in 1816 (see December
29); *'The Treason of the Blue Books'* - The Report of the Commission of Inquiry
into the State of Education in Wales - was published in 1847; Frederick William
Gibbins, philanthropic Quaker industrialist, tinplate magnate and MP, was born
in Neath in 1861 (see July 30); Death in Patagonia in 1899 of Abraham
Matthews of Llanidloes, minister and historian; In 1920, the Disestablishment of
the Church in Wales Bill came into force. Anglicanism was no longer the official
religion of Wales; Last flight from Cardiff's Pengam Moors airport, as Cardiff
Airport was transferred to Rhoose in 1954 (this gave the Vale of Glamorgan, an
area that Stan Awbery MP wanted designated as a National Park, airports at
Llandow, St Tathan and Rhoose, with a polluting power station on the beautiful
site of the ancient port of Aberthaw); In 1963, there was another sabotage
attempt at Trywerin Reservoir; 1970 saw the Pontypridd 'School of Mines'
designated as the Polytechnic of Wales; In 1974 there was the bizarre
reorganisation of Wales' 13 ancient counties into 8; In 1995, the Welsh Folk
Museum, for some unknown reason, was redesignated the Museum of Welsh Life;
Cardiff Harbour Authority took over the Cardiff Bay barrage and lake in 2000

*'Perhaps it would be difficult to point out any other country in the world in which the
peasantry and lower classes feel such an interest in literary and intellectual pursuits as
the people of Wales do.'* (-1824 Mold Eisteddfod speech) ... *'I have no hesitation in
asserting that the Welsh language at the present day to the Welsh peasant is a much more
cultivated and literary medium of knowledge than the English is to an Englishman of the
same class ... Show me another language in the world in which such a body of
knowledge is found in the hands of the common people! Show me another race of man
on the face of the earth among whom the labouring classes are the entire patrons of the
press.'* (1826 Brecon Eisteddfod speech) - Rev. Thomas Price (Carnhuanawc)

*On this day...*

....................................................................................................................

....................................................................................................................

....................................................................................................................

....................................................................................................................

....................................................................................................................

# April 2

Troops were called into Denbigh to stop rioting in 1795; Death in 1877 of the pioneer bone-setter Thomas Rocyn Jones of Manordeifi; Edward Thomas Chapman of Pontlottyn, serving with the Monmouthshire regiment, won the Victoria Cross in Germany in 1945; An earthquake with its epicentre in mid-Wales, measured 5.2 on the Richter Scale, a British record in 1990

*'Raisins, currants, and venison*
*Roasted - this is no boast - and bitterns...*
*Above Ireland the sky's pitch black*
*From the smoke of Anglesey's kitchens'* - Lewys Glyn Cothi (fl. 1447-1486)

*On this day...*

.........................................................................................................................

.........................................................................................................................

.........................................................................................................................

# April 3

Holy Day of Bishop Richard (1253) at Chichester. Reginald de Grey was captured by Glyndŵr at the Battle of Ruthin in 1402, and a ransom note delivered to Parliament. The hated baron, the cause of the war, was taken into imprisonment at Dolbadarn Castle; George Herbert*, divine and poet, was born in Montgomeryshire in 1593; Death of Thomas Edwards of Llanefydd (Twm o'r Nant), poet, in 1810, aged 71; John Ormond Thomas, poet and film-maker, born in Dunvant in 1923 (see May 4); Cardiff Bay Development Corporation was set up in 1987

*'Let all the world in every corner sing,*
*My God and King.*
*The heavens are not too high,*
*His praise may thither fly:*
*The earth is not too low,*
*His praises there may grow.*
*Let all the world in every corner sing,*
*My God and King.*
*The church with psalms must shout,*
*No door can keep them out:*
*But above all, the heart*
*Must bear the longest part.*
*Let all the world in every corner sing,*
*My God and King'*
*- 'Antiphon', by George Herbert*

*On this day...*

.........................................................................................................................

.........................................................................................................................

.........................................................................................................................

## April 4

*FEAST DAY OF SAINTS* CYNIDR AP GWYNLLIW 6th century at Aberysgir, Llangynidr, Glasbury, Kenderchurch (also December 8); TEYRNOG 6th century (also September 25) at Llandyrnog; MERIN (see January 6); and GONERI (see July 18). The diocese of Swansea and Brecon was created in 1923; The brilliant rugby league star Lewis Jones was born in Gorseinon in 1931; 'The Times' reports in 1998 that Ron Davies MP, the Welsh Secretary, wishes to 'drop' the Welsh flag, the oldest national flag in the world. The South-African Welsh Minister Peter Hain agrees that the flag should be 'modernised'

*'The Welsh language is a vast drawback to Wales and a manifold barrier to the moral progress and commercial prosperity of Wales ... Whether in the country or among the furnaces, the Welsh element is never found at the top of the social classes ... his language keeps him under the hatches.'* - 1847 Report on Education in Wales, 'The Treason of the Blue Books' (*Brad y Llyfrau Gleision*)

*On this day...*

..................................................................................................................................

..................................................................................................................................

..................................................................................................................................

## April 5

*FEAST DAY OF SAINTS* DERFEL GADARN 6th century at Llanderfel; and BRYCHAN c. 390 - c. 450 (also 6); approximate date of PALM SUNDAY, SUL Y BLODAU (Flower Sunday). Francis Kilvert and Rev John Fisher noted the South Wales habit of dressing graves with flowers on Sul y Blodau. In 1859, 26 miners died in flooding at Chain Colliery, Neath; In 1891 the first language census showed the number of Welsh-speakers to be 1,685,614; The miners' leader Arthur Horner was born in Merthyr Tudful in 1895; T.E. Ellis, nationalist and Liberal politician, died in Cannes, aged 40 in 1899 (see February 16); Bette Davis, film-star, was born in 1908; The surreal village of Portmeirion was first opened to the public in 1926; Billy the Seal died in 1939, having lived in the pool at Cardiff's Victoria Park for 27 years; Petula Clark received one of the West End's greatest ovations at the closing curtain of 'Sunset Boulevard' in 1997

*'Three things which strengthen a man to stand against the whole world:*
*Seeing the quality and beauty of truth;*
*Seeing beneath the cloak of falsehood, and*
*Seeing to what ends truth and falsehood come.'* - from the Welsh Triads of Virtues

*On this day...*

..................................................................................................................................

..................................................................................................................................

..................................................................................................................................

# April 6

FEAST DAY OF SAINT BRYCHAN (see 5); OLD LADY DAY. Christening in 1774 at Abererch of John Elias, the most powerful preacher of his age (see June 8); In 1835, Edward Morgan was hanged at Monmouth for his role in the 'Scotch Cattle' disturbances; Death of Stephen Davies (1790-1858) of Prestatyn, poet, buried at Galltmelyd (Meliden); J.G. Parry Thomas, who went on to hold the world land-speed record, was born in Wrexham in 1884; In 1896, the Snowdon Mountain Railway opened; The BBC National Orchestra of Wales made its first broadcast in 1928; The wonderful 'miner-poet' Idris Davies* died at Rhymney in 1953 (see January 6); The Welshpool and Llanfair Light Railway reopened in 1963

*'They sold apples and geese and ponies
In the fair upon the moor
On fine September evenings
Years and years ago…
They cursed and laughed and haggled
Until the deals were done,
And lifted pots of beer
Against the autumn sun…
And the wily folk worked wonders
Upon the moor of old,
But the florins lasted longer
Than they who bought or sold…
And now the moor is silent,
With rougher winds to freeze
The lips of a Rhymney poet
Making bargains with the breeze.' - Idris Davies, 'Waun Fawr'

*On this day…*

...................................................................................................................................................
...................................................................................................................................................
...................................................................................................................................................

# April 7

FEAST DAY OF SAINTS BRYNACH* d570 at Cwm-yr-Eglwys, Nevern, Penllin, Llanfyrnach, Llanfernach, Henry's Moat, Llanboidy, Pontfaen, Lavernock; KING DOGED 6th century (also 22, and July 23, 27) at Llandoget; GORAN 5th century? at Goran, Bodmin; GWRNERTH 6th century at Welshpool (Trallwng); LLYWELYN 6th century at Welshpool; and GONERI (see July 18). Birth in 1866 of Charles Granville Bruce, Ghurka commander and mountaineer (see July 12); Birth at Llangiwg in 1873 of John Dyfnallt Owen, poet, writer, journalist and Archdruid of Wales (see December 28); Alfred George Edwards, Bishop of St Asaf, was elected first Archbishop of Wales in

1920; Cliff Morgan, the Cardiff, Wales and Lions outside-half, and sports broadcaster, was born in Trebanog in 1930; Rugby's new National Stadium was finished on the site of the Arms Park in 1984, but demolition began less than 13 years later, on March 16th, 1997, to make way for the Millennium Stadium - Cardiff RFC, on the ground alongside it, retained the Arms Park name

*'Nevern, signed with David's cross and Brynach's,
lay hushed and innocent. We stood
in the sunny churchyard. Tower and trees
rippled with heat-haze, as if a tiny breeze
passed over baptismal water
in a golden font. On Carn Ingli above,
Brynach walked with angels, the afternoon
was a pause in their conversation....' - Lines from Ruth Bidgood's 'At Nevern'

**On this day...**

....................................................................................................................................................
....................................................................................................................................................
....................................................................................................................................................

# April 8

FEAST DAY OF SAINT DYFAN 2nd century (also May 24 with Ffagan) at Merthyr Dyfan; Holy Day of Griffith Jones, priest and teacher (1761). In 1421, Mareddud ab Owain Glyndŵr accepts the King's Pardon, 20 years and 6 months after the Glyndŵr Rebellion began. He refused it in 1416 and 1417; In 1646 Ruthin Castle surrendered to Parliamentarians; Griffith Jones of Llanddowror, the man who made Wales the most literate nation in the world, died in 1761; Birth in 1880 of Thomas Thomas at Penygraig, Rhondda, first British middle-weight boxing champion, who trained with a bull (see August 13); Terry Nation, script-writer who also created the 'Daleks', born in Cardiff in 1930 (see March 9); Hywel Bennett, actor, born in Garnant, Amman Valley in 1944; Jack Howells won an Oscar in 1963 for the best short documentary, 'Dylan Thomas'; Death in 1963 of Clough Williams-Ellis, architect and creator of Portmeirion, 62 years and 3 days after his village was opened to the public; The novelist Richard Vaughan died in 1983

'Palace, n. A fine and costly residence, particularly that of a great official. The residence of a high dignitary of the Christian Church is called a palace; that of the Founder of his religion was known as a field, or wayside. There is progress.' - Ambrose Gwinnett Bierce, The Devil's Dictionary, 1911

**On this day...**

....................................................................................................................................................
....................................................................................................................................................
....................................................................................................................................................

# April 9

FEAST DAY OF SAINTS MADRUN & ANHUN 5th century at Minster, Trawsfynydd (also June 9, October 19). Lucy Walter's son James Duke of Monmouth was born in 1649 at Rotterdam; The Confederate armies of Jefferson Davis surrendered at Appomattox in 1865; Death of John Pughe (*Ioan ab Hu Feddyg*), physician and scholar, who translated 'The Physicians of Myddfai', in 1874; In 1917, at the Battle of Arras, the great poet Edward Thomas was blown to pieces on Easter Monday (see March 3); Frank Lloyd Wright*, the great American architect, died in 1959

*'*He was in league with the stones of the field and he taught his children to work hard until the valley blossomed like a garden. His New Wales. He planted a small world within the world that is again within other worlds, without end.'* - Frank Lloyd Wright recalling his US-immigrant grandfather

*On this day...*

............................................................................................................................................

............................................................................................................................................

............................................................................................................................................

# April 10

FEAST DAY OF SAINT ENDA (see April 30). Death in Paris in 1410 of Bishop William Trevor of St Asaph, diplomat for Owain Glyndŵr and arch-enemy of Henry IV and V; Death in 1630 of William Herbert, 3rd Earl of Pembroke, '*the pillar of the realm*', of apoplexy; Chartist Memorial Day, commemorating the democratic People's Charter of 1838; Captain Bernard Warburton-Lee of Maelor won the Second World War's first Victoria Cross at Narvik in 1940, on HMS Hardy; Wales played their last rugby match at Swansea in 1954; In 1957, work had been completed on Llandaff cathedral after the German bombing, and Epstein's statue of Christ in Majesty was consecrated, and the nave re-hallowed

'*It is interesting from its (Snowdon's) connection with history; it was to Snowdon that Vortigern retired from the fury of his own subjects, caused by the favour which he showed to the detested Saxons. It was here that he called to his counsels Merlin, said to be begotten on a hag by an incubus, but who was in reality the son of a Roman consul by a British woman. It was in Snowdon that he built his castle, which he fondly deemed would prove impregnable, but which his enemies destroyed by flinging wild fire over its walls; and it was in a wind-beaten valley of Snowdon, near the sea, that his dead body decked in green armour had a mound of earth and stones raised over it. It was on the heights of Snowdon that the brave but unfortunate Llewelyn ap Griffith made his last stand for Cambrian independence; and it was to Snowdon that that very remarkable man, Owen Glendower, retired with his irregular bands before Harry the Fourth and his numerous and disciplined armies, soon however to emerge from its defiles and follow the foe, retreating less from the Welsh arrows from the crags, than from the cold, rain and starvation of the Welsh hills... Who when he thinks of Snowdon does not associate it with the heroes of romance, Arthur and his knights?'* George Borrow, Wild Wales, 1862

**On this day...**

......................................................................................................................................

......................................................................................................................................

......................................................................................................................................

## April 11

*DEATH OF LLYWELYN FAWR, Llywelyn ap Iorwerth ab Owain Gwynedd* - in 1240, Llywelyn the Great*, Prince of Aberffraw and Lord of Eryri, died peacefully as a monk in Aberconwy, aged 67; 1241 - death at Abbey Dore, of Cadwgan, former Bishop of Bangor, placed in the see by the influence of his lord Llywelyn ab Iorwerth in 1212; Gilbert de Clare began constructing Caerffili Castle in 1268; Birth in 1722 to a Welsh mother of Cristopher Smart, madman and poet (see May 20); In 1862 Charles Evans Hughes was born - in 1916 he was narrowly defeated for the Presidency of the USA by Woodrow Wilson; In 1893, 63 miners were killed in an underground fire at the Great Western Pit, Pontypridd; Mel Charles, John's younger brother, scored 4 goals against Northern Ireland at Ninian Park in 1962; Cerys Matthews, formerly of Catatonia, born in Canton, Cardiff, in 1969; At Wembley Stadium in 1999, Tom Jones performed *'Delilah'* before the game where Scott Gibbs scored *'that try'* for Wales to fortunately beat England 32-31 and prevent their attaining the 'Grand Slam'

*\*'The following day he went in search of the ancient Abbey of Maenan but found little evidence of its existence. The foundations of the abbey had been discovered a few years previously by Lord Newborough, the then owner of the land. This had been the original Cistercian Abbey of Aberconwy established in the last decade of the 12th century by the monks of Stata Florida in Cardiganshire. It was removed to Maenan by Edward I in 1283 to make room for the building of his new castle at Conwy. The Abbey was demolished completely at the Dissolution and the timber and stones removed and used to repair the castle at Caernarfon.'* - John Parker, 'A Tour of Wales and its Churches', 1862. Edward symbolically built Conwy Castle upon the tomb of Llywelyn the Great

**On this day...**

......................................................................................................................................

......................................................................................................................................

......................................................................................................................................

# April 12

FEAST DAY OF SAINT IESTYN 6th century (also October 10, April 19, August 14) at Llaniestyn, Brittany; Holy Day of Bishop George Augustus Selwyn, missionary (1878). Robert Davies besieged at Gwysaney by William Brereton's Parliamentarians in 1645; Rowland Laugharne took the Royalist Aberystwyth Castle in 1646; Birth in 1790 of William Davies Evans at St Dogmael's, inventor of the tri-coloured light for shipping and 'the Williams Gambit' in chess (see August 3); First rugby international at Cardiff's Arms Park in 1884, Wales beating Ireland; Death in 2000 of the naturalist Ronald M. Lockley, who was born in Cardiff

*'As for the Diet of the Briton, it is not very delicate, neither is he curious in it; for if he sould, his Appetite perhaps might cure his Nicety, and by pleasing his palate, he may starve his Belly. A good Mess of Flummery, a Pair of Eggs he rejoices at as a Feast, especially if he may close his stomach with toasted Cheese; a Morsel of which he hath great Kindness for. You may see him pictured sometimes with a Crescent of Cheese and his Hat adorned with a Plume of Leeks: Good edible Equipage! Which, when Hunger pinches, he makes bold to nibble; he first eats his Cheese and his Leeks together, and for second Course, he devours his Horse.'* - 'A Collection of Welsh Travels and Memoirs of Wales', John Torbuck, 1738

*On this day...*

..........................................................................................................................

..........................................................................................................................

..........................................................................................................................

# April 13

FEAST DAY OF SAINTS CARADOG OF LLANCARFAN (d.1124) at Lawrenny, Haroldston East (also April 14); and GWYNNO (see October 26) in Scotland. Death in 1679 of the soldier Sir Thomas Morgan of Llangattock, who served in the Thirty Years War and for Parliamentary forces in the Civil War; In 1723 the Tal-y-Foel ferry sank near Caernarfon, with 33 drowning; Death in 1863 of Sir George Cornewall Lewis (see April 21); Death of Daniel Silvan Evans near Lanwrin in 1903 (see January 11); Birth at Tredegar in 1941 of Margaret Price, leading soprano; Death of Gwyn Thomas, writer, in Cardiff in 1969 (see July 6)

*'A peacock should be skinned, then the skin, feathers, head, wings and tail should be kept in one piece. According to Sion ab Ifan, Squire of Tref Drystan near Brecon in the mid-16th century and a typical Renaissance scholar-gentleman, the best way to do this was to make a small incision in its head, then through a quill blow quickly away between the skin and the flesh until the skin lifts away from the flesh. Roast the peacock in a sitting position. When cold, place on a dish with vinegar and powdered lombard (Lombardy mustard); then wind the skin and feathers, complete with tail, around the roasted bird.'* - 'Food of the Bards', Dr Enid Roberts

............................................................................................
............................................................................................
............................................................................................

# April 14

FEAST DAY OF SAINT CARADOG (see 13). In 1188 Giraldus Cambrensis ended his crusading journey around Wales; Around this date in 1212 King John hung several Welsh hostages, including the 7 year-old son of Maelgwn Gwynedd; Newport received its charter as a borough in 1385; The Act of Union between England and Wales was given Henry VIII's assent in 1536; Aberystwyth Castle was captured by Parliamentarians in 1646; John Evans* of Waunfawr, the great American explorer of the Missouri, was christened in 1770 (died May 1799); The poet, dramatist and eisteddfodwr Sir Albert Evans-Jones (Cynan) was born at Pwllheli in 1895 (see January 26); 'Black Friday' in 1921, when the dockers and railwaymen decided not to support the Miners' Strike which started on April 15th; Roy Vernon, the Wales football star, was born at Holywell in 1937; The Tenovus Cancer Research Centre, financed by Welsh businessmen and the Welsh people, opened at Cardiff's University Hospital of Wales in 1969; Dorothy Squires died in 1998

*'In my letter of 13th inst., I enclosed you a map of a Mr (John) Evans, a Welshman, employed by the Spanish government for that purpose, but whose original object I believe had been to go to search of the Welsh Indians said to be up the Missouri. On this subject a Mr Rees of the same nation established in the Western part of Pennsylvania will write to you.' - letter from President Jefferson in January 1804 to Meriwether Lewis before the Lewis and Clark Expedition

............................................................................................
............................................................................................
............................................................................................

# April 15

FEAST DAY OF SAINT BISHOP PADARN 5th-6th century (also 16, 17, 20, May 15, June 20, September 23, November 1) - Paternus, a Founder Saint of Brittany is remembered at Llanbadarn, Trefeglwys, Vannes. The novelist Emyr Humphries was born at Prestatyn in 1919; In 1921 coal miners across Great Britain with-held their labour. Wages had been reduced by 40-50% for the quarter of a million coal workers across Wales. The miners held out until June, but by the beginning of 1922, were working for half-pay; In 1946, the Welsh National Opera staged its first full productions; Tommy Cooper died, on stage, in 1984

*'I would sooner go to Hell than Wales'* - Herbert Asquith MP, 1905

*On this day...*

## April 16

*FEAST DAY OF SAINT PADARN* (see 15). Baron Aberdare born in 1815 at Duffryn, near Aberdare (see February 25); Sidney Gilchrist Thomas, steel innovator, was born in 1850; Birth in 1881 at Tregarth of Sir Ifor Williams, Welsh scholar and author (see November 4); The death in 1929 of Sir John Morris Jones, scholar, grammarian and poet, at Llanfairpwllgwyngyll; Death in 1938 of Sir William Price, who founded United Dairies; Cardiff's last trolley bus ran in 1966

*'In Wales no one begs. Everyone's home is open to all, for the Welsh generosity and hospitality are the greatest of all virtues. They very much enjoy welcoming others to their homes. When you travel there is no question of asking for accommodation or of their ofering it: you just march into a house and hand over your weapons to the person in charge. They give you water so that you may wash your feet and that means you are a guest. With these people the offering of water in which to wash one's feet is an invitation to stay. If you refuse the offer, it means that you have only dropped in for refreshment during the early part of the day and do not propose to stay the night.'* - - Giraldus Cambrensis, 'The Description of Wales', 1193/1194

*On this day...*

## April 17

*FEAST DAY OF SAINTS* DUNWYD (see August 17); GWERYDD (ARVIRAGUS?) 1st century? at St Donat's (Llanwerydd). Henry Vaughan, the metaphysical poet, was born at Llansantffraed in 1622; Thomas Brigstocke, the portrait painter, was born in Carmarthen in 1809 (see March 11); Death in 1919 of the honoured missionary Timothy Richard, whose name *'Li T'i-mo-tai'* was a household word in China (see October 10); In 1993, Steve Robinson of Cardiff won the WBO Featherweight Title

*'Cinnamon, saffron and incense,*
*Stag broth and raisins and currants,*
*And Lowri has, as I have heard,*
*Cloves and canel* (a type of cinnamon), *oranges and mace.*
*Hundreds of apples are carried here,*
*And walnuts and pears and wine.'* - lines written by Tudur Aled (fl.1480-1526) about Dolgynwal, Ysbyty Ifan, Betws-y-Coed

*On this day...*

..........................................................................................................................................

..........................................................................................................................................

..........................................................................................................................................

# April 18
FEAST DAY OF SAINT NECTAN (see February 14); TRADITIONAL DATE OF BIRTH OF JESUS (also March 28 and May 29). Death of 'Judge Jeffries' in prison in 1699 (see May 15); Death of the King's Harpist, Edward Jones, in 1824 (see March 29); Conwy Railway Bridge opened in 1848; The Welsh football star Roy Paul was born at Ton Pentre in 1920; Wales' sadly missed 'Empire Pool' was opened in 1958

*'... like a growing child I am now trying to master a new language - the Welsh language. I learn Welsh not only in order to know the riches of Welsh literature ... but in order to come nearer to the soul of the Welsh.'* - Kate Bosse-Griffiths, 1942

*On this day...*

..........................................................................................................................................

..........................................................................................................................................

..........................................................................................................................................

# April 19
FEAST DAY OF SAINT IESTYN (see April 12) in Brittany. Richard Price, Wales' greatest thinker, honoured in America and France, died in 1791; In 1823 Anna Laetitia Waring, hymn-writer, was born near Neath; Death in 1874 of the architect Owen Jones (see February 15); The novelist Richard Hughes was born in 1900; Gus Risman of Cardiff became the oldest man to appear in a rugby league cup final in 1952, when his team Warrington won - he was 41; Billy Meredith of Manchester City, Manchester United and Wales, football's first superstar, died in 1958 (see July 28)

*Falstaff: 'My own knee! When I was about thy years, Hal, I was not an eagle's talon in the waist; I could have crept into any alderman's thumb-ring. A plague of sighing and grief! It blows a man up like a bladder. There's villainous news abroad: here was Sir John Bracy from your father: you must to the court in the morning. That same mad fellow of the north, Percy, and he of Wales, that gave Amaimon the bastinado and made Lucifer cuckold, and swore the devil his true liegeman upon the cross of a Welsh hook - what a plague call you him?*
*Poins: 'Owen Glendower.'* - William Shakespeare, Henry IV, Part I

**On this day...**

..................................................................................................................

..................................................................................................................

..................................................................................................................

# April 20

FEAST DAY OF SAINTS BEUNO d.642 (also 21) at Aberffraw, Llanfeuno, Dolbenmaen, Clynnog Fawr, Llanycil, Gwyddelwern, Betws, Berriew; CALLWEN 6th century (also July 6) at Cellan; and PADARN (see 15). TRADITIONAL ALL SAINTS DAY - before the 9th century, this was the traditional date. Not until the 12th century did it move to November 1st in Wales. In 1776, John Stuart was created Baron Cardiff of Cardiff Castle, and later became the Earl of Windsor and Marquis of Bute; In 1836, the Festiniog Railway opened; John Jones (Shoni Sguborfawr), Rebecca Rioter, was conditionally discharged in 1858, almost fifteen years after his arrest and transportation to Tasmania; In 1871 W.H. Davies, the tramp-poet, was born in Newport; BP opened its oil terminal in Milford Haven in 1978; East Moors Works, Cardiff, stopped producing steel in 1978

*'Who would have thought my shrivelled heart*
*Could have recovered greenness? It was gone*
*Quite underground - as flowers depart*
*To see their mother-root when they have blown,*
*Where they together*
*All the hard weather,*
*Dead to the world, keep house unknown'* - George Herbert

**On this day...**

..................................................................................................................

..................................................................................................................

..................................................................................................................

# April 21

FEAST DAY OF SAINTS BEUNO* (died 642, see 20); DYFNAN 5th century (also April 22, 23, 24) at Llandyfnan; and GWYNDAF HEN (see November 6). Henry VII (Henry Tudor) died in 1509; Birth in 1806 of Sir George Cornewall Lewis, Palmerston's Secretary of State for War (see April 13); In 1877, 5 miners were rescued from Porth's Tynewydd Colliery after being entombed for 10 days; Sir David Treharne Evans, Mayor of London, born in Llantrisant in 1849 (see August 14); George V opened the first part of the National Museum of Wales in 1927; Tessie O'Shea died in Leesburg, Florida in 1995

*'When Saint Beuno lived at Clynnog, he used to go regularly to preach at Llanddwyn on the opposite side of the water, which he always crossed on foot. But one Sunday he accidentally dropped his book of sermons into the water, and when he had failed to recover it a gylfin-hir, or curlew, came by, picked it up, and placed it on a stone out of reach of the tide. The saint prayed for the protection and favour of the Creator for the gylfin-hir; it was granted, and so nobody ever knows where that bird makes its nest.' - from Baring-Gould and Fisher, 'Lives of the British Saints', 1907

*On this day...*

.................................................................................................
.................................................................................................
.................................................................................................

# April 22

FEAST DAY OF SAINTS DYFNAN (see 21); and DOGED (see April 17); The warrior Sir Rhys ap Thomas, Lord of Dinefwr, was made a Knight of the Garter in 1505; Birth in 1789 at Llanymynech of Richard Roberts, inventor (see March 11); Megan Lloyd George born in 1902; Death of the politician Llywelyn William Williams in 1922 (see March 10); A record 57,800 watch Cardiff versus Arsenal at Ninian Park in 1953; Ryan Davies, the comedian died of asthma in Buffalo, New York State, in 1977, aged 40 (see January 22)

'For I will consider my Cat Jeoffrey
For he is the servant of the Living God duly and daily serving him.
For at the first glance of the glory of God in the East he worships in his way.
For this is done by wreathing his body seven times around with elegant quickness.
For then he leaps up to catch the musk, which is the blessing of God upon his prayer.
For he rolls upon prank to work it in.
For having done duty and received blessing he begins to consider himself.
For this he performs in ten degrees.
For first he looks upon the forepaws to see if they are clean.
For secondly he kicks up behind to clear away there.

*For thirdly he works it upon stretch with the forepaws extended.*
*For fourthly he sharpens his claws by wood.*
*For fifthly he washes himself.*
*For sixthly he rolls upon wash.*
*For seventhly he fleas himself, that he may not be interrupted upon the beat.*
*For eighthly he rubs himself against a post.*
*For ninthly he looks up for his instructions.*
*For tenthly he goes in search of food.*
*For having considered God and himself he will consider his neighbour.'* - opening lines of 'Jubilate Agno' by Cristopher Smart (1722-1772)

*On this day...*

.................................................................................................

.................................................................................................

.................................................................................................

# April 23

*FEAST DAY OF SAINT* IFOR 4th or 5th century at Ferns?; and GEORGE d. c. 300 - the Lebanese patron saint of England. Death in 1695 at Llansantffraed of Henry Vaughan, the poet; Death in 1816 of the landowner and man of letters Thomas Johnes of Hafod (see August 20); In 1841, the Taff Vale Railway between Merthyr and Cardiff opened; Death in 1880 of the cleric-poet Robert Thomas (see August 11); In 1887 the poet and folk-historian John 'Ceiriog' Hughes died in Caersws, and is buried in Llanwnog (see September 25); Cardiff City won the FA Cup in 1927, beating Arsenal at Wembley. It was the first Cup Final to be broadcast, the the only time the Cup has left England; In 1947, the 39-man crew of the 'Santampa' and the 8-man crew of the Mumbles Lifeboat perished off Sker Point, Porthcawl; Pete Ham of Swansea, co-writer of 'Without You', committed suicide 4 days before his 28th birthday, in 1975

*'Ni edrych angau pwy decaf ei dalcen'* - *'Death does not consider who is fairest of forehead.'*

*On this day...*

.................................................................................................

.................................................................................................

.................................................................................................

# April 24

*FEAST DAY OF SAINTS* MEUGAN (see September 24); and DYFNAN (see 21). In 1848, the first public excursion train crossed the Conwy Bridge; In 1916, Jimmy Wilde of Tylorstown won the World Flyweight Championship, and held it for 7 years, longer than any other boxer; Death at Pistyll in 1950 of Thomas Jones, the priest whose goldmine supplied the wedding ring for Princess Elizabeth in 1947

*'Guests who arrive early in the day are entertained until nightfall by girls who play to them on the harp. In every house there are young women just waiting to play for you, and there is certainly no lack of harps. Here are two things worth remembering: the Irish are the most jealous people on earth, but the Welsh do not seem to know what jealousy is; and in every Welsh court or family the menfolk consider playing on the harp to be the greatest of all accomplishments.'* - Giraldus Cambrensis, 'The Description of Wales', 1193/1194

*On this day...*

## April 25

*FEAST DAY OF SAINTS* MADOG MORFRYN 6th century at Leitrim; and MARK *1st century* - Farming work was traditionally prohibited on this day. The defenders of Castell y Bere surrendered to Edward I in 1283, and Dafydd ap Gruffydd escaped to the mountains; In 1599, Oliver Cromwell a.k.a. Oliver Williams, Lord Protector, was born; In 1649 Colonel John Poyer, governor of Pembroke Castle, was executed by Parliamentary firing squad at Covent Garden; Mary Ann Edmunds (nee Jones), diarist and educationist, was born at Carmarthen in 1813 (see March 10); In 1891 William Hope married Iris Towns of Cardiff - their son Bob became a comedian (see May 29); Cardiff City lose 1-0 to Sheffield Wednesday in the FA Cup Final at Wembley in 1925; In 1925, two landing craft sank in heavy seas off Milford Haven in 1943, with 78 soldiers drowning; The actor John Griffiths (John Ogwen) was born near Bangor in 1944; Death of 4th Marquess of Bute, responsible for restoration of Cardiff and Caerffili castles, in 1947; In 1952, the Prudential Building in Cardiff (now the Hilton Hotel) is built on the ruins of Greyfriars Monastery and the 1317 grave of Llywelyn Bren, an act of planning vandalism that cut the superb Civic Centre away from the view of Queen Street; 'The Guardian' reported in 1996 that Ronson was moving its cigarette lighter production from Korea to Wales, as wages were much lower, at around £8,000-£10,000, compared to £10,000-£12,000.

*'The Brigantes indeed, when a few who were beginning hostilities had been slain and the rest pardoned, settled down quietly but on the Silures neither terror nor mercy had the least effect; they persisted in war and could be quelled only by legions encamped in their country. That this might be the more promptly effected, a colony of a strong body of veterans was established at Camulodunum on the conquered lands, as a defence against the rebels, and as a means of imbuing the allies with a respect for our laws. The army*

*then marched upon the Silures, a naturally fierce people and now full of confidence in the might of Caractacus (Caradog), who by many an indecisive and many a successful battle had raised himself far above all the other generals of the Britons. Inferior in military strength, but deriving an advantage from the deceptiveness of the country, he at once shifted the war by a stratagem to the territory of the Ordovices, where, joined by all who dreaded peace with us, he resolved on a final struggle.'* - from Tacitus Book XII, 'The Campaigns of Publius Ostorius Scapula and Aulus Didius, AD48-54

**On this day...**

..................................................................................................................................................

..................................................................................................................................................

..................................................................................................................................................

# April 26
*FEAST DAY OF SAINT GWYDDALUS* (May 9 New Style) at Llanwyddalus. Around this time the traitor Dafydd Gam was captured by Glyndŵr's forces in 1412 - he was later personally ransomed by Henry IV and died fighting for the English at Agincourt; A.G. Jones-Williams and N.H. Jenkins made the first non-stop flight from Britain to India in 1929

*'Caractacus selected a position for the engagement in which advance and retreat alike would be difficult for our men and comparatively easy for his own, and then on some lofty hills, wherever their sides could be approached by a gentle slope, he piled up stones to serve as a rampart. A river too of varying depth was in his front, and his armed bands were drawn up before his defences. Then too the chieftains of the various tribes went from rank to rank, encouraging and confirming the spirit of their men by making light of their fears, kindling their hopes, and by every other warlike incitement. As for Caractacus, he flew hither and thither, protesting that that day and that battle would be the beginning of the recovery of their freedom, or else everlasting bondage. He appealed, by name, to their forefathers who had driven back the dictator Julius Caesar, by whose valour they were free from the Roman axe and tribute, which still preserved inviolate the persons of their wives and children. While he was thus speaking, the host shouted applause; every warrior bound himself by his national oath not to shrink from weapons or violence.*

*Such enthusiasm confounded the Roman general. The river too in his face, the ramparts, the frowning hilltops, the stern resistance and masses of fighting men daunted him. But his soldiers insisted on battle, exclaiming that valour could overcome all these factors; and the prefects and tribunes stimulated the ardour of the legionaries. Ostorius by a survey having ascertained the inaccessible and the assailable points of the position, led on his furious troops, and crossed the river without difficulty. When he reached the barriers, as long as it was a fight with missiles, the wounds and slaughter fell mainly upon our soldiers; but when he had formed the military testudo* (-the 'tortoise' fomation whereby the legionaries sheltered unter their shields-), *and the rude, ill-compacted*

wall of stones was torn down, and it was an equal hand-to-hand engagement, the barbarians retired to the heights. Yet even there, both light and heavy-armed soldiers rushed to the attack; the first harassed the foe with missiles, while the latter closed with them, and the opposing ranks of the Britons were broken, destitute as they were of the defence of breast-plates or helmets. When they faced the auxiliaries, they were felled by the swords and javelins of our legionaries; if they wheeled around, they were again met by the sabres and swords of the auxiliaries. It was a glorious victory; the wife and daughter of Caractacus were captured, and his brothers too were admitted to surrender.'
- from Tacitus, Book XII 'The Campaigns of Publius Ostorius Scapula and Aulus Didius, AD48-54

**On this day...**

.......................................................................................................................................................

.......................................................................................................................................................

.......................................................................................................................................................

# April 27

*FEAST DAY OF SAINTS* CYNIDR AP RHIEGAR 6th century at Maelienydd; and NOE (NWY) 6th century? (also July 6, November 8) at Newlyn, Skenfrith, Pontivy. In 1402, three armies assembled at Chester, Shrewsbury and Hereford, to attack Owain Glyndŵr's forces; In 1404 Prince Henry is made lieutenant in North Wales, with 500 men-at-arms and 3000 archers; On this day Philip the Bold, Duke of Burgundy died in Paris, severely harming Glyndŵr's hopes of any peace with England; In 1405, the 5th royal invasion force assembles at Usk under Prince Henry; Death in 1584 of David Lewis of Abergafenni, first principal of Jesus College, Oxford; Death in 1867 of Lord Llanover (see November 8); The last horse races were held at Ely Race-Course in 1939; Pete Ham of Badfinger born in Swansea in 1947 (see April 23 and November 23); Death in 1955 of William Ambrose Bebb (see July 4)

'There is seldom safety for the unfortunate, and Caractacus, seeking the protection of Cartimandua, Queen of the Brigantes (in North Yorkshire), was put in chains and delivered up to the conquerors, nine years after the beginning of the war in Britain. His fame had spread thence, and travelled to the neighbouring islands and provinces, and was actually celebrated in Italy. All were eager to see the great man, who for many years had defied our power. Even at Rome the name Caractacus was no obscure one; and the emperor (Claudius), while he exalted in his own glory, enhanced the renown of the vanquished. The people were summoned as to a grand spectacle; the praetorian cohorts were drawn up under arms in the plain in front of their camp; then came a procession of the royal vassals, and the ornaments and neck-chains that the king had won in wars with other tribes, were displayed. Next were to be seen his brothers, his wife and daughter; last of all, Caractacus himself. All the rest stooped in their fear to abject supplication; not so the king, who neither by humble look or speech sought compassion.

*When he was set up before the emperor's tribunal, he spoke as follows:*
*"Had my moderation in prosperity been equal to my noble birth and fortune, I should have entered this city as your friend rather than as your captive; and you would not have disdained to receive, under treaty of peace, a king descended from illustrious ancestors and ruling many nations. My present lot is as glorious to you as it is degrading to myself. I had men and horses, arms and wealth. What wonder if I parted with them reluctantly? If you Romans choose it to lord over the world, does it follow that the world is to accept slavery? Were I to have been at once delivered up as a prisoner, neither my fall nor your triumph would become famous. My punishment would be followed by oblivion, whereas, if you save my life, I shall be an everlasting memorial of your clemency." Upon this the emperor granted pardon to Caractacus, to his wife, and to his brothers.'* - from Tacitus, Book XII 'The Campaigns of Publius Ostorius Scapula and Aulus Didius, AD48-54

*On this day...*

..................................................................................................................................

..................................................................................................................................

..................................................................................................................................

# April 28

FEAST DAY OF SAINT GWENOLE (WINWALOE) (see March 3). Rhys ap Gruffydd ap Rhys ap Tewdwr, 'The Lord Rhys', died in 1197 and was buried in St David's Cathedral; 1603 saw the great funeral procession of Elizabeth I; In 1645, Royalists defeated Parliamentarians at Newcastle Emlyn; James Monroe, the Welsh-American US President, was born in 1758; Godfrey-Charles Morgan, Viscount Tredegar, was born at Rhiwperra Castle in 1831, and went on to take part in the Charge of the Light Brigade and to become a patron of Welsh culture (see March 11); Sir Benjamin Hall, husband of Lady Lanover, after whom Big Ben was named, died in 1867; Last horse races at Cardiff's Ely Racecourse in 1939; Death in 1989 of Aled Vaughan, writer and broadcaster, at Llanwnda

*'The Senate was then assembled, and speeches were delivered full of pompous eulogy on the capture of Caractacus. It was as glorious, they said, as the display of Syphax by Scipio, or of Persea by Lucius Paulus, or indeed of any captive prince by any of our generals to the people of Rome. Triumphal distinctions were voted to Ostorius, who thus far had been successful, but soon afterwards met with reverses; either because, when Caractacus was out of the way, our discipline was relaxed under an impression that the war was ended, or because the enemy, out of compassion for so great a king, was more ardent in their thirst for vengeance. Instantly they rushed from all parts on the camp-prefect, and legionary cohorts left to establish fortified postions among the Silures, and had not speedy succour arrived from towns and fortresses in the neighbourhood, our forces would then have been totally destroyed. Even as it was, the camp-prefect, with eight centurions, and the bravest of our soldiers, were slain; and shortly afterwards, a*

*foraging party of our men, with some cavalry squadrons sent to their support, was utterly routed. Ostorius then deployed his light cohorts, but even thus he did not stop the flight, till our legions sustained the brunt of the battle. Their strength equalised the conflict, which after a while was in our favour. The enemy fled with trifling loss, as by now the day was on the decline. Now began a series of skirmishes, for the most part like raids, in woods and morasses, with encounters due to chance or to courage, to mere heedlessness or calculation, to fury or lust to plunder, under directions from the officers, or sometimes even without their knowledge. Conspicuous above all in stubborn resistance were the Silures, whose rage was fired by words rumoured to have been spoken by the Roman general, to the effect, that as the Sugambri had been formerly destroyed or transplanted into Gaul, so the name of the Silures ought to be blotted out. Accordingly they cut off two of our auxiliary cohorts, the rapacity of whose officers let them make incautious forays; and by liberal gifts of spoil and prisoners to the other tribes, they were luring them too into revolt, when Ostorius, worn out by the burden of his anxieties, died, to the joy of the enemy, who thought that a campaign at least, though not a single battle, had proved fatal to a general whom  none could despise. The emperor, on hearing of the death of his representative appointed Aulus Didius in his place, so that the province might not be left without a governor. Didius, although he arrived quickly, found matters far from prosperous, for the legion under the command of Manlius Valens had meanwhile been defeated, and the disaster had been exaggerated by the enemy to alarm the new general, while he again magnified it, to gain more glory by quelling the movement or have a fairer excuse if it lasted. This loss too had been inflicted on us by the Silures, and they were scouring the country far and wide, until Didius harried and dispersed them.'* - from Tacitus, Book XII 'The Campaigns of Publius Ostorius Scapula and Aulus Didius, AD48-54

**On this day...**

...................................................................................................................................

...................................................................................................................................

...................................................................................................................................

## April 29

FEAST DAY OF SAINTS ENDELLION 5th-6th century at St Endellion's, Lundy Island, Tregony; SENAN d. 660; and SANNAN (see March 1). Julia Ann Hatton, Ann of Swansea, born in 1764; In 1926, J.G. Parry Thomas set a new world landspeed record at Pendine Sands, of 171mph; In 1941, 26 people were killed in Cwmparc, Rhondda in German air-raids. 41 were killed in Cardiff and a land-mine blew a crater 15 feet deep and 45 feet across in the grounds of Cardiff Castle; Death in 1966 of William Ewart Williams at Pasadena; The novelist Richard Hughes died near Harlech in 1976

*'In the consulship of Caesonius Paetus and Petronius Turpilianus, a serious disaster was sustained in Britain, where Aulus Didius, the emperor's legate, had merely retained our*

*existing possessions, and his successor Veranius, after having ravaged the Silures in some trifling raids, was prevented by death from extending the war... Now, however, the country was in the hands of Suetonius Paulinus, who in military knowledge and popular favour, which allows no-one to be without a rival, vied with Corbulo, and aspired to equal the glory of the recovery of Armenia by the subjugation of Rome's enemies. He therefore prepared to attack the island of Mona (-Anglesey, the centre of European druidism-) which had a powerful population and was a refuge for fugitives. He built flat-bottomed vessels to cope with the shallows and uncertain depths of the sea (-the Menai Straits-). Thus the infantry crossed, while the cavalry followed by fording, or, where the water was deep, swam by the sides of their horses. On the shore stood the opposing army with its dense array of armed warriors, while between the ranks dashed women, in black attire like the Furies, with hair dishevelled, waving firebrands. All around, the Druids, lifting up their hands to heaven, and pouring forth dreadful imprecations, scared our soldiers by the unfamiliar sight, so that, as if their limbs were paralysed, they stood motionless and exposed to wounds. Then urged by their general's appeals and mutual encouragement not to quail before a troop of frenzied women, they bore the standards onwards, smote down all resistance, and wrapped the foe in the flames of his own brands. A force was next set over the conquered, and their groves, devoted to inhuman superstitions, were destroyed.'* - from Tacitus, Book XII 'The Campaigns of Publius Ostorius Scapula and Aulus Didius, AD48-54, just before the rising of Boudicca.

*On this day...*

..................................................................................................................................................

..................................................................................................................................................

..................................................................................................................................................

# April 30

FEAST DAY OF SAINTS AMWN DDU c. 480-540 at Llanilltud Fawr; BRIOC c. 440-530 (also May 1) at Llandyfriog, Founder Saint of Brittany; CYNWYL (see January 5); and ILAN at Eglwysilan, St Ilan, Trefilan; BELTANE EVE. With the Feast of Oimelc, the greatest night for drinking for the Celts – in other words, a Spring New Year's Eve; The death of the Celtic Goddess of Winter. In Germany Walpurgis Night when witches ride on broomsticks and he-goats; Birch trees were cut down across Wales for use as maypoles*. In 1401, Hotspur claimed to have fought Glyndŵr on this day at Cadair Idris, and so did John Charlton, Lord of Powys elsewhere in Wales, possibly at Machynlleth. (Glyndŵr's brother Tudor looked like him,which may explain the discrepancy); In 1417, Maredudd ab Owain Glyndŵr finally acepted a pardon from Henry V, 17 years after the war's start; Birth in 1770 of David Thompson, son of David and Ann ap Thomas, who explored North America; Chartist disturbances at Llanidloes started in 1839; David Jacobs, gold medallist swimmer in the 1912 Olympics, was born in Cardiff in 1888; In 1926 Coal-miners were locked out of pits after refusing to work an extra hour a day with a 13% pay cut - the precursor of the General Strike from May 3; Death of Bob Owen in 1962 at Llanfrothen - Cymdeithas Bob Owen keeps his memory alive

*Francis Kilvert wrote on this day in 1870, about the custom of the Welsh villagers in his curacy: *'This evening being May Eve I ought to have put some birch and wittan (mountain ash, rowan) over the door to help keep out the "old witch". But I was too lazy to go out and get it. Let us hope the old witch will not come in during the night. The young witches are welcome'.*

**On this day...**

30

........................................................................................................................................

........................................................................................................................................

........................................................................................................................................

# MAY - MAI
## Mae (Breton), Miz Me (Cornish)

## May 1

FEAST DAY OF SAINTS PHILIP AND JAMES 1st century; ASAF (ASAPH, ASA) 6th-7th century (also 5 and 11), Feast from April 30-May 2 at St Asaph's, Llanasa; BAGLAN AB ITHEL HAEL 6th century (also 2, 3) at Baglan; TYFRIOG 6th century at Llandyfriog, Little Lidney; CORENTIN* (see November 2); UST and DYFNIG 6th century at Llanwrin (before Gwrin); GWRIN 6th century (also November 1) at Llanwrin, Wrinstone; BRIOC (see April 30); CALAN HAF (the first day of Summer), when bonfires were held across South Wales until the 19th century; ASCENSION DAY (now moveable); BELTANE To the Celts, the First Day of Summer. Cattle were driven from shelter to grass and twin bonfires were lit for the cattle to pass between, to protect them from evil.The Chief festival for well-worship, a practice outlawed by Henry VIII; The busiest time of the year for Fairies and spirits to affect us. There are hundreds of May Day traditions still extant. At Puck's Dale near Crickhowell a door leads into the fairy kingdom. In Somerset, dew will cure freckles; Maypole Raiding was extremely popular in Wales; DIPPING DAY in Cornwall, Dippy day was when people were sprinkled with dew water to bring them luck; Traditionally the best day for fishing, in Wales. William Latham Bevan, who held the living of Hay-on-Wye for 56 years, was born in 1821; Richard Bell, MP and Taff Vale trade-union leader (born Penderyn, Brecon in November 1859) died in 1930; Mary Harris (Mother) Jones born in 1830; Western Mail first published in 1869; Birth in 1873 in Dowlais of Harry Evans, composer, musical director and conductor (see July 23); Birth in 1880 of Thomas Michael Jones (Thomas Michaeliones) at Pen-y-Groes, Caernarfon, priest and Graigwen goldmine owner (see April 24); In 1916 Gwynllyn Samuel Newton Ford, whose parents came from Tonypandy, was born, later known as Glenn Ford, the Hollywood film star; Ray Smith, the actor, was born in Trealaw, Rhondda in 1936; Cardiff City lost 2-3 at home in the European Cup-Winners' Cup to Hamburg in 1958, having drawn 1-1 away (If Cardiff again becomes a Premiership club, Wales' international profile will rise measurably)

*'One day St Corentin received a visit from two eminent saints and he was in despair. He had flour, and could give them pancakes for dinner, but pancakes, before it was understood how to season them with sugar, nutmeg and lemon, were thought very insipid. He went to the fountain to look at his fish. If he broiled for his visitors the entire fish he would have killed his golden goose. But he found the spring full of plump eels! He cooked them for dinner in light wine, and his vistors left, licking their lips, and glorifying God for having given them so dainty a meal'. - Baring-Gould's 'Lives of the Saints' 1877 - the Reverend Kilvert's diary entry for this day in 1870

*On this day...*

..................................................................................................................................

..................................................................................................................................

..................................................................................................................................

## May 2

FEAST DAY OF SAINTS GWYNIO 6th century (also March 2) at Llanwynio; and GENYS 6th century? (also 3, and July 19) at Launceston, Trigg Minor. The will was proved in 1575 of Humfrey Toy, the Carmarthen merchant who paid for the printing of the Welsh translations of the new Testament and The Book of Common Prayer; Death of the soldier and writer Morris Kyffin in Dublin in 1598; Hester Lynch Piozzi (Mrs Thrale) died in 1821; Birth at Camrose in 1847 of John Mathias Berry, whose three sons were created peers (see January 9, September 17, June 23 and May 7); Death in 1852 at Nevern of John Jones (Tegid, see February 10); Birth in 1880 of the poet Isaac Daniel Hooson at Rhosllanerchrugog (see October 18); Death in 1885 of the musician-composer Henry Brinley Richards (see November 13)

*'Welcome, graceful greenwood choir,*
*Summer's month of May, for longing is mine.*
*Strong knight of loving favour,*
*Green-chained master of the wild wood;*
*Friend of love and birds,*
*The lore of lovers and their kinsmen;*
*Courier of nine-times-twenty rendezvous,*
*Favourer of honoured meeting.*
*And great it is, by Mary, that he,*
*May, perfect month, is coming,*
*With his mind set, claiming warm respect,*
*On the conquest of every green glen.'*
Extract from 'May and January' by Dafydd ap Gwilym (c.1320-1380), trans. R.M. Loomis

*On this day...*

.......................................................................................................................
.......................................................................................................................
.......................................................................................................................

## May 3

FEAST DAY OF SAINTS CARADOG FREICHFRAS 6th century at Porthskewett, Caerwent; GLYWYS 6th century at Merthyr Mawr, St Gluvias, Coedkernew, Newton Nottage; GENYS (see 2); and BAGLAN (see 1); CROUCHMAS DAY - A festival where people bowed (crouched) to the Holy Cross - this was 'Unlucky Cross-Mass' or 'Avoiding Day', celebrating the finding of the True Cross by Elen in 326. In 1230, Llywelyn the Great hanged William de Braos for intriguing with Joan, Llywelyn's wife, thus ending the main line of the most treacherous Marcher dynasty; 1926 - the General Strike* begins, with over 250,000 Welsh miners staying away from the pit-heads. The TUC called off the strike after just 9 days, but Welsh miners do not return until the end of 1926; Mary Hopkin born at Pontardawe in 1950; 1958 saw the first Festival of Wales; Death of Cardiff novelist Howard Spring in 1965

*'Among brown hills and black hills
And hills bleak and bare
They have given us hovels
And a bed and a chair
And told us to labour
And not to desire
The cake of the countess,
The wine of the squire

But here we come marching
And ready to dare
The wrath of the gamblers
Who have dirtied the air,
And here we come singing
The songs of our ire,
And with torches of beauty
To set cities on fire.' - verse 42 of 'The Angry Summer 1926' by Idris Davies

*On this day...*

..............................................................................................................................................

..............................................................................................................................................

..............................................................................................................................................

# May 4

FEAST DAY OF SAINTS ALLGO 5th - 6th century (first Sunday in May, see Nov 27) at Llanallgo; KING YNYR GWENT 5th - 6th century at Abergavenny, Caerwent; and MELANGELL* (see 28). William Morgan of Bridgend, a pioneer of scientific life insurance and nephew of Richard Price, died in 1833; Charles Stewart Rolls, youngest son of Lord Llangattock, first met Henry Royce in 1904; Last race meetings held at Monmouth racecourse in 1933 and at Cowbridge in 1939; Death in 1958 of the missionary Christy Davies (see July 16); John Ormond, poet, died in Cardiff in 1990, aged 67 (see April 3); In 1996, 'The Western Mail' reported that non-manual pay for Welsh men is £57 per week less than in England, and for women £27. Dafydd Wigley MP reported that EU funding to Wales was less than that for England, and that Ireland, a far richer country, received £478 per person per year, compared to a Welsh person's £45.

*'Mil engyl a Melangell
Trechnant lu fyddin y fall'
(Melangell with a thousand angels*

*Shall triumph over the whole power of Hell)* - lines written in the 1680 Parish Register

*On this day...*

....................................................................................................................

....................................................................................................................

....................................................................................................................

## May 5

FEAST DAY OF SAINTS ASAF (see April 1); HYDROC 6th century at Lanhydrock; and BRITO at Trier. Royalist forces including Dafydd Gam overcome Glyndŵr's army at Pwll Melyn, near Usk in 1405 - John ap Hywel, Abbot of Llantarnam is among those slain. Owain Glyndŵr's almost identical brother Tudor is also killed, and the English believe that they have killed Glyndŵr. Glyndŵr's eldest son Gruffudd is taken to the Tower of London, to die there in 1411; Birth in 1861 of Sir John Edward Lloyd, historian and editor (see June 20); Birth in the Amman Valley in 1882 of Daniel Powell Williams (Pastor Dan), founder and first President of the Apostolic Church, the only Welshman to establish a world-wide church (see February 13); Britain's first motorway tunnel opened at Newport in 1967; The brilliant Ruthin driver Tom Pryce, was killed in the South African Grand Prix in 1977; The 'Iron Ring' of Edward I's castles around Gwynedd, at Harlech, Beaumaris, Caernarfon and Conwy, was designated a UNESCO World Heritage Site in 1988; The Empire Pool was closed in 1998, with no Olympic-size swimming pool to replace it in Wales

'Tri enllyn iechyd - mel, memyn a llaeth' (Three sauces of life - honey, butter and milk).
'Tri enllyn afiechyd - cig, cwrw ac aesel' (Three sauces of sickness - meat, beer and vinegar).

*On this day...*

....................................................................................................................

....................................................................................................................

....................................................................................................................

## May 6

FEAST DAY OF SAINTS GLYWYS (1st Sunday in May, see May 3); and EDWARD JONES at London, St Asaf. In May, 1404, Glyndŵr sent the famous letter to Charles VI of France, referring to Owain Llawgoch's service to France, and asking for assistance, signed 'Owynus dei gratia princeps Wallie' (Owain, the the grace of God, Prince of Wales); In 1774, John Elias*, the most powerful preacher of his time in Wales, was christened in Abererch (see June 15); Birth at Llanrug in 1828 of General Sir Hugh Rowlands, first Welshman to win the

Victoria Cross (at Inkerman in the Crimean War - see August 1); Johnny Morris died in 1999, aged 82

*Then, stretching his hand out as though he were holding them in it, and casting a glance over the crowd, he (John Elias) shouted at the very highest volume of his voice, "Who will take them? Who will take them? Who will take them?" Then in an instant his whole nature was convulsed; his eyes flashed and he made a most odd movement; he turned his face towards his left, and in a rather low voice and yet distinct enough for the whole congregation to hear, he said, "I thought I heard the Devil at my elbow saying "Knock them down to me; I will take them." .... And then he turned again to his left and pointing with his right forefinger at his left elbow, he moved it up and down, once, twice, thrice, and then shouted with tremendous force until his voice echoed through the town, "I was going to say, Satan, that you could have them: but...." and he raised his eyes towards heaven and with a victorious, yet tender voice, he cried "I hear Jesus shouting, "I will take them, I will take them; to wash them of their filth, to sober them in their drunkenness; to purify them of all their uncleanness with my own blood."'.' - Owen Thomas describing John Elias preaching against drunkenness at a mass meeting at Holyhead in 1824

*On this day...*

......................................................................................................

6 ......................................................................................................

......................................................................................................

# May 7

FEAST DAY OF SAINT SANCTAN 6th century (also 9) at Llansannan, Kilnasantan. St Dyfrig's relics are taken from Ynys Enlli (Bardsey Island) to Llandaf Cathedral in 1120; Rice Powell pardoned from the death penalty by Parliamentarians in 1649; Varina Banks Howell, 'The First Lady of the Confederacy' was born in 1826; In 1839, the Chartist leader Henry Vincent was arrested and gaoled in Monmouth; Birth in 1883 of James Gomer Berry, newspaper magnate who became 1st Viscount Kemsley (see February 6 and May 2); Death in 1886 from a microbe, of the pathologist Timothy Lewis (see October 31); Sir Huw Pyrs Wheldon was born in Prestatyn in 1916 (see March 14); In 1960 Gladys Mary (Mai) Jones, pianist, entertainer, producer, who wrote the music to 'We'll keep a Welcome in the Hillsides', died in Newport, aged 61 (see February 16); The author of 'Off to Philadelphia in the Morning', Jack Jones, died in Cardiff in 1970 (see November 23); In 1988, a world record attendance of 56,000 for a club game, saw Llanelli beat Neath, in the WRU Cup Final in Cardiff

'Brain, n. An apparatus with which we think we think. That which distinguishes the man who is content to be something from the man who wishes to do something. A man of great wealth, or one who has been pitchforked into high station, has commonly such a headful of brain that his neighbours cannot keep their hats on. In our civilization, and *under our republican form of government, brain is so highly honoured that it is rewarded by exemption from the cares of office.'* - Ambrose Gwinnett Bierce, The Devil's Dictionary, 1911

*On this day...*

.......................................................................................................................

.......................................................................................................................

.......................................................................................................................

## May 8

*FEAST DAY OF SAINT* MIHANGEL/MICHAEL (also September 29 is Michaelmas) - Many Welsh churches were renamed by the Normans, but some were original Mihangel dedications; *WORLD RED CROSS DAY; Furry Day at Helston, Cornwall, which celebrates the 'feriae', or festival.* (This may stem from the Welsh *'fory'* or tomorrow, signifying that the dance is carried on until the morrow). Death in 1176 of David Fitzgerald, son of Gerald of Windsor and Nest, who was bishop of St David's from 1148; The Battle of St Ffagans in 1648 saw the Royalists routed, and hundreds of Welshmen transported to Barbados; Ann Maddocks, the Maid of Cefn Ydfa, was christened Ann Thomas at Llangynwyd in 1704 (see June 6); Death of the Chartist leader Zephania Williams of Argoed, in Tasmania in 1874 - he had been transported in 1840 after the original sentence of hanging, drawing and quartering had been commuted; Birth in 1885 of Robert Owen (Bob Owen, Croesor) at Llanfrothen, historian and legend in his own lifetime (see April 30); VE Day was celebrated across Wales in 1945

*'Before I was crooked of back,*
*I was skilful with my words.*
*My exploits were famed.*
*The men of Argoed were always behind me.*

*Before I grew crooked of back,*
*I was bold.*
*I was welcome in the mead-halls*
*Of Powys, Paradise of Wales*

*Before I grew crooked of back,*
*I was magnificient.*
*My spear was the first to draw blood.*
*Now I am bent. I am weary. I am pitiful.'* - Llywarch Hen, 7th century

*On this day...*

.......................................................................................................................

.......................................................................................................................

.......................................................................................................................

# May 9

FEAST DAY OF SAINT SANCTAN (see 7); TUDGLID 6th - 7th century at Llanwrtyd Wells; TUDWG 6th century at Llandudwg (Tythegston), Plessala; MELYD at Melidan; MYFOR at (possibly) Merthyr Mawr, Llan; and GWYDDALUS (see April 23); the traditional date for calving in Wales. In 1191 Walter de Clare founded Tintern Abbey, the first site for Wales' favourite order, the Cistercians; The artist Kyffin Williams was born at Llangefni in 1918; Death of John Fisher in 1930, buried at St Asaf Cathedral (see January 5); Joseph E. Davies, diplomat and holder of America's greatest civilian award, the Medal of Merit, died in 1958 and is buried in Washington Cathedral (see November 29)

Francis Kilvert wrote on this day in 1870: *'Now the various tints of green mount one over another in the hanging woods of Penllan above the dingle. Over the level line of brilliant larch green rises the warmer golden green brown of the oaks. But the most brilliant green of all is the young green of the beeches. The brilliance of the beeches is almost beyond belief. The turtles (doves) were trilling softly and deeply in the dingles as I went up the steep orchard. The grass was jewelled with cowslips and orchises. The dingle was lighted here and there with wild cherry, bird cherry, the Welsh name of which being interpreted is "the tree on which the Devil hung his mother". The mountains burned blue in the hot afternoon and the air felt quite sultry as I climbed the hill.'*

***On this day...***

..................................................................................................................................

..................................................................................................................................

..................................................................................................................................

# May 10

Treaty signed between Owain Llawgoch, heir to the nation of Wales, and Charles V of France in 1322; Welsh archers win the Battle of Poitiers in 1356; Owain Glyndŵr holds a conference at Dolgellau in 1404, and sends ambassadors to the French Court of Charles VI; Death in 1828 of Major-General Lewis Davies (born at Llanbadarn Fawr in 1777), hero of the Peninsular War; In 1837, 21 miners died at Plas-yr-Argoed Colliery, Mold; In 1852, 65 miners died in an explosion at Middle Dyffryn Colliery, Mountain Ash; In 1852, 27 miners were drowned in an inundation of quicksand in the Gwendraeth Valley; Approx. death date of Sorobabel Davies of Llandilo (1806-1877), schoolmaster, Baptist minister and Australian newspaper proprietor, in Melbourne; Jefferson Davis and his wife Varina Howell were captured in 1865; Mumbles Pier opened in 1898; Death in 1899 of Willaim Jones of Ruthin, successor to Henry Richard as secretary to the Peace Society; Death of H.M. Stanley (John Rowlands) in 1904

*'And as I was green and carefree, famous among the barns*
*About the happy year and singing as the farm was home,*
*In the sun that is young once only,*

*Time let me play and be*
*Golden in the mercy of his means,*
*And green and golden I was huntsman and herdsman, the calves*
*Sang to my horn, the foxes on the hills barked clear and cold,*
*And the sabbath rang slowly*
*In the pebbles of the holy streams.'*
- Dylan Thomas, second verse of 'Fern Hill'

*On this day...*

.............................................................................................................................................

.............................................................................................................................................

.............................................................................................................................................

## May 11

FEAST DAY OF SAINTS TUDY (also 9 and 20) at St Tudy, Loc Tudy; and
ASAF (see May 1). Cromwell captured Chepstow Castle in 1648; Birth at
Aberystwyth in 1826 of the theologian David Charles Davies, principal of
Trefecca College (see September 26); Birth in 1880 of David Davies, 1st Baron
Davies of Llandinam, MP, benefactor and campaigner for peace (see June 16); In
1897, Marconi transmitted the world's first radio message over water, from
Lavernock Point to Flat Holm (an alternative date is May 13) The first sentence,
in Morse Code,was 'So be it, let it be so.'; RAF St Athan was bombed in 1941

*'The liking of Welshmen for Welshmen is very strong, and not only when they meet on*
*foreign soil, as in London, but in their own land. They do not, I suppose, love their*
*neighbours more than other men do, but when they meet a fellow-countryman for the*
*first time they seem to have a kind of surprise and joy, in spite of the commonness of*
*such meetings. They do not acquiesce in the fact that the man they shake hands with is*
*of their race, as the English do. They converse readily in trains: they are all one family,*
*and indeed if you are Welsh, not only can you not avoid meeting relatives, but you do*
*not wish to.'* - Edward Thomas, 'Wales', 1905

*On this day...*

.............................................................................................................................................

.............................................................................................................................................

.............................................................................................................................................

## May 12

FEAST DAY OF SAINT CYNGAR (see November 7) in Brittany, MAY EVE,
OLD STYLE, which was called *Cynnull y Ferfain (Gather the Vervain)* to hang
around the neck to ward off nightmares. A plaque outside the Owain Glyndŵr
Hotel in Corwen reads *'The first Eisteddfod to which the public were admitted was held*

at this Hotel on 12th May 1789'; Birth of Sarah Jacob 'the Welsh fasting girl' in 1857 (see December 17); In 1926, the Trades Union Council* declared an end to the General Strike, betraying the Welsh miners, who stayed on strike; In 1941, 32 people were killed at Pembroke Dock during German air-raids; A black day for Wales when Wylfa Nuclear Power Station was opened in 1972 on Anglesey (see November 24 and 25); 1999 saw the first meeting of the National (British) Assembly at Cardiff Bay, with little power compared to its Scottish counterpart possibly because 8 leading Cabinet members Blair (PM), Brown (Chancellor), Cook (Foreign), Robertson (Defence), Irvine (Lord Chancellor), Smith (Culture), Darling (Social Security), and Dewar (Scotland) were all Scottish. In the 21-person Cabinet, Welsh interests were represented by Alan Michael.

'*They had forged a revolutionary weapon without having a revolutionary intent' - Aneurin Bevan, speaking of the TUC decision in 1926

**On this day...**

.......................................................................................................................

.......................................................................................................................

.......................................................................................................................

# May 13

FEAST DAY OF SAINTS MAEL & SULIEN 6th century at Cwm, Corwen. Thomas Williams, 'The Copper King', was born at Llansadwrn in 1737 (see November 30); The great Welsh architect John Nash of Cardigan, died in 1835; The first tollgate, at Efailwen near St Clears, was destroyed in 1839 by Rebecca Rioters*; The painter Sir Frank Francois Guillaume Brangwyn was born in Bruges in 1867, the greatest decorator of his time (see June 11); Birth in 1887 of Sir David John James, businessman and philanthropist (see March 7); The actor Glyn Houston unveiled the South Wales Miners' Memorial at Trehafod's Rhondda Heritage Park in 2000

*After we had left the gate I asked John Jones whether he had ever heard of Rebecca of the toll-gates. "Oh yes," said he; "I have heard of that chieftainess." "And who was she?" said I. "I cannot say, sir; I never saw her, nor anyone who had seen her. Some say that there were 100 Rebeccas, and all of them men dressed in women's clothes, who went about at night, at the head of bands to break the gates. Ah, sir, something of the kind was almost necessary at that time. I am a friend of peace, sir, no head-breaker, house-breaker nor gate-breaker, but I can hardly blame what was done at that time, under the name of Rebecca. You have no idea how the poor Welsh were oppressed by those gates, aye, and the rich too. The little people and the farmers could not carry their produce to market owing to the exactions at the gates, which devoured all the profit and sometimes more. So that the markets were not half supplied, and people with money could frequently not get what they wanted. Complaints were made to the Government, which not being attended to, Rebecca and her byddinion made their appearance every *night, and broke the gates to pieces with sledge-hammers, and everybody said it was gallant work, everybody save the keepers of the gates and the proprietors…"* - George Borrow, 'Wild Wales', 1862

*On this day…*

..................................................................................................................................

..................................................................................................................................

..................................................................................................................................

## May 14

FEAST DAY OF SAINTS MATTHIAS 1st century; and ENDDWYN at Llanenddwyn. Welsh archers fought for de Montfort at the Battle of Lewes in 1264, where Fulk Fitz Warin IV of Whittington was killed; Robert Owen, *'the modern world's first Socialist'*, born at Newtown in 1771 (see November 17); Alcwyn Caryni Evans, antiquary, born in Carmarthen in 1828 (see March 11); Death of Jean Rhys in 1979; Mabon (William Abraham, see June 14) died in 1922 at Pentre, Rhondda, aged 79; John Hughes, composer of Cwm Rhondda, died at Llantwit Fardre in 1932 (see November 22); Sian Phillips was born near Gwaun-cae-Gurwen in 1934; Megan Lloyd George, Wales' first female MP, died in 1966; The actor Hugh Griffith died in 1980

*'Over the great old-fashioned door of Court Evan Gwynne hung the sprigs of birch and wittan (rowan), the only remnants of the old custom I have noticed this May. The sprays had been hanging since May Eve and were rather withered.'* - Kilvert's Diary, this day in 1870

*On this day…*

..................................................................................................................................

..................................................................................................................................

..................................................................................................................................

## May 15

FEAST DAY OF SAINTS CENEU 5th century at Llangenneu under Llangattock; and PADARN (see April 15); Holy Day of Edmwnd Prys, priest, poet and translator (1624); Holy Day of John Davies, priest and translator (1644). Death at Mallwyd in 1644 of the scholar and translator Dr John Davies (see March 16); Birth in 1645 of George Jeffreys at Acton, Wrexham, who became Earl of Flint and 1st Baron Jeffreys of Wem (see April 18); Richard Wilson, *'Founder of British Landscape Painting'* died at Llanferres in 1782; Death in 1870 of Major-General Charles Hinde of Pen-y-bryn, who served with distinction in the East India Company, the Turkish and Indian armies; Jimmy Wilde, possibly the world's greatest-ever boxer, was born in Tylorstown in 1892 (see March 11); In

1902, 230 Welsh colonists left Patagonia to setttle in Manitoba; Death in 1920 of Sir Owen Morgan Edwards - his account of wearing the 'Welsh knot' at school is immensely moving (see December 26); Llyn Brianne reservoir dam opened in 1973

On this day in 1403, Prince Henry wrote from Shrewsbury to Henry V: '*We were lately informed that Oweyn de Glendourdy caused to assemble his force of rebels and others of his adherents, a great number, purposing to over-ride and also to fight, if the English people should resist his purpose, and thus he boasted to his people; whereupon we took our people and went to a place of the said Oweyn, well built, which was his principal mansion called Saghern (Sycharth), where we supposed that we should have found him if he had been willing to have fought in the manner as he said; but upon our arrival there we found no-one; hence we caused the whole place and many other houses of his tenants in the neighbourhood to be burnt, and then we went directly to his other place at Glyndourdy (Glyndyfrdwy) to seek for him there. We caused a fine lodge in his park to be burnt, and all the country thereabout, and we lodged there at rest all that night... and then we went to the commote of Edeirnion in the county of Merioneth, and there we caused a fine well inhabited country to be burnt; and then we went to Powys, and in want of food for the horses we made our people carry oats for them*'.

**On this day...**

..................................................................................................................

..................................................................................................................

..................................................................................................................

# May 16

FEAST DAY OF SAINTS BRENDAN c.486-575 at Llancarfan, Clonfert; GEREINT 6th century at Magor, Cilgerran; CARANNOG (see 27); and CARADOG (see April 13). Death in 1667 of Robert Vaughan, who collected the famous Hengwrt Library; David Edward Hughes, physicist and inventor born at Corwen in 1831 (see January 22); Felicia Hemans, author of '*The Boy Stood on the Burning Deck*' died in 1835; Death at Llandudno of Sir William Lloyd in 1857 (see December 29); Sir Leonard Twiston Davies, patron of the arts who helped found the Museum of Welsh Life at St Ffagans, was born in 1894 (see January 8); Death in 1963 of the politician Ted Williams at Bridgend; Sir Lewis Casson, actor, died in 1969 (see June 3)

Glendower: '*Cousin, of many men
I do not bear these crossings. Give me leave
To tell you once again that at my birth
The front of heaven was full of fiery shapes,
The goats ran from the mountains, and the herds
Were strangely clamorous to the frighted fields.
These signs have mark'd me extraordinary;*

*And all the course of my life do show*
*I am not in the roll of common men.*
*Where is he living, clipp'd in with the sea*
*That chides the banks of England, Scotland, Wales,*
*Which calls me pupil, or hath read to me?*
*And bring him out that is but woman's son*
*Can trace me in the tedious ways of art*
*And hold me pace in deep experiments.'* - William Shakespeare, Henry IV Part I

*On this day...*

.................................................................................................................

.................................................................................................................

.................................................................................................................

## May 17

*FEAST DAY OF SAINTS* CATHAN late 6th century at Llangathen; and MADRUN 6th century (also May 21) at Madron; In Welsh tradition, the traditional date for Noah entering the Ark. Dolly Pentreath, the last Cornish speaker, baptised in Paul, Cornwall in 1714; 'Tithe War' riots at Llanefydd in 1888; Last race at Newport racecourse in 1948; The Rhondda's last explosion in 1965 killed 31 miners at the Cambrian Colliery (see March 10); Death of Cardiff's Hugh Cudlipp, journalist, press magnate and Chairman of the Mirror Group, in 1998

*'Mae'r oll yn gysegredig... It is all sacred. Every hill and every valley. Our land is a living thing, not a grave of forgetfulness under our feet. Every hill has its own history, every locality its own romance, every part of the landscape wears its own particular glory. And to a Welshman, no other country can be like this. A Welshman feels that the struggles of his forefathers have sanctified every field, and the genius of his people has transformed every mountain into hallowed ground. And it is feeling like this that will make him a true citizen.'* - Sir Owen M. Edwards

*On this day...*

.................................................................................................................

.................................................................................................................

.................................................................................................................

## May 18

*FEAST DAY OF SAINT* NECTAN (see February 14). Execution in 1554 of William Thomas, Italian scholar and formerly advisor to Edward VI, for his part in Wyatt's Conspiracy. He was the first man to advocate the teaching of English in English schools, 30 years before Mulcaster; Bertrand Russell, the philosopher, mathematician, pacifist and Nobel Prize winner, was born in Trellech, Monmouthshire, in 1872; Birth in 1899 of David James Jones (Gwenallt*) at Pontardawe, lecturer, conscientious objector, nationalist and supreme poet (see December 24); 1921 saw Glamorgan's first county championship cricket match at the old Arms Park; In 1943, 43 people died in Cardiff and Dinas Powys during German air-raids; Death in 1966 of Sir Daniel Thomas Davies of Pontycymer, physician to the Royal Family from 1938; In the Rhondda in 1979, Annie Powell became the first Communist mayor in Britain

*Marxism for us was a much better gospel than Methodism. It was a real gospel; a religion, a social religion, and we were ready to live for it, to sacrifice ourselves for it, yes, and to die for it. Who on earth would lift a finger on behalf of Calvinism? To us Capitalism was a living thing. We could see before our eyes the poverty, the starvation and the hunger, the filth of the hovels, mothers growing old before their time, the fierce cruelty of the soldiers and the policemen during strikes, doctors writing "tuberculosis" on death certificates instead of "silicosis" to save the company paying compensation to the families, and the bodies carried home after the accidents. They brought my father's body... they brought him home burnt to death by the molten metal, an accident which could have been avoided. During the funeral sermon, when the minister said this was the will of God I let loose inside me every haulier's oath I could remember and spat them out at his sermon and his God. And when they sang at the graveside "Bydd Myrdd o Rhyfeddodau" (There Will Be a Multitude of Wonders) I sang, in my own heart The Red Flag.' - Gwenallt

On this day...

## May 19
FEAST DAY OF SAINT PUDENTIANA 1st - 2nd century in Rome. Ascension Day is around this time, and a Welsh proverb recorded in the 14th century says 'Do not take your coat off before Ascension Day'. In 1665, John Trevor, MP for Denbigh, became Wales' first Speaker of the House of Commons; Birth in Cilgerran in 1790 of the itinerant preacher Thomas Rhys Davies (see June 26); John Blackwell (born Pontwerwyl, Mold, 1797), poet and cleric, died in 1840 at Maenordeifi; William Ewart Gladstone died at Hawarden Castle in 1898; Death in 1922 of Thomas Powell of Llanwrtyd, Celtic scholar; Percy Bush, the great rugby player, died in Cardiff in 1955 (see June 23)

'An empiricist of our own century, Bertrand Russell, has provided a more grotesque example. A chicken which experiences every day that it gets fed when the farmer's wife comes over to the chicken run will finally come to the conclusion that there is a causal link between the approach of the farmer's wife and feed being put into its bowl.' "But *one day the chicken doesn't get its food?."* 'No, one day the farmer's wife comes over and wrings the chicken's neck.' *"Yuck, how disgusting!"* 'The fact that one thing follows another thus does not necessarily mean there is a causal link. One of the main concerns of philosophy is to warn people against jumping to conclusions. It can in fact lead to many different forms of superstition.' - Jostein Gaarder, 'Sophie's World', 1995

**On this day...**

...........................................................................................................................

...........................................................................................................................

...........................................................................................................................

# May 20

FEAST DAY OF SAINTS AMO (ANNO) at Llananno, Newborough; and TUDY (See May 11); in the 37th, 38th and 39th days after Easter, the Rogation Days. Welsh girls *'processioned'* wearing garlands of milkwort to ensure good dairy pastures. The flower is called Blodyn Llaeth (milk flower), and also Llysiau Crist (Christ's Herb). Evan Evans (Ieuan Fardd* or Ieuan Brydydd Hir), poet, unrivalled scholar and cleric, was born in Lledrod, Ceredigion in 1731 (see August 4); Death in 1771 of Kit Smart, the poet (see April 11); Death in 1926 of the great scholar Thomas Rees (see May 30)

*\*'I cannot without the utmost indignation observe the unnatural behaviour of the modern Welsh clergy and gentlemen of the principality of Wales. They have neither zeal for religion nor the interest of their country at heart. They glory in wearing the badge of their vassalage, by adopting the language of their conquerors, which is a mark of the most despicable meanness of spirit and mind lost to all that is noble and generous; and our clergy contrary to their oaths, perform divine services in a language, that one half of the congregation does not understand; and thus they rob those of the means of grace that pay them their tithes. This is no better than mere popery.' - Ieuan Fardd*

**On this day...**

...........................................................................................................................

...........................................................................................................................

...........................................................................................................................

# May 21

FEAST DAY OF SAINTS COLLEN 7th century (also May 31) at Llangollen, and in Brittany; CONSTANTINE the GREAT d. 337 at Rome; ELEN (with son Constantine) (see August 18) at Rome; MARCHAN 6th century at Llan Marchan; and MADRUN (see 17). Jac Glan-y-Gors (John Jones), the satirist and radical, died in London in 1821 (see November 10); Joseph Parry , hymn-writer, composer, was born in Merthyr Tudful in 1841. On this day also in 1862, he married Jane Thomas in Dannville, Pennsylvania (see February 17); The poet Leslie Norris was born in 1921 at Merthyr Tudful

*'At 6 o'clock we left Chester for Llangollen. We walked up through the town to the Hand Hotel, stopping for a moment on the fine quaint old grey stone bridge of Dee with its sharp angled recesses, to look down into the clear rocky swift winding river, so like the Wye. As we came near the Hand we heard the strains of a Welsh harp, the first I ever heard. The harper was playing in the hall the air 'Jenny Jones'. I would have come all the way to Llangollen on purpose to hear the Welsh harp. This is the only hotel in Wales where a Welsh harper can be heard. I stood by him entranced while he played Llwyn-Onn and the Roaring of the Valley, and several of the other guests in the house gathered around his harp in the corner of the hall. The harper was a cripple and his crutch rested by his side against a chair. He was a beautiful performer and he was playing on a handsome harp of sycamore and ash, which he had won as a prize at an Eisteddfod. He told me there were very few people now who could play the Welsh harp, and the instrument was fast going out of use. The young people learn the English harp which is much easier being double stringed instead of treble stringed. The Welsh harp has no silver string and it is played from the right shoulder. Sir Watkin keeps no harper. His sister does, and her harper is the brother of old Pugh of Dolgellau who took me up Cader Idris. The Llangollen harper said he knew him and thought him a good harper, but his brother whom he also knew and who is dead was much better, the first harper in Wales.'*
- Kilvert's Diary, this day in 1871

*On this day...*

.....................................................................................................................

.....................................................................................................................

.....................................................................................................................

# May 22

FEAST DAY OF SAINT ELEN LLUYDDOG 4th century (also August 25) at Llanelen, Bletherston, Caernarfon (Segontium). Birth in 1859 of Jonathan Ceredig Davies, traveller, writer, publisher and collector of folk-lore, at Llangunllo (see March 29); Death of Evan William Evans at Ithaca, New York State, in 1874 (see January 6); First issue of 'Y Cymro', the Welsh newspaper in 1890, edited by Isaac Foulkes (see November 2 and 9); HTV (Harlech) took over commercial television from TWW in 1968; Keidrych Rhys, poet and critic, died in 1987

*'In desire, in lust, in transgression,*
*It is time to make for*
*the land of your final retreat.*
*Seven saints, seven score, seven hundred*
*Gone in one convocation*

*With Christ the Blessed*
*Dread*
*They do not suffer'* - lines from 'Maytime Thoughts', a 13th century Welsh poem

*On this day...*

.........................................................................................................................
.........................................................................................................................
.........................................................................................................................

## May 23

FEAST DAY OF SAINT ABBOT PEDROG d.590 (also June 4, September 14, October 1) at Padstow, Y Ferwig, Mwnt, Llanbedrog, St Petrox, Bodmin. St Dyfrig's relics are re-interred in Llandaf Cathedral in 1120, after being brought on a 16-day journey from Ynys Enlli (Bardsey Island); Riots by lead miners and colliers at Rhuddlan in 1740, because of low wages and high food prices; The 9th Lancers are called into Denbigh in 1888 to enforce the sale of farms; Death in 1928 of Baron Buckland (see September 17); Jack Petersen of Cardiff won the British Light-Heavyweight Title in 1932; In 1970, the Britannia Bridge over the Menai Straits was severely damaged by fire

*'Sundays, workdays - he was not a weakling -*
*There were saucers, utensils of silver;*
*Cellars of gold with jewels on them:*
*And where else are there better goblets for wine?'* - lines from a poem to the lord of Penrhyn, Llandygai, by Dafydd Llwyd (c.1420-c.1500) of Mathafarn, from Dr Enid Roberts' 'Food of the Bards'

*On this day...*

.........................................................................................................................
.........................................................................................................................
.........................................................................................................................

## May 24

FEAST DAY OF SAINTS DYFAN AND FFAGAN 2nd century (Dyfan also April 8) at Merthyr Dyfan, St Ffagan's, Llanmaes. Birth of Betsi Cadwaladr (Elizabeth Davies), Crimean nurse, at Llanycil, Bala in 1789 (see July 17); Birth of Joseph Parry*, composer, at Chapel Row, Georgetown, Merthyr in 1841; Death in 1901 of 81 miners at Universal Colliery, Senghenydd; Pendyrus Male Voice Choir was formed in 1924; Death at Aberystwyth in 1926 of Sir John Williams, cultural benefactor (see November 6); The last trawler landed fish at Cardiff in 1956

*'Paham mae dicter, O Myfanwy,
Y llenwi'th lygaid duon di,
A'th ruddiau tirion, O Myfanwy,
Heb wrido wrth fy ngweled I
Pa le mae'r wen oedd ar dy wefus,
Fu'n cynnau cariad ffyddlon ffol?
Pa le mae sain dy eiriau melys,
Fu'n denu nghalon ar dy ol?
Myfanwy, boed yr oll o'th fywyd,
Dan heulwen ddisglair canol dydd,
Ar boed I rosyn gwridog iechyd,
I ddawnsio ganmlwydd ar dy rudd,
Anghofia'r oll o'th addewidion,
A wneist I rywun eneth ddel,
A dyro'th law Myfanwy dirion,
I ddim ond dweud y gair Ffarwel.' - Joseph Parry*

**On this day...**

....................................................................................................................

....................................................................................................................

....................................................................................................................

## May 25

*FEAST DAY OF SAINTS* MAELand SULIEN (see 13). Mansel Bussey, MP and Parliamentary commander, buried at Briton Ferry in 1699; John Frost, Chartist leader, born at the Royal Oak Inn, Newport in 1784; Death in 1946 of the poet, author and editor Ernest Percival Rhys (see July 17); Work began on this day on the Cardiff Bay Barrage in 1994, and exactly six years later to the day, in 2000, the excellent water bus service began

'As to my latter end I go,
To meet my Jubilee,
I bless the good horse Bendigo
Who built this tomb for me' - epitaph on the gravestone of R.J. Lloyd-Price at Llanfor, the man who founded Bala whisky and organised the world's first sheepdog trial, referring to his huge winning bet on a race-horse which won the Derby

**On this day...**

....................................................................................................................

....................................................................................................................

....................................................................................................................

# May 26

FEAST DAY OF SAINTS LLEURWG MAWR c.120-c.190 (martyred on December 3) at St Mellons (Llanlleurog); FFAGAN (see February 10); and RUFUS PUDENS at Rome, the martyred husband of Gwladys Claudia ferch Caradog. In 1401, Henry V disbanded his huge army that had failed to subdue Wales; Elizabeth I allowed the famous Caerwys Eisteddfod to take place in 1567; Birth in 1750 of William Morgan at Bridgend, who made the first company valuation (The Equitable) and was the first man to produce x-rays; Birth in 1837 of Henry Hicks at St Davids*, physician and geologist (died November 18, 1899); The first greyhound races were held at Cardiff's Arms Park in 1928; *'Fanfare for Four Trumpets'*, written by Karl Jenkins of Penclawdd (composer of *Adiemus*) opened the National (British) Assembly of Wales in 1999

*'*Ty Gwyn is situated above Porth Mawr, and about two miles from St David's. It stands on the south slopes of Carn Lidi, the purple rocks above it springing out of the heath, with here and there a gorse bush, like a puff of flame breaking out of the crannies in the rock. Below it, near the sea, are the foundations of the church of Ty Gwyn, the cradle of Christianity among the southern Irish, now trodden underfoot by sheep and oxen, that wander over the wide cemetery where lie thick, in narrow coffins of unshaped stones, the bodies of the inmates of that earliest Mission College in Britain. When we visited the spot in 1898, the farmer had torn up the grave slabs of the tombs in the cattle yard, and the drainage of his cow stalls and pig styes soaked into the places where bodies of the ancient fathers of the British and Irish churches had crumbled to dust.'* - Mrs Dawson, writing in Archaeologia Cambrensis in 1898

*On this day...*

..............................................................................................................................................................

..............................................................................................................................................................

..............................................................................................................................................................

# May 27

FEAST DAY OF SAINTS CARANNOG 6th century (also May 16) Llangrannog, Crantock, Llandudoch, Chernach, Carantec; ELEN (see August 18); MELANGELL (see 28); and GARMON of MAN (see July 1); Birth in 1874 of David Walters (*Eurof*) near Ammanford, minister and writer (see September 24); Death in 1923 of the rugby international Charles Prytherch Lewis of Llanwrda, who won a 'triple Blue' at Oxford, winning the hurdles, hammer-throwing and playing cricket; Stanley Baker, film actor and director, was knighted in 1976; In 2000, Wales beat the French Barbarians in the world's first ever indoor rugby game at the Millennium Stadium

*'At the top of Jacobs ladder met Miss Sandell with the Morrell children carrying home from their ramble a beautiful rich nosegay of wild flowers. They had found the bog bean, the butterwort, milk-wort in four varieties, butterfly orchis, mouse ear, marsh valentine,*

*marsh buttercup, hawkweed fumitory, yellow pimpernel, yellow potentilla. The children showed me what I never found out for myself or knew before, that the bog bean grows in the wern below Great Gwernfydden. And I have walked 14 miles for that flower, when it grew close by. Miss Sandell taught me more about these flowers in ten minutes than I have learnt from books in all my life. She knows a great deal about flowers. She does not know the comfrey or yellow hill-violet, some of which I promised to bring her from the Warren Hill today.'* - Kilvert's Diary, this day in 1871

**On this day...**

..........................................................................................................................

..........................................................................................................................

..........................................................................................................................

## May 28

*FEAST DAY OF SAINTS* ABBESS MELANGELL d.641 (also May 27 and January 31) at Pennant Melangell*; GARMON of MAN (see July 1); and SAMSON (died, see July 28); *WHITSUNDAY QUARTERDAY in SCOTLAND*. In 1259, Maredudd ap Rhys Grug was tried by his peers for defecting from Llywelyn to the king, and imprisoned in Cricieth Castle; *The Birth of Owain Glyndŵr in 1349 or 1354;* In 1356 Owain Llawgoch survived the carnage of Poitiers, fighting for the French; Birth of David Jones (of Wallington), historian and genealogist, at Llanbleddian in 1834 (see July 11); John Bowen of Llanllawer near Fishguard (born November 21, 1815), missionary and Bishop of Sierra Leone, died in Freetown in 1859; Dan Isaac Davies of Llandovery, pioneer of Welsh teaching in schools, died in 1887; ); Freddie Welsh (Frederick Hall Thomas) lost his world lightweight title in New York in 1917; 1944 saw Cardiff's last air-raid; Donald Watts Davies of Treorchy, the man who made the Internet possible, died in 1999

*'Why, Lord, did you make Cwm Pennant so lovely,
And the life of an old shepherd so short?'* - Eifon Wyn (Eliseus Williams) 1867-1926

**On this day...**

..........................................................................................................................

..........................................................................................................................

..........................................................................................................................

## May 29

*FEAST DAY OF SAINTS* DYFRIG c.485-c.546 (also November 4 and 14, March 11) at Mochras, Moccas, Archenfield, Hentland, Whitchurch, Madley, Caldey Island; ERBIN (see January 13); JOHN PENRY (executed at St Thomas a Watering in Surrey 1593) at Llangammarch Wells; TRADITIONAL DATE

OF BIRTH OF JESUS (also March 28 and April 18). The architect of Portmeirion, Clough Williams-Ellis, was born in 1883; Bob Hope, comedian, born Leslie Towns Hope in 1903 - his parents had lived in Barry and Newport (see April 25); The actress and script-writer Mary Diana Morgan was born in Radyr, Cardiff in 1910 (see December 9)

*'Three things it is everyone's duty to do:*
*Listen humbly,*
*Answer discreetly,and*
*Judge kindly'* - from the Welsh Triads of Virtues

**On this day...**

.................................................................................................................

.................................................................................................................

.................................................................................................................

# May 30

*FEAST DAY OF SAINTS* CADOG 7th century at Centule; and TUDCLYD at Penmachno. Death in 1884 of Sir Henry Bartle Frere, hero of the Indian Mutiny, who was born at Llanelly Hill, Breconshire in 1815; Birth of Thomas Rees, principal of Bala-Bangor College, pacifist and scholar, at Llanfyrnach in 1869 (see May 20); In 1912 Hugh Griffith was born in Marian Glas, Anglesey, and later won an Oscar for his part in Ben Hur; In 1929, Megan Lloyd George became Wales' first female MP, for Anglesey, and Aneurin Bevan was first elected as an MP; In the 1929 General Election, Plaid Cymru had its first candidate

On this day In 1403, Prince Henry wrote to Henry IV *'... the rebels hear every day if we are paid, and they know well that without payment we cannot continue; and they strive to raise all the forces of North Wales and of South Wales to over-ride and destroy the March and the counties adjoining thereto; and there is no resistance here, so they well acccomplish their malice; and when our men have retreated from us, it is necessary that we should by all means retreat into England, there to be disgraced forever... and at present we have very great expenses and have made all the pawning we are able of our little jewels to destroy them, for two of our castles, Hardelagh (Harlech) and Lampadern (Aberystwyth) are besieged and have been for a long time, and we must rescue the march around us with the third body (army) against the entry of the rebels (of Glyndŵr)*

**On this day...**

.................................................................................................................

.................................................................................................................

.................................................................................................................

## May 31

FEAST DAY OF SAINTS WINNOW (see October 25); and COLLEN (also 21). In 1257, a Norman army from Carmarthen was repelled at Dinefwr Castle (see June 2); The castle and walled town of Tenby under Rice Powell, surrendered to Horton and Cromwell in 1648; In 1865, 163 Welsh people sailed from Liverpool on the Mimosa for the new Welsh colony in Patagonia; In 1962 the High Court ruled that election nomination papers in Welsh were valid; Sadly, the excellent Welsh Industrial and Maritime Museum in Cardiff Bay was closed in 1998 - a shameful event, but thankfully Swansea has resurrected the museum in its bay area

'When the young year wakes germ and grain,
With the young year he comes again;
When the blue corn-flower's in the wheat,
And barley-ears wave green and sweet;
When sings the lark above the lea,
And finch and linnet on the tree -
Comes back to us our welcome guest,
At holiday and patrons' feast.
Oh would that every month were May,
And every hour a holiday:
Would I could see about the sky
All the year round the swallows fly;
Could see them still, from spring to spring,
Around our chimney on the wing!' - Lines from the Breton poem 'The Swallows', trans. Tom Taylor

**On this day...**

....................................................................................................

....................................................................................................

....................................................................................................

# JUNE - MEHEFIN
## (Mid-Summer)
### Even (Breton), Miz Epham (Cornish)

## June 1

*FEAST DAY OF SAINTS* GWEN TIERBRON 5th - 6th century at Whitchurch Canicorum; EUDDOGWY (see July 2); and TEGLA (see October 15). The great Crumlin Viaduct opened in 1857; In 1920, Alfred George Edwards was enthroned first Archbishop of Wales at St Asaf's Cathedral (see November 2); The submarine Thetis sank off Anglesey in 1939, with 99 drowning; Jonathan Pryce, film and theatre actor, born in Holywell in 1947; The world's first scheduled helicopter service started in 1950, between Cardiff, Wrexham and Liverpool

*'Though the nation be said to be unconquered and most loving liberty, yet it was never mutinous, and please your majesty, but stout, valiant, courteous, hospitable, temperate, ingenious, capable of all good arts, most lovingly constant, charitable, great antiquaries, religious preservers of their gentry and genealogy, as they are zealous and knowing in religion.'* - Ben Jonson (1572-1637), 'For the Honour of Wales'

**On this day...**

## June 2

*FEAST DAY OF SAINT* BODFAN (see January 2). In 1257 the Norman army retreating from Dinefwr (see May 31) were defeated by Maredudd ap Rhys and Maredudd ab Owain, at Cymerau, near Pont-ar-Gothi*; In early June, 1401, Glyndŵr was surrounded in the Hyddgen Valley, 12 miles from Aberystwyth, by a superior force of English and Flemings, but won an impressive victory; Eleanor Butler, one of the 'Ladies of Llangollen' died in 1829; The Merthyr Rising, unprecedented in British history, started in 1831, with around 24 deaths occurring over the next 4 days; The hymn-writer David Charles died in 1834; Riots in Mold in 1869; Birth near Carmel in 1893 of the economist David James Davies (see October 11); Death of John Viriamu Jones, first President of University College Cardiff, in 1901; Collapse of Cleddau Bridge, with 4 dead, in 1970; Pope John Paul II visited Wales in 1982

*\*'More than 3000 Englishmen fell that day... very few if any of the armed knights survived that battle'* - a monastic chronicler at Talyllychau (Talley Abbey)

**On this day...**

# June 3

FEAST DAY OF SAINTS CWYFAN 6th century (also 7) at Llangwyfan, Dyserth, Glendalough; TUDWAL BEFR 5th century at Llanstadwel, St Tudwal's Island, Tudweiliog; and MERIADOC (see 7). In 1659, the Dissenter Morgan Llwyd died; On this day in 1831, about 20 people were shot dead in The Merthyr Rising by the Argyll and Sutherland Highlanders; Jefferson Davis, President of the Confederate States of America, was born in 1808, and the day is still officially celebrated in four southern states (see December 5); In 1867 the Barmouth Viaduct opened; Birth of Hugh Robert Jones, founder of the Welsh National party, in Deiniolen in 1894 (see June 17); Jim Driscoll wins the European featherweight title in 1912; Memorial Service at Westminster Abbey for Sir Lewis Casson, who was still acting aged 91 (see May 13 and October 26)

*'Ychydig a wneid am y nef, pe diffoddid uffern' - 'Little would be done about heaven if hell fire were extinguished.'*

**On this day...**

...................................................................................................................................

...................................................................................................................................

...................................................................................................................................


# June 4

FEAST DAY OF SAINTS NINNOC 6th century at Ploemur, Scaer; PEDROG (see May 23); and GUDWAL (see 6). Caernarfon Castle surrendered to Parliamentarian forces in 1646; Death in 1835 of William Owen Pughe (see August 7); Death in 1960 of the artist Margaret Lindsay Williams (see June 18)

*'A process in the weather of the world*
*Turns ghost to ghost; each mothered child*
*Sits in their double shade.*
*A process blows the moon into the sun,*
*Pulls down the shabby curtains of the skin;*
*And the heart gives up its dead.'* - Dylan Thomas, final verse of 'A Process in the Weather of the Heart'

**On this day...**

...................................................................................................................................

...................................................................................................................................

...................................................................................................................................

# June 5

FEAST DAY OF SAINT TUDNO 6th century (also November 31) at Llandudno. The Royalists were routed at the Battle of Y Dalar Hir, Llandegai, in 1648; Wales beat the football world champions, West Germany, 1-0 in 1991

'Upon Sundays and holidays the multitude of all sorts... meet in sundry places either on some hill or on the side of some mountain where their harpers and fiddlers sing them songs of the doings of their ancestors, namely, of the wars against the kings of this realm and the English nation, and then do they recite their pedigrees at length how each of them is descended from those of their old princes. Here also do they spend their time in hearing some part of the lives of Taliesin, or Merlin, Beuno, Cybi, Garmon and such other intended prophets and saints of the country.' - excerpt of a spy's report from Snowdonia to the Council of Wales and the Marches, c.1590

*On this day...*

..................................................................................................................

..................................................................................................................

..................................................................................................................

# June 6

FEAST DAY OF SAINTS GUDWAL d. 603 (also 4, 7) at Finstall, Worcester, Gulval, Finistere, Ghent, St Malo; GURWAL (see 12); and PEDR (see 29). In 1282 Gilbert de Clare's Norman forces were so badly beaten by Llywelyn's troops near Llandilo that he was stripped of his command of royal forces; Ann Maddocks, 'The Maid of Cefn Ydfa' buried at Llangynwyd in 1727; John Bradford of Betws Tir Iarll (born 1706), inspiration of Iolo Morganwg, was buried in 1785; The painter Ceri Richards born at Dunvant in 1903; Merthyr Tudful granted borough status in 1905; South Wales Borderers land on Normandy beaches in 1944

'Something must be done. You may be sure that all I can do for you, I will.' Edward VIII, 1936, to Welsh miners during The Great Depression. Three weeks later he abdicated.

*On this day...*

..................................................................................................................

..................................................................................................................

..................................................................................................................

# June 7

FEAST DAYS OF SAINTS BISHOP MERIADOC 6th century (also June 3 and 9) at Camborne, Vannes; CWYFAN (see 3); GUDWAL (see 6); and COLMAN (see November 20). Death aged 54 at Sempringham of Princess Gwenllian in 1337, after 54 years in captivity; By this day in 1831, Merthyr Tudful was back under the forces of law and order after the Merthyr Rising on June 3; Lord Justice Sir William James of Merthyr Tudful died in 1881; Death of Samuel Davies (2nd), Wesleyan Methodist Minister, at Amlwch in 1891; Tom Jones was born in Trefforest in 1940

On this day in 1983, the Labour leader Neil Kinnock made a prophetic speech at Bridgend, at a time when Wales was still relatively prosperous vis-à-vis England: *'If Margaret Thatcher wins on Thursday she will become more a leader than a Prime Minister.*

*That power produces arrogance, and when it is toughened by Tebbitry and fawned upon by spineless sycophants, the boot-licking tabloid Knights of Fleet Street and placemen in the Quangos, the arrogance corrupts completely.*

*If Margaret Thatcher is re-elected as Prime Minister on Thursday, I warn you.*

*I warn you that you will be quiet when the curfew of fear and the gibbet of unemployment makes you obedient.*

*I warn you that you will have pain – when healing and relief depend upon payment.*

*I warn you that you will have ignorance - and then talents are untended and wits are wasted, when learning is a privilege and not a right.*

*I warn you that you will have poverty – when pensions slip and benefits are whittled away by a government that won't pay in an economy that can't pay.*

*I warn you that you will be cold – when fuel charges are used as a tax system that the rich don't notice and the poor can't afford.*

*I warn you that you must not expect work – when many cannot spend, more will not be able to earn. When they don't earn, they don't spend. When they don't spend, work dies.*

*I warn you not to go out into the streets alone after dark or into the streets in large crowds of protest in the light.*

*I warn you that you will have defence of a sort – with a risk and at a price that passes all understanding.*

*I warn you that you will be home-bound – when fares and transport bills kill leisure and lock you up.*

*I warn you that you will borrow less – when credit, loans, mortgages and easy payments are refused to people on your melting income.*

*If Margaret Thatcher wins on Thursday –*
*I warn you not to be ordinary*
*I warn you not to be young*
*I warn you not to fall ill*
*I warn you not to get old'*


**On this day...**

# June 8

FEAST DAY OF SAINT EUGRAD 6th century (also January 6) at Llaneugrad, Treouergat. In 1287 Rhys ap Maredudd, Lord of Dryslwyn, rose in revolt against Edward I - he was captured in 1291 and executed at York (see Jan 20 and September 5); Sarah Siddons died in 1831; Death in 1841 at Llangefni of the preacher John Elias (see May 6); Birth in 1859, at Beaufort near Ebbw Vale, of Thomas Richards MP, miners' leader and Privy Councillor; Frank Lloyd Wright, one of the world's greatest architects, was born in 1867; Death of Gerard Manley Hopkins in 1889; Brecon Mountain Railway opened in 1980; In 1982, 39 Welsh Guardsmen were killed, and 79 (including Simon Weston) injured on the 'Sir Galahad' at Bluff Cove in the Falklands War

*'The Royal Variety Performance which made last Sunday the longest Sabbath since the Lord's first Day of Rest, must be republicanism's most powerful secret weapon.'* - Gwyn Thomas, in a letter in The Western Mail about a televised broadcast when there was only one TV channel

*On this day...*

........................................................................................

........................................................................................

........................................................................................

# June 9

FEAST DAYS OF SAINTS ANNUN (ANHUN) with MADRUN 5th century (also October 19, April 9) at Trawsfynydd; and MERIADOC (see 7). Thomas Tomkins 'II' of St Davids, organist and composer, died in 1656; Birth of Samuel Davies (1st'), Wesleyan Methodist Minister at Cilcain in 1788; Death in 1886 of the ironmaster Edward Williams (see February 10); Clifford Evans of Senghenydd, actor-director, died in 1985 aged 73

*'He who cleans his teeth with the point of his knife, shall soon clean them with the haft'* - from the 14th century 'Book of Iago ap Dewi'

*On this day...*

........................................................................................

........................................................................................

........................................................................................

# June 10

FEAST DAY OF SAINT RHYCHWYN (also June 12 and first Sunday after June 21) at Llanrhychwyn. Glyndŵr's forces attack Archenfield in 1404; In 1710, the Welsh Jacobite 'Society of the White Rose' was founded; In 1869, 53 miners died at Ferndale Colliery, Rhondda; Birth in 1883 of Margaret Haig Thomas,

Viscountess Rhondda (see July 20); The opera-singer Adelina Patty married in Ystradgynlais in 1886; In 1971, the formation of the Sports Council for Wales was announced

In 1403, on this day, Richard Kingeston, Archbishop of Hereford, wrote to Henry IV *'The Welsh rebels in great numbers have entered Archenfield, and there they have killed the inhabitants and ravaged the country to the great dishonour of our king and the insupportable damage of the country. We implore you to consider this very perilous and pitiable case and to pray to our sovereign Lord that he will come in his royal person or perhaps send some person with sufficient power to rescue us from the invasion of the rebels. Otherwise we will be utterly destroyed, which God forbid: whoever comes will as we are led to believe have to engage in battle, or will have a very severe struggle with the rebels. And for God's sake remember that honourable and valiant man, the Lord of Abergavenny, who is on the very point of destruction if he is not rescued.'*

*On this day...*

..........................................................................................................................................

..........................................................................................................................................

..........................................................................................................................................

# June 11

*FEAST DAYS OF SAINTS* BARNABAS 1st century; and TEILO (see February 9). Troops were called in to the' Tithe War' at Bodfari in 1887; In 1941, the 'Baron Carnegie' was sunk by German aircraft off Strumble Head, with 25 dying; The first Llangollen International Music Festival began in 1947; The artist Sir Frank Brangwyn died in 1956 (see May 13); In 1969 the Royal Regiment of Wales was formed from the merger of the South Wales Borderers (formed 1689), and the Welch Regiment (formed 1719)

*'Exception, n. A thing which takes the liberty to differ from other things of its class, as an honest man, a truthful woman, etc. "The exception proves the rule" is an expression constantly upon the lips of the ignorant, who parrot it from one another with never a thought of its absurdity. In the Latin, "Exceptio probat regulam" means that the exception tests the rule, puts it to the proof, not confirms it. The malefactor who drew the meaning from this excellent dictum and substituted a contrary one of his own exerted an evil power which appears to be immortal.'* - Ambrose Gwinnett Bierce (1842 - missing in Mexico 1913), The Devil's Dictionary, 1911

*On this day...*

..........................................................................................................................................

..........................................................................................................................................

..........................................................................................................................................

# June 12

FEAST DAY OF SAINTS GURWAL 6th century (also 6) at Guer; and RHYCHWYN (see 10). Birth in 1282 at Abergwyngeryn of Princess Gwenllian ferch Llywelyn ap Gruffudd, taken to live in captivity at Sempringham for 54 years; Birth in 1823 of John Roberts, for 21 years the world billiards champion; The Welsh National War Memorial unveiled in Cardiff in 1928; John L. Lewis, Welsh-American miners' leader, died in 1969; Nicolette Milnes-Walker sets off from Dale, Pembrokeshire, to cross the Atlantic in 1971 (see July 26)

'... suspicion was the greatest enemy which the National party must face. Suspicion comes readily to Welshman. Because of the watertight pockets of countryside in which he has dwelt so long he is wary of those who live across the mountain, for, often developing in different directions, neighbouring districts have not seen eye to eye. Overriding this internal distrust was the general suspicion in which the people over the border were held, a suspicion which successive races - Jutes, Angles, Romans and Normans - had done their worst to justify. Any Welsh political party which hoped to gain general backing must therefore disarm the mistrust which the native people have been taught by history to use as a protective shield against threats both within the country and outside it.' - Thomas Firbank, 'A Country of Memorable Honour' 1953

*On this day...*

..............................................................................................................................................................
..............................................................................................................................................................
..............................................................................................................................................................

# June 13

FEAST DAY OF SAINTS ELERI 6th century at Gwytherin; SANNAN (see March 1); and ARMEL (see Aug 16). Llywelyn Bren is fully pardoned by the King in 1317, and his estates restored; In 1941, the ferry St Patrick was sunk by German aircraft of Strumble Head, with 30 killed; Last train across the Crumlin Viaduct in 1964; Harry Secombe knighted in 1981

'Men went to Catraeth with the dawn,
Their ardour shortened their lives.
Before their hair turned grey, death came to them...
The warriors arose, they assembled;
Together, with one accord, they attacked.
Short were their lives, long their kinsmen's grief for them.
They slew seven times their number of the English (Saxons).
By fighting they made women widows,
Many a mother with a tear on her eyelid...
The warband of Mynyddog, famous in battle,
They paid for their mead-feast with their lives,
Caradog and Madog, Pyll and Ieuan,
Gwgon and Gwion, Gwyn and Cynfan,*

*Peredur, armed with steel, Gwawrddur and Aeddan,*
*Attackers in the fight, with shattered shields;*
*And although they were slain, they slew,*
*Not one returned to his homeland...*
*Three hundred golden-torqued warriors attacked*
*Defending their land, with cruel slaughter;*
*Although they were slain, they slew,*
*And until the end of the world they shall be praised...'*
- Lines from the 7th century epic poem 'Y Gododdin' - Catraeth has always been placed at the inland Catterick, but the place-name actually means Cad-Traeth, Battle-beach

*On this day...*

## June 14

FEAST DAY OF SAINT TEGWEL (see DOGMAEL, October 31). In 1645, after the battle of Naseby, over 100 Welsh-speaking Royalist wives were slaughtered by Parliamentarians, who thought they were *'foreign spies'*; In 1646, the Parliamentarians took Beaumaris Castle; Thomas Pennant, trravel writer, naturalist and nationalst, born at Whitford near Holywell in 1726 (see December 16); William Abraham (Mabon*), MP and first President of the South Wales Miners' Federation was born in 1842 at Cwmafan; Lloyd George's maiden speech to Parliament in 1890

*'Great hero of Labour, live coal of the platform, gifted soul, genial of nature, brave and beloved, the shield of our rights, honest visionary with a wide heart. From the tower of his forehead, fire flowed - for the truth, and his eloquence will be remembered by the whole nation.'* - tribute to Mabon from the Archdruid Dyfed

*On this day...*

## June 15

FEAST DAY OF SAINTS CENEU 5th century at Llangeneu; MEWAN d.c.590 (also June 21) at Saint Meen-le-Grand, St Mewan, Megavissey; TRILLO 5th-6th century (also June 16, 24, 25, 26) at Llandrillo, Llandrygarn; and NON (see March 3). In 1215, the Magna Carta was signed by King John, ceding power to

Llywelyn Fawr (Llywelyn ab Iorwerth) and the English Barons, and respecting Welsh law; Sir Mathew Cradock, royal official, died in 1531, and was buried in Swansea; The Calvinistic Methodist and famous preacher John Elias died in 1841, and is buried at Llanfaes, near Beaumaris (see May 6); Birth in 1851 of Ernest Howard Griffiths at Brecon, physicist, FRS and second principal of the University College of South Wales and Monmouthshire (see March 3); Captain Scott's Expedition left Cardiff in the Terra Nova for the South Pole in 1910; First branch of the Women's Institute began at Llanfairpwllgwyngyll in 1915 (an alternative date in August 11); In 1941, the RAF took over Fairwood Common, Gower*, as a fighter station; Death in 1954 of Viscount Camrose (see June 23); In 1955 Tom Jones, the founder of Coleg Harlech, died

*'An old woman who kept a little inn on the Gower gathered her hops wild from the hedges, drying them in bags from the kitchen ceiling, and by this economy was able to brew an 18-gallon cask of beer for 1 shilling and 6 pence. A shilling was paid for 14 lbs of barley, which was sprouted for 5 days before being boiled and steeped, 4 pence was spent on balm (yeast) and additionally, and somewhat mysteriously, half-an-ounce of Bristol twist tobacco was added, for colour and flavour, for two pence. A man who had drunk this brew in his youth told me: "When you'd had 4 pints of it, you were drunk".' John Waters, quoted in 'Prince of Ales', by Brian Glover

*On this day...*

...........................................................................................................................

...........................................................................................................................

...........................................................................................................................

# June 16

*FEAST DAY OF SAINTS* CURIG 6th century (also February 17) at Llangurig, Capel Curig, Porthkerry, Llanilid, Newport, Locquirec; ELIDON (see September 1); JULIOT (ILUD) (also nearest Sunday to June 29) at Luxulyan, Tintagel, St Juliot, Lanteglos; and ISMAEL 7th century (also 25) at St Ismael's. Gruffudd ap Cynan, king of all Wales, defeated Leofgar, bishop of Hereford in a battle in 1056 in the Machawy Valley; The Battle of Stoke Field in 1487, when Henry Tudor and Sir Rhys ap Thomas defeated an army of German and Irish soldiers, with 7000 dead. They were supporting the impostor Lambert Simnel, whom Henry spared; Birth of Robert Davies (Cyndeyrn), musician and composer near Henllan, Denbigh in 1814; In 1865, 38 miners died at New Bedwellty Colliery, Tredegar; Birth in 1902 of the great poet, dramatist and nationalist James Kitchener Davies near Tregaron (see August 25); In 1933, 7 men and 4 women were found guilty at Monmouth and imprisoned, for rioting over the employment of blackleg miners; Death in 1944 of Lord Davies of Llandinam (see May 11)

*Glendower: 'Three times hath Henry Bolingbroke made head*

*Against my power; thrice from the the banks of Wye*
*And sandy-bottomed Severn have I sent him*
*Bootless home and weather-beaten back.'* - William Shakespeare, Henry IV Part I

*On this day...*

..............................................................................................................................

..............................................................................................................................

..............................................................................................................................

# June 17

*FEAST DAY OF SAINTS* BRIAVEL at St Briavels; MYLLIN d. 696 at Llanfyllin
- thought to have introduced baptism by immersion; HUARVE 6th century at St
Herve; and NECTAN (see February 14). In 1497 at the Battle of Blackheath, Sir
Rhys ap Thomas took Lord Audley prisoner; Gabriel Goodman of Ruthin died in
1601 aged 83, and was buried in Westminster Abbey - he assisted in the
production of William Morgan's Bible, and founded Christ's Hospital and a
grammar school in Ruthin; Willam Alexander Madock, builder of Tremadoc, was
born in 1773; In 1837, 20 miners died at Henwain Colliery, Blaina, Gwent;
Holyhead's new harbour was opened in 1880; Sir David Brunt was born at
Nantyglo in 1886, an outstanding meteorologist after whom the *Brunt Period* (the
fundamental period of atmospheric oscillation) is named (see February 5); Death
in 1930 of Hugh Robert Jones, founder of the Welsh Nationalist Party and 'Y
Ddraig Goch' (see June 3); Death in Buenos Aires in 1952 of Alberto Williams,
composer (born 1862); John Cowper Powys, writer, died at Blaenau Ffestiniog in
1963 (see October 8)

*'From time immemorial Wales has been divided into three more or less equal parts.*
*When I say equal I mean in value rather than in size. These are Gwynedd, or North*
*Wales; South Wales, called in Welsh Deheubarth, which really means Right-Hand*
*Wales, a sub-section of which, containing seven cantrefs, has been given the name*
*Demetia or Dyfed; and Powys, which is in the middle and stretches eastwards. The*
*reason for this three-fold division is as follows. Rhodri Mawr (820-878), or Roderick*
*the Great, who ruled over all Wales, had three sons, Merfyn, Anarawd and Cadell. He*
*gave North Wales to Merfyn, Powys to Anarawd and South Wales to Cadell. The*
*people agreed to this arrangement, and so did all three brothers, for, although South*
*Wales was by far the largest region, it was much the least attractive, for it was ruled by*
*a large number of local chieftains, called "uchelwr" in Welsh, who were in constant*
*rebellion and hard to control. Cadell's brothers predeceased him and in the end he ruled*
*over all Wales. So did his successors down to the time of Tewdwr. Tewdwr's successors*
*in their turn were, like him, rulers of the whole of Wales; Rhys ap Tewdwr, Gruffydd*
*ap Rhys and Rhys ap Gruffydd, who is the present prince.'* - Giraldus Cambrensis,
'The Description of Wales', 1193-1194

*Norwegian Church at Cardiff Bay - Cathy Crompton*

*Cardiff Bay - Cathy Crompton*

*'Cardiff Bay' - Cathy Crompton*

*The Pierhead Building Cardiff Bay - Cathy Crompton*

*Lock Keepers Hut - Cardiff Docks - Martin S. Green*

*Pierhead Building, Cardiff Bay - Martin S. Green*

*Penarth Pier - Martin S. Green*

*Penarth Pier - Martin S. Green*

*Ffont-y-gari Bay at low tide - Martin S. Green*

*Nash Point Lighthouse - Martin S. Green*

*Cold Knap - Martin S. Green*

*Norwegian Church, Cardiff Bay - Cathy Crompton*

*Tenby Harbour and Town - Wales Tourist Board Photo Library*

*Llandudno Beach and Seafront - Wales Tourist Board Photo Library*

*The Tube, Cardiff Bay - Cardiff Marketing*

*Cardiff Bay - Cardiff Marketing*

*The Norwegian Church, Cardiff Bay - Cardiff Marketing*

*Sculpture at Margam Park - Martin S. Green*

*The Millennium Stadium, Cardiff - Wales Tourist Board Photo Library*

*Snowdonia near Dolgellau - Wales Tourist Board Photo Library*

*Snowdonia, Cader Idris - Wales Tourist Board Photo Library*

*Castle of the Winds, between Glyder Fawr and Glyder Fach - Cathy Crompton*

*Snowdon from Glyder Fawr - Cathy Crompton*

*Herding Sheep - Cathy Crompton*

*"Chip off the Old Block" - Cathy Crompton*

*Checking over a new born calf - Cathy Crompton*

........................................................................................................

........................................................................................................

........................................................................................................

# June 18

FEAST DAY OF SAINT MAWAN 6th century at St Maughan's, St Meugan. The will was proved in 1558 of the mathematician and inventor of *pi*, Robert Recorde of Tenby; Sir Thomas Picton, hero of Waterloo, died in 1815 in the battle, having been gravely wounded previously at Quatre Bras; Birth at Barri in 1888 of Margaret Lindsay Williams, artist (see June 4); Birth in 1890 of Aneurin Iolo Williams, author and art historian (see January 18); Birth in 1902 of Morgan Phillips at Aberdare, General Secretary of the Labour Party (see January 15); In 1923, Jimmy Wilde lost his World Flyweight Title; In 1928, Amelia Earhart became the first woman to fly the Atlantic, when she landed her seaplane off Burry Port; Delia Smith, 'the matron saint of English cooking', born in Monmouth in 1941 - her mother was Etty Lewis from Twyn and Llwyngwril; The Irish Sea was officially designated the Celtic Sea in 1974; Wales finished 3rd in the 1987 Rugby World Cup, beating Australia

A small tombstone in Ystrad Fflur, Strata Florida Abbey, reads *'The left leg and part of the thigh of Henry Hughes, Cooper, was cut off and interred here, June 18, 1756'*. The rest of Henry emigrated to the USA

........................................................................................................

........................................................................................................

........................................................................................................

# June 19

FEAST DAY OF SAINT LLIDNERTH 6th century. Alternative date of birth in 1282 of Gwenllian (see June 12), and the death of her mother Eleanor de Montfort, which sparked Llywelyn's decision to join his brother Dafydd's rebellion against Edward I; Henry Humphries Lloyd, leading miltary engineer, died in Belgium in 1783; John Gibson R.A., the great sculptor was christened in Conwy in 1790 (see August 13); Carmarthen Workhouse was destroyed in 1843 by Rebecca Rioters because of the Poor Law Amendment Act; First German air-raid on Cardiff in 1940; Wales unluckily lost to Brazil 1-0 in the World Cup semi-final in Sweden, John Charles being too badly injured to play

*'The juice of the leek is good against the vomiting of blood. It is good for women who desire children to eat leeks. Take leeks and wine to cure the bite of adders and venomous beasts. The juice of leeks and mothers' milk is good against pneumonia. The juice with*

*goat's gall and honey in equal parts, put warm into the ear, is good for deafness. It will relieve wind of the stomach, and engender strange dreams'* - 'Meddygon Myddfai', 13th century

*On this day...*

......................................................................................................

......................................................................................................

......................................................................................................

# June 20

*FEAST DAY OF SAINTS* ALBAN 3rd century (also June 17, 22 and July 22) at Caerleon, St Alban's ; GOVAN 6th century (also March 26) at St Govan's; ARFON and JULIUS (see July 1); PADARN (see April 15); GWENOLE (see March 3); and NOVATUS at Rome; *MIDSUMMER EVE - celebrated by the Celts.* The will was administered in 1656 of Sir Robert Mansell of Penrice, admiral, MP and glass manufacturer; Thomas Essile David (*Dewi Wyn o Esyllt*), poet, born in Dinas Powys in 1820; Death in 1882 of David Thomas, who made the world's first 'anthracite' iron in America (see November 3); Ernest John (Johnny) Morris, children's TV entertaner, born in Newport in 1916; The historian Sir J. E. Lloyd died in 1947 (see May 5)

'Holl amrantau'r ser ddywedant,
Ar hyd y nos:
Dyma'r ffordd I fro gogoniant,
Ar hyd y nos.
Golau arall yw tywyllwch,
I arddangos gwir brydferthwch,
Teulu'r nefoedd mewn tawelwch
Ar hyd y nos.

'Every star in heaven is singing,
All through the night;
Hear the glorious music ringing
All through the night,
Songs of sweet aethereal lightness
Wrought in realms of peace and whiteness,
See, the dark gives way to brightness,
All through the night' - John Ceiriog Hughes (1832-1887), first verse of 'Ar Hyd y Nos'

*On this day...*

......................................................................................................

......................................................................................................

......................................................................................................

## June 21

FEAST DAY OF SAINTS CIWG 6th century at Llangiwg; RIOC fl. 450 at Trefiagat, Rigat; CERI 1st - 2nd century at Porthkerry, Fontygari, Kerry?; and MEWAN (see 15). THE LONGEST DAY - Celebrated by the Celts when villagers stayed up all night to see the spirits of those to die in the year to come. Iorwerth, abbot of Talley, was consecrated Bishop of St Davids at Staines, 6 days after Llywelyn the Great had signed the Magna Carta and secured Wales in 1215; Inigo Jones, the founder of Classical English Architecture, died in 1652; Iolo Morganwg* holds the first Gorsedd of Bards at Primrose Hill 1792; Sir John Rhys, Celtic scholar, born in 1840 at Cwmrheidol (see December 17); In 1848, 11 miners died at Victoria Colliery, Ebbw Vale; Death in 1908 of the novelist 'Allen Raine', born Anne Adelisa Evans in Newcastle Emlyn; Doctor Jack Matthews, Cardiff and Wales centre alongside Bleddyn Williams, born in 1920 at Bridgend

*'Iolo, old Iolo, he who knows
The virtues of all herbs of mount or vale...
Whatever lore of science or of song
Sages and bards of old have handed down' - Robert Southey

On this day...

## June 22

FEAST DAY OF SAINTS AARON (AIHRAN) early 6th century at Pleumeur-Gautier, St Malo; CELER 7th century ? (also 21 - 29) at Beddgelert, Llangeler; and GWENFREWI martyred (see September 19). In 1265, Simon de Montfort granted Llywelyn the Great* the services of the Lord of Whittington, in return for his support; The Battle of Pilleth, near Knighton, 1402, when Glyndŵr's army defeated the English and captured Earl Mortimer and Sir Thomas Clanvowe for ransom. Possibly 2000 English died at the site, also known as Bryn Glas, including Sir Kinard de la Bere, Sir Walter Devereux and Sir Robert Whitney and their retinues; In 1664, Katherine Philips, 'The Matchless Orinda' died; Charles Nice Davies, linguist, soldier and minister, died at Brecon in 1842; Gwen John, artist, was born in Haverfordwest in 1876 (see September 18); Birth in 1880 at Llangennech of Rhys Gabe, Llanelli, Wales and Cardiff rugby three-quarter (see September 15); Henry Wayne Davies ('Naunton Wayne'), the actor, born in Llanwonno in 1901 (see November 17); Death in 1930 of the singer Mary Davies (see February 27)

*'Though the legend is known to most people I shall take the liberty of relating it... Llywelyn ab Iorwerth during his contests with the English had encamped with a few followers in the valley, and one day departed with his men on an expedition, leaving his infant son in a cradle in his tent, under the care of his hound Gelert, after giving the child

its fill of goat's milk. Whilst he was absent a wolf from the neighbouring mountains, in quest of prey, found its way into the tent, and was about to devour the child, when the watchful dog interfered, and after a desperate conflict, in which the tent was torn down, succeeded in destroying the monster. Llywelyn returning in the evening found the tent on the ground, and the dog, covered with blood, sitting beside it. Imagining that the blood with which Gelert was besmeared was that of his own son devoured by the animal to whose care he had confided him, Llywelyn in a paroxysm of righteous indignation forthwith transfixed the faithful creature with his spear. Scarcely, however, had he done so when his ears were startled by the cry of a child from beneath the fallen tent, and hastily removing the canvas he found the child in its cradle, quite uninjured, and the body of an enormous wolf frightfully torn and mangled lying near. His breast was now filled with conflicting emotions, joy for the preservation of his son and grief for the fate of his dog, to whom he forthwith hastened. The poor animal was not quite dead, but presently expired, in the act of licking his master's hand. Llywelyn mourned over him as a brother, buried him with funeral honours in the valley, and erected a tomb over him as a hero. From that time the place was called Beddgelert (Gelert's Grave)' - George Borrow, 'Wild Wales', 1862

**On this day...**

.....................................................................................................................................................

.....................................................................................................................................................

.....................................................................................................................................................

# June 23
*FEAST DAY OF SAINTS* CELER (see 22); and RHYCHWYN (see 10). In 1217, Reginald de Braos defected from Llywelyn to the Crown, and Llywelyn Fawr ravaged his lands in Brecon and Gower; In 1314, Dafydd ap Llywelyn was chosen Bishop of St Asaf, succeeding Llywelyn ap Llywelyn; In 1864, the railway to Aberystwyth was opened; Percy Bush, Cardiff and British Lions rugby star, born in Cardiff in 1879 (see May 19); Birth in 1879 of William Ewart Berry, owner of The Sunday Times, Financial Times and the Daily Telegraph, who became 1st Viscount Camrose (see June 15 and May 2); In 1894, 290 men and children were killed in an explosion at the Albion Colliery, Cilfynydd; The monument to Llywelyn ein Llyw Olaf was unveiled at Cilmeri* in 1956

*'He bled to death like a pelican of disaster,
And independent Wales with him...
We come today like an army to the place in Cilmeri
Where not one bone of our Prince remains;
But here is blood, and the blood of his Wales,
The Wales of St David and King Hywel and God.'
- lines translated from Gwenallt's 'Llywelyn Ein Llyw Olaf (Llywelyn Our Last Prince)

..........................................................................................................

..........................................................................................................

..........................................................................................................

# June 24

FEAST DAY OF SAINTS TRILLO (see 15); and CELER (see 22); MIDSUMMER QUARTERDAY; ST JOHN THE BAPTIST 1st century; some Celtic rites like jumping fire embers were transferred to the Eve and Night of St John. In 1401, the Tudor brothers handed back Conwy Castle to Hotspur, with nine rebels executed, and the others including the Tudors pardoned and set free.

*'Some of the worst cases of hardship I've known have been in homes where the father was trying to keep six children on £2 5s a week and was too proud to accept help off anyone..... When you're on shift you fall out for twenty minutes and eat bread and butter, or bread and cheese which your wife puts in your food tin..... One day we were sitting like this talking when Bill didn't answer..... He'd fainted....... So I lifted him and carried him to the pit bottom to send him home, but before I did this I gathered up his food tin. There wasn't a crumb in it ! He'd been sitting there in the dark pretending to eat, pretending to me − his pal − Now that's what I call pride.'* A South Wales miner in conversation with H.V. Morton, reported in 'In Search of Wales' 1932

*On this day...*

..........................................................................................................

..........................................................................................................

..........................................................................................................

# June 25

FEAST DAY OF SAINTS AMPHIBALUS d. 287 at Caerleon; ISMAEL (see 16); TYFODWG 6th century at Llantrisant, Llandyfodwg; NON (see March 3); PAUL (see 30); SELYF (see February 1). Possible date of the murder of Sir Thomas Vaughan by Richard III in 1483 - all of Edward IV's counsellors were executed between 13 and 25 June, before they could swear in Edward V, a fact conveniently overlooked by those who say that Richard did not murder the princes in the Tower; The film actor Roger Livesey was born in Barri in 1906 (see February 4)

*'Until I was eighteen I suppose I had hardly ever left Wales: and I remember that my strongest desire was to leave it for what I imagined to be the less constricted, less narrow, less puritanical life of other countries. Since then I have not lived in Wales except for very brief periods. I have lived in England and abroad, and I confess that by now I am much fonder of my country than before: and my people seem to me to possess more of*

*those qualities I admire, of passion, intelligence, individualism, and of natural devotion to culture than almost any other I have known.'* - Goronwy Rees, 1938

*On this day...*

..............................................................................................................................

..............................................................................................................................

..............................................................................................................................

# June 26

FEAST DAY OF SAINTS TWROG 6th century (also August 15) at Llandwrog, Maentwrog; SIMAUS d.550 at St Cieux; and CEITHO, CELYNEN, GWYN, GWYNNORO, GWYNOG 6th century at Llanpumsaint. Agents of the Crown visited Margam Abbey to strip its valuables and assess its worth in 1536 - two months later the lead of its roof had been melted down; Death in Swansea in 1859 of Thomas Rhys Davies of Cilgerran, an itinerant preacher who preached 13,145 times across Wales; Birth in 1885 at Llansawel of David John Williams, writer (see January 4); In 1999 the Millennium Stadium was opened, and Wales beat South Africa, the world champions, for the first time

*'Again and again from his rough pony's back our leader*
*signalled with his hazel-staff of office*
*four, breathless, to lay down your coffin,*
*four, fresh in strength, to bear you,*
*up the old sledge-ways, the sinew-straining tracks,*
*the steps of Rhiw Gelynen and Rhiw'r Ych.'*
Lines from 'Burial Path' by Ruth Bidgood

*On this day...*

..............................................................................................................................

..............................................................................................................................

..............................................................................................................................

# June 27

FEAST DAY OF SAINTS CENYDD (see July 5) and CELER (see 22). 'The Welsh College', Jesus College, Oxford, founded in 1571; Death of the industrialist Richard Crawshay in 1810; 1906 saw the equal highest recorded earthquake in Britain at Swansea (see July 19), at 4.8 on the Richter Scale; The poet Vernon Watkins born in Maesteg in 1906 (see October 8); First German air-raids on Swansea, and on North Wales, at Broughton

*'The people of the dominion of Wales have and do daily use a speech nothing like nor consonant with the mother tongue used within this realm... No person or persons that use the Welsh speech or language shall have or enjoy any manor, office or fees within*

*the realm of England, Wales or other of the King's dominions upon pain of forfeiting the same offices or fees unless he or they use and exercise the speech or language of the English'* The Act of Union, 1536

***On this day...***

........................................................................................................

........................................................................................................

........................................................................................................

# June 28

*FEAST DAY OF SAINTS* AUSTOL (AUSTELL) d. 627 at St Austell, St Meen; CELER (see 22) and MYLLIN (see 17). Dafydd ap Gruffudd, last Prince of Wales, was captured on the slopes of Cadair Idris in 1283 and executed 3 months later; Sir Robert Jones, first President of the International Society of Orthopaedic Surgery, was born at Rhyl in 1857 (see January 14 and the entry for Hugh Owen Thomas, August 23); In 1865, major gold deposits were found at St David's Lode, Clogau Mine, near Dolgellau; In 1960, an explosion at Six Bells, Abertillery, killed 45 men; Sabotage explosion on Liverpool's water pipleine from the River Dee in 1968; In 1976, Sir Stanley Baker died of cancer at Malaga, exactly a month after being knighted (see February 28)

*'Five-hundred men, ordinary men, chosen accidentally from among the unemployed'* - David Lloyd George, referring to the House of Lords in a 1909 speech

***On this day...***

........................................................................................................

........................................................................................................

........................................................................................................

# June 29

*FEAST DAY OF SAINTS* EURGAIN 6th century at Llaneurgain (Northop); TRINIO 6th century (also 28 and 30) at Llandrinio, Melverley, Llandyssilio; PEDR 5th - 6th century at Llanbedr; and CIWG 6th century at Llangiwg. Death of the civil libertarian, philosopher and pamphleteer David Williams of Eglwysilan, honoured in France, in 1816; Birth in 1834 of Robert Davies (*Asaph Llechid*), musician, near Bethesda in 1834 (see August 29); In 1889 John Hughes died in St Petersburg. He founded one of Russia's first ironworks with Welsh workers at Donetsk, which was originally called Yuzovska in his honour.

*'Three sureties of happiness for a man:*
*Good habits, amiability*

*And forebearance'* - from the Welsh Triads of Virtues

*On this day...*

.......................................................................................................

.......................................................................................................

.......................................................................................................

## June 30
*FEAST DAY OF SAINTS* JULIOT (ILLUDIANA) Nearest Sunday to 29, see June 16) and PAUL d. 65 (also 25, 29 and January 24). In 1688, Arthur Herbert of Montgomery sailed to Holland to ask William of Orange to take over from James II; The great scholar, botanist, antiquary, philologist and geologist Edward Lhuyd died in 1709; Death in 1851 of Thomas Phillips, educational benefactor who served in Australia and India (see July 6); In 1969, 6 members of the Free Wales Army were found guilty in Swansea of offences under the Public Order Act; In 1986, the last coal was taken from Maerdy Colliery

*'Traha a threisio'r gweinion a ddifa'r etifeddion'* - *'The oppression of the weak is the destruction of heirs.'* - Welsh proverb

*On this day...*

.......................................................................................................

.......................................................................................................

.......................................................................................................

# JULY - GORFFENNAF
## (Completion Month)
### Mezevennik (Breton), Mis Gorephan (Cornish)

## July 1

FEAST DAY OF SAINTS ARFON (AARON) d.287 (also June 20, July 3) at Caerleon, Newport, Llanharan; JULIAN (JULIUS) d. 287 (also June 20, July 3) at Caerleon, Newport, Llanharan, St Julians; DAVID (See March 1) in Brittany; CEWYDD (See 15); SIMON ZELOTES (See October 28); and GOULVEN (see 8); Glyndŵr's Tywi Valley Campaign in 1403, when 8000 troops took English-held castles including the stronghold of Carmarthen; Meibion Glyndŵr holds an annual march at Abergele; Conwy Suspension Bridge opened in 1826; From 1888, the first Monday in every month was free from work for miners, 'Mabon's Day', fought for by William Abraham (see June 14); Birth at Ebbw Vale in 1890 of Sir Edward John (Ted) Williams, miner and Labour MP for Ogmore (see May 16); Birth in 1915 of the poet Alun Lewis at Aberdare (see March 5); In 1941, 37 people died in Newport in German air-raids; In 1948 the Welsh Folk Museum, the foundation of Dr Iorwerth Peate, opened at St Ffagans (now renamed The Museum of Welsh Life); In 1969 Charles Philip Arthur George Saxe-Coburg-Gotha-Schleswig-Holstein-Sonderburg-Glucksburg (a.k.a. Windsor) was designated Prince of Wales at the symbol of the monoglot French Edward I's power, Caernarfon Castle; Two members of Mudiad Amddiffyn Cymru were killed at Abergele when their anti-Investiture explosives detonated prematurely in 1969

*'Remember that God who made men also ordained nations; to destroy a nation is only one grade less of a disaster than to destroy the whole of mankind, and to destroy the language of a nation one grade less of a disaster than to destroy the nation itself... It pleased God to reveal that He made people as nations... Remember that you are people of the same blood as the English and the Boers and the Kaffirs and the Chinese. Be therefore ready to render them all the rights that you would wish for yourselves. Remember also that you are a nation, through God's ordinance. Do therefore all you can to maintain the nation as a nation, by maintaining its language, and all other valuable things that may pertain to it. If you are not faithful to your country and your language and your nation, how can you expect to be faithful to God and humanity? Do not be ashamed of those things which distinguish you from other nations; and if you wish to imitate the nation next to you, imitate her in those things in which she excels, but not her pride, her arrogance, her boastfulness, her love of war, her frivolity, her narrowness of thought and her lack of empathy with other nations.'* - Robert Ambrose Jones (Emrys ap Iwan), 1903

#### On this day...

# July 2

FEAST DAY OF SAINTS EUDDOGWY (OUDOCEUS) 545-616 at Llandaf, Llandogo; TYRNOG 6th century (also October 3) at Clonmore, Tregantarec, Ploudaniel; and AMPHIBALUS (see June 25). In 1403, Henry Dwn's men were besieging Dinefwr Castle for Owain Glyndŵr - Dinefwr and Carreg Cennen soon fell

*'The heralds of Nonconformity found minds fertile to germinate the seed of their instruction. "Away with our traitor leaders and their Church sycophants," the people cried. They accepted Nonconformity as a weapon to break spiritual bondage, and speedily found the new tool to be a new master. Their traditional gaiety left the Celts. They plagued themselves with the terrors of the new dogmas. They wore repentance like a hair-shirt to exorcise devils by which, perhaps, they had never been possessed. They lay shivering in the shadows, and shrank from the sunlight in which Jesus had expounded his philosophy.'* - Thomas Firbank, 'A Country of Memorable Honour' 1953

*On this day...*

.............................................................................................

.............................................................................................

.............................................................................................

# July 3

FEAST DAY OF SAINTS PEBLIG 4th-5th century at Llanbeblig; AARON and JULIUS (see 1); GARMON of MAN (see July 31) on the Isle of Man (Manaw); NON (see March 3); and THOMAS *1st century*. Death in 1749 of the mathematician William Jones FRS of Llanfihangel Tre'r Beirdd, Anglesey, the originator of the *pi* sign; Death of Davis Castellhywel in 1827, buried in Llanwenog (see February 14); Birth of William Henry (W.H.) Davies, the *'tramp-poet'* in Pillgwenlly (properly Pwll-Gwynlliw after the 6th century saint), Newport in 1871; In 1901, 11 miners died at Old Coal Pit, Nantyglo; Death at Llanwern in 1918 of David Alfred Thomas, first Viscount Rhondda; Rheidol hydro-electric plant opened in 1964; Death in 1951 of Gwendoline Davies (see February 11); Swansea was made a city in 1969; The novelist Kate Roberts* died in 1971

*\*'And the people who were left at home began to ask themselves and ask each other what it all meant. They understood what hard times meant. They had suffered wrongs and injustices in the quarries: the oppression of the masters and the owners, the oppression of bribery and of favouritism. They had seen their friends and children killed at work, but they had never before seen their sons taken away from them to be killed in war. Since the quarry-cabin was closed, the forum of discussion shifted to the Sunday School where they tried by every means to explain and understand what was happening... They no longer believed that the purpose of the war was to protect small nations, or that it was the war to end war, and neither did they believe that one country was more to blame than another... In the depths of their being, they believed by this that someone was*

*making money out of it, the same people who exploited them in the quarries and sucked their blood to turn it into gold for their own use. These were the people who desired to delay the return of peace.'* - lines from Kate Roberts, 'Traed Mewn Cyffon' (Feet in Chains), 1936

*On this day...*

..................................................................................................................

..................................................................................................................

..................................................................................................................

## July 4

FEAST DAY OF SAINTS ILUD (see JULIOT, June 16); and MARTIN (see November 11). James I knighted Sir Sackville Trevor of Denbigh in 1604, for capturing four Spanish ships; In 1776, 56 men signed the American Declaration of Independence, drafted by the Welsh-American Thomas Jefferson*. As many as 18 of the signatories were of Welsh descent; George Everest, after whom Mount Everest is named, was born at Gwernvale, Powys in 1790; Birth in 1807 of Robert John Pryse, man of letters, at Llanbadrig (see October 3); In 1815 Henry Paget of Plas Newydd was made the 1st Marquess of Anglesey for his bravery at Waterloo, where he lost his leg; Death of the Welsh-American Presidents Thomas Jefferson (1826), John Adams (also 1826) and James Monroe (1831); Birth in 1894 at Goginan of William Ambrose Bebb, historian, writer and nationalist politician (see April 27); Alex Templeton, jazz pianist, born in Cardiff in 1910

*'When a man has cast a longing eye on them (offices), a rottenness begins in his conduct'* Thomas Jefferson 1799

*On this day...*

..................................................................................................................

..................................................................................................................

..................................................................................................................

## July 5

FEAST DAY OF SAINTS CENYDD 6th century (also August 1 and June 27) at Llangennith, Senghenydd, Caerphilly, and Brittany; and MWYNEN (MORWENNA) (see August 14). Owain Glyndŵr* besieged Carmarthen on this day in 1403, fresh from overseeing the siege of Carreg Cennen Castle, and on his way to sack Llansteffan and Newcastle Emlyn castles; In 1415, Owain Glyndŵr and his son Maredudd refused royal pardons from Henry V; In 1450, Mathau Goch (Mathew Gough) of Maelor was killed on London Bridge by Jack Cade's rebels. Born around 1400, he was known as the great warrior *'Matago'* in Europe, and fought at Cravant (1434), Verneuil (1424) and until 1449 in France, when Normandy was lost. He had the honour of addressing the English troops on the eve of the Battle of Formigny in 1449; In 1775, Sarah Siddons was born at the 'Shoulder of Mutton' Inn, Brecon; In 1836, Evan Herber Evans, great preacher and Principal of Bala-Bangor College at Bangor, was born in Newcastle Emlyn (see December 30); John Romilly Allen (see July 9) died in London in 1907; Philip Madoc, actor, born in Merthyr Tudful in 1934

*On this day in 1403, John Scudamore, holding Carreg Cennen against Glyndŵr's forces, wrote: '*Glyndŵr lay last night at Dryslwyn Castle with Rhys ap Gruffudd, and there I was and spoke to him upon Wales and prayed for a safe conduct under his seal, to send home my wife and her mother and their company and he would none grant me'*. Richard Kyngeston, Bishop of Hereford wrote to King Henry IV on the evening of this day: '*For God's Love my liege, Lord, think on yourself, and your estate, or by troth all is lost else, but and ye come yourself with haste, all others will follow after. On Friday last, Carmarthen town is taken and the castle yolden (yielded) by Roger Wigmore and the Castle Emlyn is yolden, and slain of Carmarthen more than 50 persons. Written in right haste on Sunday; and I cry your mercy and put me in your high grace that I write so shortly; for by my troth I vowe you, it is needful.*'

*On this day...*

.............................................................................................................
.............................................................................................................
.............................................................................................................

# July 6
*FEAST DAY OF SAINTS* DARERCA d. 518 at Killeavy; ERFYL 6th century? at Llanerfyl; GREDFYW 6th century (also November 11) at Llanllyfni; CALLWEN 5th - 6th century (also April 20 , November 1) at Cellan; GWENFYL 5th - 6th century (also November 1) at Gwynfil; NOE (NOYALE) see April 27; IAGO (see 24); and GWETHENOC (see 24). Carmarthen Castle surrendered to Owain Glyndŵr in 1403; The Battle of Sedgemoor in 1685, when the Duke of Monmouth was defeated by the forces of James II; Birth in 1760 of Thomas Phillips at Llandegley, surgeon and founder of Llandovery College (see June 31); Birth in 1821 of Henry Hussey Vivian at Singleton Park, Swansea, who made Swansea '*the metallurgical centre of the world*' (see November 28); Glamorgan County Cricket Club formed in 1888; Gwyn Thomas, writer, wit, born in Cymmer, Rhondda in 1913; Nancy Griffith, folk-singer, born in 1954; Aneurin Bevan MP died at Chesham, Bucks in 1960 (see November 15)

*'Iago Prytherch is my name, though, be it allowed,*
*Just an ordinary man of the bald Welsh hills,*
*Who pens a few sheep in a gap of cloud.*
.................................................................
*His clothes, sour with years of sweat*

*And animal contact, shock the refined,*
*But affected, sense with their stark naturalness.*
*Yet this is your prototype, who, season by season*
*Against siege of rain and wind's attrition,*
*Preserves his stock, an impregnable fortress*
*Not to be stormed even in death's confusion.*
*Remember him, then, for he, too, is a winner of wars,*
*Enduring like a tree under the curious stars.'*
Extracts from 'A Peasant' by R.S. Thomas

**On this day...**

............................................................................................................................................

............................................................................................................................................

............................................................................................................................................

## July 7

FEAST DAY OF SAINTS EFRDDYL (see August 6); GOULVEN (see 8); and DOGED (see April 7). In 1403, the Sheriff of Herefordshire broke Glyndŵr's siege of Brecon; In 1914, Frederick Hall Thomas (Freddie Welsh) of Pontypridd won the World Lightweight Boxing Championship; In 1950, Glamorgan won the County Championship for the first time, beating Middlesex at the Arms Park pitch; Geraint Evans, the opera star, was knighted in 1969

*'In a few minutes we were descending in the cage. The water from the sides of the shaft dripped steadily on us, and soon we were at the bottom, more than 1000 feet from the surface. We were led along a passage to a central gallery, from which branched out various galleries leading to all parts of the mine. Soon a number of men passed us, and about 6.15 a collier rose and started the hymn, "Guide me, O Thou Great Jehovah". At once it was caught up by a large number of voices, and the music was simply awe-inspiring. Then another rose and offered up prayer that God would bless them and keep them all day, and that He would put pure thoughts and good desires in their hearts, and help them to do their day's work for His sake.*
*After that a Welsh hymn was sung...By this time several hundred men had gathered in the various galleries, and altogether there were more than 300 colliers, out of nearly 500 employed in the pit, at the prayer-meeting. A lad recited with exquisite effect the fifteenth chapter of John, in Welsh, and the melody of his utterance came like a musical ripple on the air. From out of a gallery, like a voice from the unseen, came an address on the power of God to keep and save; which was followed by the hymn "Come ye that love the Lord"...One felt the joy of the Lord surging through the hearts of the colliers. A Church clergyman from Durham prayed in English, and cited the 39th Psalm... When he came to the words... "The darkness and the light are both alike to thee", then the presence of God overshadowed us as a glorious blessing, and though in the gloom,*

*lit up only by the feeble lights of the Davy lamps, we could scarcely distinguish the features of man, we felt that we were in the hollow of God's hand and full of joy unspeakable... It was an awe-inpiring sight to see the lamps gleaming out of the blackness of the galleries; to hear the echoes of the musical choruses of the Welsh hymns ringing through the pit. Promptly at 7 the service ended, and the colliers wended their way down the tunnels into the darkness, singing with gladness praises unto God. When we reached the top of the shaft, day was just coming in over the mountains, and we felt that a newer day had dawned in the darkness underground, whose light was the Lamb.'*
- description of a Pit in Pontypridd' from 'The Baptist Times', 1905

**On this day...**

..............................................................................................................................................

..............................................................................................................................................

..............................................................................................................................................

# July 8

FEAST DAY OF SAINT GOULVEN 6th century (also 1 and 8) at Goulven, Goulien. Possible death date in 1335 of Gruffydd ap Rhys ap Gruffydd ab Ednyfed (Gruffydd Llwyd), who suppressed Roger de Mortimer's revolt in 1322; Elihu Yale*, founder of the University, died in 1721, and is buried in Wrexham; Statue of David Lloyd George unveiled outside the National Museum of Wales by Harold MacMillan in 1960

*'Born in America, in Europe bred,*
*In Africa travell'd, and in Asia wed,*
*Where long he liv'd, and thriv'd; at London dead.*
*Much good, some ill, he did; so hope's all even,*
*And that his soul, thro' mercy's gone to Heaven.*
*You that survive, and read, take care*
*For this most certain exit to prepare:*
*Where blest in peace, the actions of the just*
*Smell sweet, and blossom in the dust.'*
1721 epitaph in Wrexham Church to Elihu Yale, the founder of Yale University

**On this day...**

..............................................................................................................................................

..............................................................................................................................................

..............................................................................................................................................

## July 9

FEAST DAY OF SAINT CEWYDD* (see 15). In July and August 1401, Prince Henry led an army through Bala to Harlech to subdue Glyndŵr, while Glyndŵr headed in the opposite direction to take Radnor Castle, Montgomery Castle and the surrounding areas; In 1447 the great soldier Sir Gruffudd Vaughan of Guilsfield was executed by Sir Henry Grey at Powys Castle, after being attracted there by the offer of safe conduct; Death at Cardiff in 1617 of Sir John Herbert, lawyer, diplomat and secretary of state to Elizabeth I, after a duel; Birth in Cardiff Prison in 1787 of Taliesin ab Iolo, poet and author (see February 16); John Romilly Adams, the archaeologist was born in 1847, descended from the Allens of Cresselly; Howard Winstone won the European featherweight title in 1966

*'Gwlad Vrychan am Vorgan vydd
Ail I gawod wyl Gewydd
Deugain niau davnau dwvr
Ar ruddiau yw'r aweddwvr'
- lines from a 15th century elegy by Lewys Glyn Coth to Morgan ap Dafydd Gam, referring to the fact that St Cewydd predated Swithun by centuries as a rain-saint ('Brychan's land will be like a shower on Cewydd's feast-day. Forty drops of water on cheeks (tears) will be the downpour'.)

*On this day...*

## July 10

FEAST DAY OF SAINT CEWYDD (See 15). After defeat at the battle of Northampton in 1460, Queen Margaret fled to Harlech Castle, after which she was protected by the Earl of Pembroke, Jasper Tudor at Denbigh Castle; The Gorsedd held its first meeting in Wales, at Carmarthen in 1819; The popular singer Donald Rhys Hubert Peers was born in 1908 in Ammanford (see August 9); July 10th and 11th were the climax of the Battle of Mametz Wood which began on July 7 in 1916, where there were 4000 casualties amongst Lloyd George's 'Welsh Army'*, the 38th Division; The Offa's Dyke Footpath was opened in 1971 at Knighton

*Siegfried Sassoon wrote as the 38th gathered for its assault at Mametz: 'Our little trench under the trees was inundated by a jostling company of exclamatory Welshmen. They were mostly undersized men, and as I watched them arriving at the first stage of their battle experience I had a sense of victimisation. Two days later, the Welsh division, of which they were a unit, was involved in massacre and confusion.' Robert Graves wrote in the aftermath of the battle: 'Mametz Wood was full of dead of the Prussian Guards reserve, big men, and of Royal Welsh and South Wales Borderers of the new army battalions, little men... There was not a single tree in the wood unbroken... There had

*been bayonet fighting in the wood. There was a man of the South Wales Borderers and one of the Lehr regiment who had succeeded in bayoneting each other simultaneously.'*

*On this day...*

## July 11

*FEAST DAY OF SAINT CYWAIR* at Llangywair. Pembroke Castle was captured by Cromwell in 1648, and Laugharne, Powell and Poyer sentenced to death; The Welsh-American President, John Quincy Adams, was born in 1767; Death in 1795 of the diarist William Thomas at Michaelston-super-Ely (see July 29); Birth of Sir William Robert Grove in 1811 at Swansea, noted scientist and lawyer; In 1905, 119 men were killed at the National Colliery, Wattstown, Rhondda; In 1886, Ernest Thompson Willows, airship pioneer, was born in Cardiff; Gold found in the Gwynfynydd mine near Dolgellau in 1887; Death in 1890 of David Jones of Wallington (see May 28); In 1905, 119 men died in an explosion at the National No. 2 Pit, Rhondda; In 1941, 14 men died at the Rhigos Colliery; Death in 1971 of the poet-painter Brenda Chamberlain; Mametz memorial to the 38th (Welsh) Division dedicated in 1987

*'If you do not wish to be worse than animals, obtain learning in your own language; if you do not wish to be more unnatural than any other nation under the sun, love your language and those who love it'* - William Salesbury (c.1520-c.1584)

*On this day...*

## July 12

Holy Day of JOHN BUCKLEY JONES of Clynnog Fawr - hung, drawn and quartered on the Old Kent Road in 1598. Death in 1755 of Zachariah Williams of Rosemarket, medical practicioner, author and inventor; In 1851, Elizabeth Phillips Hughes, the educationalist was born; Henry Rolls of Monmouth, founder of Rolls-Royce cars, is the first British aviator to be killed in a plane crash in 1910, (see August 27, May 4); Death of wounds in action in 1916 of the rugby player John Lewis Williams (see January 3); Death in 1939 of Charles Granville Bruce (see April 7); Gareth Edwards, voted the world's greatest-ever rugby player, born in Gwaun-Cae-Gurwen in 1947

*"The crowd broke out into the most rapturous violence of voice and gesture... one hundred different voices in a single room produced horror in the extreme. I never experienced sound more discordant'.* The worshippers then began to jump, one after

another joining in, until everyone was jumping, and the *'person who was the happiest was he who would exert the loudest, continue the longest, and jump the highest.'* - William Hutton, 'Remarks upon North Wales' 1803, written in September 1799. He had left the tiny congregation of 16 in Llanbeblig Church to watch the Methodist 'Jumpers' sect in the village chapel

*On this day...*

....................................................................................................................................................................

....................................................................................................................................................................

....................................................................................................................................................................

# July 13

FEAST DAY OF SAINTS ENODOC (also March 7) at St Minver; DOGFAN (see 23); JUTHWARA (see December 23); and GWETHENOC (see 24). John Dee, *'the magus of his age'*, *'Black Jack'*, science pioneer, born at Beguildy in 1527 (d. December 1608); The writer Ellis Wynne* died in 1734 (see March 7); William Davies, palaeontologist, born at Holywell in 1814 (d. Feb.13, 1891); Sir Watkin Lewes of Newport, Pembrokeshire, former Lord Mayor of London, died a debtor in the London Coffee House on Ludgate Hill in 1821

*He was once known as the Good Companion and she a Gentle maiden, or easy with her body: but in this place they were given the naked names of Drunkard and Whore. "I trust," said the Drunkard, "that you will look on me with favour, since I sent many plump victims floating towards you on a flood of good beer; and when I failed to kill any more I willingly brought myself as a sacrifice to feed you". "With the Court's permission" said the Whore, "it was more than half I sent to King Death as burnt offerings, and indeed roast meat ready for his table." "Hey, hey", said Death, "all this was done to satisfy your cursed lusts and not for the sake of feeding me. Bind them both together, face to face, since they are old friends, and cast them into the Land of Darkness and let him vomit into her mouth and let her piss fire into his guts until the Day of Judgement." - lines from the 'Court of Death' trial of a youth and a maiden, in 'Visions of the Sleeping Bard' by Elis Wyn*

*On this day...*

....................................................................................................................................................................

....................................................................................................................................................................

....................................................................................................................................................................

# July 14

FEAST DAY OF SAINT ELLYW 5th - 6th century (also July 17) at Llanelieu; WELL DAY - the Celts believed that wishes made at holy wells would come true on this day; ALLIANCE BETWEEN WALES AND FRANCE - A signed Treaty of Alliance in 1404 of Charles VI of France with Owain Glyndŵr, ratifying the May Agreement; Benjamin Chidlaw was born at Bala in 1811 and died on this same day in Dolgellau in 1892, having spent 56 years establishing Sunday Schools across America; Death of Richard Davies of Llanbrynmair (Mynyddog), poet, singer and eisteddfod conductor, in 1877; Rhys Williams, British Lion and superb rugby forward, born at Cwmllynfell in 1930; Gwynfor Evans won Plaid Cymru's first parliamentary seat at Carmarthen in 1966, in the by-election after the death of Lady Megan Lloyd George

*'For I am of the seed of the Welch woman*
*and speak the truth from my heart'* - Christopher Smart 1722-1771, 'Jubilate Agno'

*On this day...*

## July 15

FEAST DAY OF SAINT CEWYDD 6th century (also July 1, 2 and second week in July) at Llangewydd, Aberedw, Dyserth, Monknash? Cewydd was the Rain Saint who predated Swithin by hundreds of years. In 1415 Gilbert Talbot was empowered by Henry V to offer Owain Glyndŵr a pardon, after 15 years of war; The great architect Inigo Jones was born in 1573; Birth in 1761 near Llanfechain of Walter Davies (Gwallter Mechain), cleric, poet, antiquary and literary critic (see December 4); In 1856, 114 men and children were killed at New Cymmer Pit, Porth, Rhondda; In 1880, 120 men and children were killed at the New Risca Colliery in Gwent

*'Unwashed colliers by the river*
*Gamble for luck the pavements hide.*
*Kids float tins down dirty rapids.*
*Coal-dust rings the scruffy willows.*
*Circe is a drab.*
*She gives men what they know.*
*Daily to her pitch-black shaft*
*Her whirring wheels suck husbands out of sleep.*
*She for her profit takes their hands and eyes.'*
Lines from 'The Rhondda', by Alun Lewis (1915-1944)

*On this day...*

## July 16

FEAST DAY OF SAINTS CYNLLO 5th century (also July 17 and August 8) at Rhayader, Llanbister, Llangynllo, Llangoedmor, Nantmel; BISHOP ISMAEL 6th century at St Ishmael's, Rosemarket, Camrose, Uzmaston; and TENENEN

(TININOR) 6th century at Leon, Ploabennec. Peter of Lee died in 1198, and Giraldus Cambrensis (c.1146 - 1223) wished to rpelace him, but was thwarted by the King; Birth at Clydach in 1878 of David Christopher (Christy) Davies, missionary to the Congo (see May 4)

*'For though the fierce enemy has ravaged your realm,*
*The old speech of Cymru he cannot o'erwhelm,*
*Our passionate poets to silence command*
*Or banish the harp from your strand.*
*Wales! Wales! Oh but my heart is with you!*
*As long as the sea*
*Your bulwark shall be,*
*To Cymru my heart shall be true.'*
Translation of the 3rd verse of the Welsh National Anthem

*On this day...*

.................................................................................................
.................................................................................................
.................................................................................................

# July 17

*FEAST DAY OF SAINTS* CYNLLO (see 16); KENELM d. 819 at Rockfield, Winchcombe; and JUTHWARA (see December 23) in Devon. Death in 1851 near Denbigh of Aneurin Owen (see July 23); Birth in 1859 of the poet and author Ernest Rhys, editor of J.M. Dent's 'Everyman's Library' (see May 25); Death in 1860 of the *'real Lady of the Lamp'*, Betsi Cadwaladr (see May 24); Abbey Steelworks, Port Talbot, opened in 1951; In 1991, the 'Evening Standard' reported Marin Amis telling A.N. Wilson that *'the South Waleyans are a particularly bitter and deracinated people'*, before beginning a 'joke' about Aberfan. *'Martin does the Welsh voice with an accuracy which reflects loathing'*

*'Whoever wants a meadow, let him keep it from St Padrig's Day (March 17th) to the Winter Calends (November 1st). A meadow is land without use except for hay, with a bank around it. That is why it is kept until the Winter Calends, because it is right to scythe it twice in a year. Meadows are forbidden to pigs because they damage the land. He who finds pigs on his meadow, let him take four legal pence in damages from their owner'* - The Laws of Hywel Dda, 10th century

*On this day...*

.................................................................................................
.................................................................................................
.................................................................................................

# July 18

FEAST DAY OF SAINTS JUTHWARA (see December 23) in Devon; and GONERI 6th century (also 19, and April 4, 7) at Gonery, Plougescent, Langoat, Plougras, Ploezal, Locarn. The Newtown Chartist Thomas Powell was released from Montgomery Gaol in 1840; Barry Dock and Railway, the brainchild of David Davies of Llandinam, opened in 1889; The Sixth Commonwealth Games started in Cardiff in 1958; Cardiff Singer of the World Competition began in 1983

'The poems of praise were an old tradition among the Celts long before the establishment of the Welsh nation ... Between the (6th century) days of Gildas and the time of Einion Offeiriad, a Welsh Christian mind had worked on this poetic tradition, and had seen it in a very different light. The praise-poem was a way of holding a mirror up to society, and especially to the leader, and - through this picture of what it and he should be - inflaming their love for that image. Wales was proud of its legal system and its rights; but in the crisis that presented itself to each generation in its turn, the maintaining of law and rights - all the benefits of society - depended upon patience, on courage, on the **character** of the leader and on loyalty to him. If he were unwise - open to vainglory, perhaps, or cowardice - he could easily bring his people under the foot of the enemy. "A braint, diffaith y weithion" ("And dignity - now it is destroyed") said Cynddelw Brydydd Mawr, after the death of Madog ab Meredudd and his son in the same year. All the passion of the period before 1282 is in the praise-poems. It was not ceremony or flattery, and society held that the status and vocation of the poet had to be protected.' - D. Myrddin Lloyd

*On this day...*

..........................................................................................

..........................................................................................

..........................................................................................

# July 19

FEAST DAY OF SAINTS GENYS (also May 2, 3) at Trigg Minor; and CYBI (last Sunday before July 25, see November 9). In 1553, Mary Tudor was crowned Queen of England; Death in 1838 of the preacher Christmas Evans at Swansea (see December 25); Lewis Edwards, theologian, died in 1887 (see October 27); Birth at Cellan in 1982 of Griffith John Williams (GJ), professor, collector and scholar (see January 10); Llyn Padarn railway line reopened in 1980; 1984 saw the equal greatest recorded earthquake in Britain on the Llŷn Peninsula (see June 27), at 4.8 on the Richter Scale

'The Welsh are afraid lest an Englishman should understand their language, and, by hearing their conversation, become acquainted with their private affairs, or by listening to it, pick up their language which they have no mind that he should know - and their very children sympathise with them. All conquered people are suspicious of their *conquerors. The English have forgot that they ever conquered the Welsh, but some ages will elapse before the Welsh forget that the English have conquered them.'* George Borrow, 'Wild Wales', 1862

*On this day...*

......................................................................................................
......................................................................................................
......................................................................................................

# July 20

FEAST DAY OF SAINT ARILD 6th century (also October 30) at Oldbury, Gloucester. William Morgan, translator of the Bible into Welsh in 1588, was consecrated Bishop of Llandaff in 1595; David Davies of Llandinam, capitalist Calvinist Methodist, died in 1890 (see July 18 and December 18); In 1917, the South Wales Miners' Federation voted to contact the labour movement in Germany to end the Great War with a united, working-class peace policy; Ruth Bidgood, poet, born at Blaendulais in 1922; William Beynon (born c.1884 in Port Talbot), former British bantam-weight champion, died in a colliery accident at Bryn, near Port Talbot, in 1932; Death in 1958 of Viscountess Rhondda (see June 12); The world's first hovercraft service started in 1962, between Rhyl and Wallasey; The Welsh Language Board was founded in 1988

*'(William Evans) then gives a reminder that Giraldus Cambrensis stated that in Anglesey there were 343 'trefs'. Evans today locates 343 of his track-bounded squares. That these had no Roman origin he proves by showing that the flank of a block, after the legal deductions laid down in old Welsh law, was 1760 yards. The Roman mile was only 1666 yards and 2 feet. It seems, then, that the statute mile used today by the English is not Roman after all, but British. The monoliths of Anglesey, says Evans, are of three heights: nine feet, six feet, and three feet respectively. The smaller the stones, the less is the distance between them. In other words, the smaller stones mark out the smaller squares, the biggest ones very large squares made up of several little ones. He instances the big monolith above Cadnant, near the Strait. From this starting-point he traces the lines of similar large stones set at four-and-a-quarter miles apart - the old quarter absorbing the cumulative deductions for tracks and King's Waste - which mark the corner boundary of superblocks which, even my arithmetic tels me, each contain sixteen of the one-mile-square plots. The theory, if correct, shows that a high degree of surveying skill was present long before the arrival of the Romans.'* - Thomas Firbank, in 'A Country of Memorable Honour' 1953

*On this day...*

......................................................................................................
......................................................................................................
......................................................................................................

# July 21

FEAST DAY OF SAINT PRAXEDES 1st - 2nd century (also 22) in R o m e ; Holy Day of Howell Harris (died 1773), preacher at Trefeca. The Battle of Shrewsbury 1403, where Glyndŵr's ally Harry Percy, 'Hotspur' was killed; Elan Valley Reservoir opened in 1904; Sir Joseph Alfred Bradney (born January 11, 1859), 'Achydd Glan Troddi' and historian of Monmouthshire, died in 1933; Oil and Gas drilling in the Celtic Sea began in 1973

'They began singing. Instead of the usual music-hall songs they sang Welsh hymns, each man taking a part. The Welsh always sang when pretending not to be scared. And they never sang out of tune.' Robert Graves describing his experiences in the First World War, in 'Goodbye to All That', 1929

**On this day...**

..................................................................................................................

..................................................................................................................

..................................................................................................................

# July 22

FEAST DAY OF SAINTS PHILIP EVANS executed 1679 (feast day October 25) at Monmouth, after being captured at Sker House, Porthcawl; and JOHN LLOYD d.1679 remembered at Penrhos - Evans and Lloyd were hung, drawn and quartered at Cardiff Castle; MAIR FADLEN 1st century (Mary Magdalene); ALBAN (see June 20); and PRAXEDES (see 21). On the nearest Sunday to this date, pilgrims come to see Gwenfrewi's holy relic at St Winifred's Well, Holywell, before triple-immersion in its waters; David Thomas Morgan, the 'Prince's Counsellor' to the Young Pretender, was hung, drawn and quartered for treason at Newgate in 1746; Howel Harris, preacher, died in 1773; In 1880, a British record 2.9 inches of rain fell in Cowbridge in 30 minutes; The great harpist Tom Bryant was born in Efeilisaf in 1882 (see January 13); The South Wales Miners' Strike* which started on July 15, ended on this day in 1915, after a visit by Lloyd George upon the 19th agreeing to a pay-rise to offset the increased costs of feeding miners' families; In 1937, Alfred George Edwards, the first Archbishop of Wales, died in 1937, aged 88, and is buried in St Asaf's Cathedral (see November 2 and June 1); The last Royal Welsh Show was held in Cardiff in 1953 before its removal to its permanent home at Builth Wells

*'It would be better to shoot 100 men in suppressing a strike rather than lose thousands in the field as a consequence of it' - Bonar Law, member of the War Coalition Government of Asquith, and leader of the Conservative Party, referring to the South Wales strike by starving miners.

## July 23

FEAST DAY OF SAINTS DOGFAN 5th-6th century (also July 13, 24); at Llanrhaiadr-ym-Mochnant; and DOGED (see April 7). In 1595 Squire Jenkin Keigwin was killed in Mousehole, Cornwall, defending his home against a Spanish invasion force; The poet and traveller Hugh Holland of Denbigh was buried in Westminster Abbey in 1633; Aneurin Owen, scholar and editor of 'The Laws of Hywel Dda' born in 1792 (see July 17); Death of Harry Evans in 1914 (see May 1); In 1930 a monument was unveiled at Pontypool's Ynysyngharad park to Evan and James James, the composers of 'Hen Wlad fy Nhadau'*; First day of the Royal Welsh Show at its new permanent home at Llanelwedd, Builth Wells, in 1963

*'Mae hen wlad fy nhadau yn annwyl i mi,
Gwlad beirdd a chantorion, enwogion o fri;
Ei gwrol ryfelwyr, gwlad garwyr tra mad,
Tros ryddid collasant eu gwaed.
Gwlad! Gwlad!
Pleidiol wyf i'n gwlad,
Tra mor yn fur
I'r bur hoff bau,
O bydded i'r hen iaith barhau.'

## July 24

FEAST DAY OF SAINTS IAGO 6th century at St Iago; GWETHENOC 6th century (then July 13 New Style, also July 6, November 5, and 7) at St Enodoc, St Goueznou; and MAELOG (see October 24). Robert Jones Derfel, socialist and poet, born Robert Jones near Llandderfel in 1824 (see December 17); In 1874, 19 miners died at Charles Colliery, Llansamlet; Death of Cadrawd in 1918, buried at Llangynwyd (see December 28)

'Brains IPA - The slogan says "It's Brains You Want". The brewery, founded in 1713, was acquired by Samuel and Joseph Brain in 1882, and is still owned by the family. The Cardiff brewery was once in the very centre of the city, but production has now moved out to a former Bass plant in a more industrial location. Brains' principal beers are known for their maltiness, but its IPA has a hoppy fragrance. It then presents a lightly malty, sweetish background flavour, before returning to the hop in an appetizing finish, with suggestions of orange zest and lemon rind. Many beers in this style have the symbols of India on the label, but Brains prefers the red dragon emblem of Wales.' - Michael Jackson, 'Great Beer Guide' of 500 international beers. Brains' draught bitter and mild ales are ordered as 'a pint of light' or 'a pint of dark'.

**On this day...**

## July 25

FEAST DAY OF SAINTS JAMES 1st century; CYNDEYRN 6th century (also August 5 and 6) at Llangyndeyrn; and MORDEYRN 5th - 6th century at Nantglyn. Death in 1201 of Gruffydd ap Rhys, prince of Deheubarth, who is buried at Strata Florida; At the battle of Banbury (Edgecote), perhaps 5000 Welshmen died in the Wars of the Roses* in 1469; Death in 1725, aged 80, of Thomas Griffiths of Llanfyrnach, first minister of the Welsh Tract Baptist Church in Delaware; W.E. Gladstone, four times Prime Minister, married Catherine Glynne of Hawarden Castle in 1839; Last public execution at Cardiff in 1857; Ifan ab Owen Edwards, founder of Urdd Gobaith Cymru, was born in 1895 at Llanuwchllyn (see January 23); Death in 1912 in Sketty of the missionary Griffith John (see December 14); In 1933, Britain's largest freshwater fish, a 388 lb sturgeon, was caught in the River Towi at Nantgaredig.

*'The Wars of the Roses were to a large extent a quarrel between Welsh Lords, who were also great English nobles closely related to the English throne ... Because mediaeval England had left half done its task of conquering Wales for civilisation (sic!), Welsh tribalism and feudalism revenged themselves by poisoning the Parliamentary life and disturbing the centralised government of its neglectful overlords. But when at length a Welsh army put a Welsh Tudor Prince upon the throne at Bosworth Field, Wales supplied a remedy for those ills in the body politic which she had helped to create.' - G.M. Trevelyan

**On this day...**

# July 26

*FEAST DAY OF SAINTS* ANNE 1st century at Llanfihangel, Malvern Wells, Trelech, Buxton; ANNA 5th - 6th century at Whitstone (Cornwall), Oxenhall (Glos); and PERIS 7th century (also December 11) at Llanberis, Llangian. In 1794, work began on the Swansea Canal; Birth in 1797 of William Bulkeley Hughes at Llanidan, lawyer, MP for Caernarfon and sometime 'father' of the House of Commons (see March 8); George Borrow, author of Wild Wales, died in 1881; In 1892, 112 men and children were killed at Parc Slip Collliery, Tondu, near Bridgend; Helen Hamilton Gardener died in 1925; Tanni Grey-Thompson, athlete, was born in Cardiff in 1969; Nicolette Milnes-Walker of Cardiff was the first woman to sail the Atlantic single-handedly non-stop, arriving at Newport, Rhode Island in 1971; Centenary celebrations of the Welsh Rugby Union in 1980

*'It was as late in the century as the 1860's before capitalists like David Davies, Llandinam, moved in (to the Rhondda Valleys), sinking shafts, building railways and docks, so that endless tons of steam coal could be shifted to Cardiff, Penarth and Barry. By the 1880's it was acknowledged that this was the best steam coal in Europe. The prosperity of the future capital of Wales was built upon black gold known as 'cardiff' in the language of many countries. It only needed one trip in a train from the Rhondda to Barry to understand that all the visual evidence of impressive wealth came from the sweat and blood of the mining community. It is hardly surprising therefore that the life of the valleys was dominated by the need of the people to hold on to a decent share of the product of their labour and if possible to increase it.'* - 'The Taliesin Tradition', Emyr Humphreys, 1983

*On this day...*

.............................................................................................................

.............................................................................................................

.............................................................................................................

# July 27

*FEAST DAY OF SAINTS* WILLIAM DAVIES d. 1593 at Llandrillo, martyred as a traitor at Beaumaris *'Syr William, seren ei wlad' (- Sir William, our country's star)*; and ARMEL (see August 16). Death of Maredudd ap Rhys Grug, Prince of Deheubarth, at Dryslwyn Castle in 1271; William Herbert, Earl of Pembroke, executed with his brother after the Battle of Banbury, at Northampton in 1469. So great were the Welsh losses in this battle that the bard Lewys Glyn Cothi called it a national calamity; In 1877, the great Chartist leader John Frost died, aged 93 (38 years after being sentenced to be hung, drawn and quartered); The Welsh Language Act received Royal Assent in 1967, allowing the use of Welsh in legal proceedings

*'... if the Saxon invasion of eastern England were a matter of peaceful coexistence over a period of years, as is increasingly thought, how could we explain the disappearance of*

the place-names (*other than those of prominent or manmade features - Roman cities, large rivers, hills, forests)? How could we account for the utter disappearance of the Celtic language from eastern England and of the Christian religion? How could we account for the fact that only a score of nouns made their way from British Celtic into Anglo-Saxon and none at all from British Latin? Why did the Saxons fail to borrow as simple a device as the potter's wheel? Why did tens of thousands of Britons flee to the Continent as early as the 460's? Why was it that the Britons who survived in the west of the island conceived a hatred of the Saxons which the passage of generations did little to abate? Why, in fact, did they refuse to preach the Gospel to their tormentors even in the early 8th century, a fact which shocked Bede?'* - E. A. Thompson, 'St Germanus of Auxerre and the End of Roman Britain', 1984

*On this day...*

..................................................................................................................................................
..................................................................................................................................................
..................................................................................................................................................

# July 28

FEAST DAY OF SAINT SAMSON d.565 (also May 28) - Samson of Dol, Founder Saint of Brittany - in Brittany and at Llanilltud Fawr. Richard II landed at Haverfordwest in 1399 from Ireland, and tried to find support across Wales to fight Henry Bolingbroke (Henry IV); After two months at sea, the first Welsh settlers arrived at Porth Madrun in Patagonia in 1865; Birth in 1874 of Billy Meredith at Chirk, the world's first football superstar (see April 19); Freddie Welsh (Frederick Hall Thomas), world champion boxer, died in 1927

In 1442, a Dunfermline monk wrote of the campagns of the English: *'against the Scots, the Welsh, the French and the Irish, they proved that they were the cruellest nation in the world.'*

*On this day...*

..................................................................................................................................................
..................................................................................................................................................
..................................................................................................................................................

# July 29

FEAST DAY OF SAINT BLEIDDIAN (LUPUS) 4th-5th century at Llanbleiddian Fawr (Llanblethian*), Llanbleiddian Fach (St Lythan's). Birth at St Fagans in 1727 of William Thomas, schoolmaster and diarist (see July 11); Possible date of the ending of Glyndŵr's second Parliament at Harlech in 1405 - Franch, Scottish, Castilian and Breton ambassadors attended. There was a 3rd Parliament at Harlech in 1406. The first was held at Machynlleth in summer

1404; John Owens (the son of Owen Owens and Sarah Humphreys of Holywell) died in 1846, leaving £100,000 to establish Owens College, which became Manchester University; In 1917, 200 miners' representatives met at Swansea to discuss establishing 'soviets' of workers and allying with the German working classes to bring peace across Europe (see July 20). The meeting was broken up by troops and armament workers

*'Our host John o' the Picton (licensee of the General Picton) simulates his neighbour Shon-y-Gwaith (John the Weaver, landlord of the King's Head) as to who shall have the best tap (finest beer), and the competition for that honour causes each of them to add an extra bushel of malt to his brewing, to gratify the village topers.' - David Jones of Wallington (1834-1890), referring to Llanblethian outside Cowbridge

On this day...

## July 30

Glyndŵr's Second Parliament ends at Harlech in 1405, having been attended by ambassadors from France, Scotland, Brittany and Castile; The Jacobite David Morgan was executed in London for treason in 1746; Frederick William Gibbins died at Llanwrtyd Wells in 1937, and is buried at Cynghordy (see April 1); Sean Moore of the Manic Street Preachers was born in Blackwood in 1970; The last greyhound races at Cardiff's Arms Park on this day in 1977, and the cinder track around the pitch was removed

'Three manifestations of humanity:
Affectionate bounty,
A loving manner, and
Praiseworthy knowledge' - from the Welsh Triads of Virtues

On this day...

## July 31

FEAST DAY OF SAINT GARMON OF MAN c.410-475 (also May 27, 28, July 13, 14, October 1 and 12) at Capel Garmon, Llanarmon, Llanfechain, St Harmon's, Pleyben, Castell Caereinion; GARMON of AUXERRE (see August 1) at Plougastell; and NEOT 9th century at St Neots; LUGHNASADHA - This *celebrated the ripening of the crops. This Irish Celtic god was known in Wales as Lleu Llaw Gyffes (The Bright One of the Skilful Hand);* In the Celtic Calendar, this was a great festivity for the gods, when women could choose husbands, sometimes for trial marriages. Prince Henry is appointed commander-in-chief for a third invasion of Wales against Glyndŵr, in 1402 - his army returns, unsuccessful, in September; The Great Orme Tramway was opened in 1902; Death in 1912 of Ellis Pierce at Dolwyddelan (see January 29); In 1917, the Victoria Cross was won on the Western Front by Pontypridd's Robert Bye, of the Welsh Guards, Nantymoel's James Davies, of the Royal Welch Fusiliers, and by Llanelli's Ivor Rees, of the South Wales Borderers; Hedd Wynn (Ellis Humphrey Evans of the Royal Welsh Fusiliers) dies of poison gas on Pilkem Ridge in Flanders on this day in 1917, and is awarded the 'Chair' posthumously at the Liverpool Eisteddfod (see September 6, January 13)

*'The common drink in those days was either buttermilk or beer. Tea or coffee was only drunk on special occasions. Not a pint of beer was imported from outside. Evey publican brewed his beer in his own back-kitchen. Now to supply these public houses, and there were about a dozen of them, and also practically every farm house in the district brewed their own beer, there had to be a big malting business. There was a malt-house in Wesley Street, another one on the Mount Road, another near the Poplars, and another large one at the Upper Tanhouse as well as others in the parish. There was always stationed at Llanfair Caereinion a government excise officer who was fully occupied in testing and supervising the malting and brewing. Large loads of barley were brought into town to be converted into malt. As good malting barley could not be grown in the uplands of Montgomeryshire and Merionethshire, the maltsters of Llanfair also supplied the requirements of the thirsty people of the Machynlleth and Dolgellau districts. Llanfair Caereinion in those days was a miniature Burton-on-Trent.'* - Charles Humphreys, c. 1850

**On this day...**

..........................................................................................................

..........................................................................................................

..........................................................................................................

# AUGUST - AWST
## Eost (Breton), Mis Est (Month of Harvest, Cornish)

## August 1

FEAST DAY OF SAINTS ALMEDHA (EILIWEDD) 5th - 6th century (also 12, March 17, October 9); GARMON OF AUXERRE d.448 (also July 31) at Auxerre, Llaniarmon yn Ial; GWINWALO d.432 at Ghent; ELLI (See August 12); RIOC (See February 6); and CENYDD (See July 5); LAMMAS - T h e pagan festival of LUG, Christianised into the Harvest Festival of 'Loaf Mass'. In Wales, LLEW was the Celtic god of light and genius, the inventor of Welsh chess, *fidchell*; GULE OF AUGUST - An old phrase across Britain, probably from the Welsh 'gwyl' meaning festival. Edward I began building a new castle at Aberystwyth in 1277; In 1406, Owain Glyndŵr held a 3rd Parliament at Harlech* Castle; In 1468, Dafydd ab Ifan ab Einion surrendered Harlech Castle to the Yorkists under Lord William Herbert, after an 8-year siege that inspired the song, '*Men of Harlech*'; In 1485, Henry Tudor, Earl of Richmond, sailed from Harfleur to conquer Richard III; In 1645, Major-General Rowland Laugharne of St Brides, Pembroke defeated Royalists at the Battle of Colby Moor near Haverfordwest; Death in 1896 of Sir William Robert Grove (see July 11); In 1802, Lord Nelson and Lady Hamilton came to Milford Haven; Birth near Llanymawddwy in 1875 of the blind harpist and singer David Roberts (Telynor Mawddwy, - see March 21); Death at Llanrug in 1909 of General Hugh Rowlands VC (see May 6); In 1914, the South Wales Miners' Federation casts doubts about the headlong rush to war, which Britain joined 3 days later - by 1918 more than 10,000,000 soldiers had been killed; Royal Assent was given in 1957 for the Liverpool Corporation to flood Trywerin - only one Welsh MP (a Conservative) had voted for the measure

*'*Robert Graves noted that ony two of the inhabitants of Harlech had hurried to enlist (in the Great War) - Graves himself and a caddie who was in trouble for stealing golf clubs. "The chapels", wrote Graves, "held soldiering to be sinful, and in Merioneth, the chapels had the last word... However, Lloyd George became Minister of Munitions in 1915, and persuaded the chapels that the war was a Crusade, and we had a sudden tremendous influx of Welshmen". ' - John Davies, 'A History of Wales'*

*On this day...*

.....................................................................................................................

.....................................................................................................................

.....................................................................................................................

## August 2

*FEAST DAY OF SAINT SIDWELLA* 5th - 6th century (also 1, July 31) at Exeter Cathedral, Llaneast. The Royalist Colonel John Bodvel (1617-1663) was given arms to 'defend his home in Wales' in 1642; 28 miners died at Cwmbach in 1845; Michael Jones defeated Ormonde's forces at Rathmines in 1649, allowing Cromwell to enter Ireland (see December 10); In 1850, the last mail stage coach left Cardiff for London. Its staging-post was the Cardiff Arms Hotel, where the Angel Hotel now stands; Myrna Loy was born Myrna Williams in 1905; Ebbw Vale's last steelworks furnace was demolished in 1978

*'Here in Wales, what can we do? We should work to make Wales free. A small country without the temptation of power, with no hope of lording it over other countries, with its good in the friendship of countries, and its society as unpretentiously of the people as only the society of small countries can be.'* - Waldo Williams

*On this day...*

...........................................................................................................................................................

...........................................................................................................................................................

...........................................................................................................................................................

## August 3

*FEAST DAY OF SAINT SETNA* 5th - 6th century (also August 4 and September 19) at Sithney, Kinsale. In 1488 Lewis of Caerleon, mathematician, Oxford don, theologian and doctor received another lucrative grant from Henry VII; The will was made in 1690 of Elis Prys, 'The Red Doctor' of Plas Iolyn, Ysbyty Ifan, *'a creature of the Earl of Leicester and devoted to all his bad designs'*; Death in 1872 of the inventor William Davies Evans in Ostend (see January 27); Ernest Thompson Willows, Cardiff airship pioneer, died in a ballooning accident in 1926; In 1952 Sir Harry Llewellyn won the equestrian gold medal in the Helsinki Olympics; The Welsh Highland Railway opened in 1980

*'One Saturday night in early March in 1937 the snow came. We often have snow in winter at Dyffryn, but it is seldom very deep, nor does it last very long. And in some way the sheep smell the threatened blizzard, and from our places in the bottom of the valley we can look up at the darkening hills and see them winding down in long white strings, so that they are soon thick along the lower land. When the snow puts down its barrage on the mountain, the victims have already fled. But this year the snow came with no warning. The most weather-wise sheep were caught in the early flurries as they made their way down to the mountain wall. There are gutters at frequent intervals in the wall, and in winter these are left open for just such occasions as this, so that the sheep can slip through and descend still farther. But that night the ewes, heavy in lamb, ploughed their way to the wall only to find the gutters buried deep, and as the animals tried to range to*

*left or right in search of an open hole the screaming wind hurled the snow in masses against the wall and buried the refugees where they stood.'* - from 'I Bought a Mountain', Thomas Firbank, 1940

*On this day...*

## August 4

*FEAST DAY OF SAINTS* BUAN late 6th century at Bodfuan; and SETNA (see 3). Welsh archers served both sides in the terrible battle of Evesham in 1265; Birth in 1811 at Abergele of the Mormon missionary Daniel Jones, who was with Joseph Smith when he was assassinated (see January 3); The last day of the 55-day siege of the Royal Welsh Fusiliers at Peking in 1900; Evan Evans, 'the greatest scholar of his age', died in 1855 (see April 20); In 1944, the Glamorgan cricket captain, England cricket player, and Wales and Cardiff rugby player, Maurice Turnbull, was killed by a sniper's bullet, serving in the Welsh Guards in Normandy - his grave is Number 3, Row 20, Plot C in the Bayeux War Cemetery; Dilys Cadwalader won the Eisteddfod Crown in 1953, the first woman to do so

*'Three antagonists of goodness:*
*Pride, Passion And Covetousness.'* - from the Welsh Triads of Virtues

*On this day...*

## August 5

*FEAST DAY OF SAINTS* CEITHO (also January 7) at Llanpumsaint (with his four brothers on January 7), Llangeitho; STINAN 6th century (also August 23) at Llanstinan, Porthstinian, St David's Cathedral; KING OSWALD d.642 at Oswestry, killed at Croes Oswallt by the Mercians; and CYNDEYRN (see July 25). In 1063, Gruffydd ap Llywelyn, the only Welshman to rule over all of Wales, was killed by treachery in Gwynedd, retreating from Harold Godwinson's Saxon armies; French and Breton allies, *'The French Expedition'*, arrived in Wales to assist Glyndŵr, taking Carmarthen and Cardigan castles, and sweeping through Glamorgan and Gwent to face King Henry near Worcester; William Cecil (Lord Burghley), *'the Architect of Elizabethan England'*, died in 1598; Haverfordwest Castle and town fell to Parliament in 1648; Sydenham Teak Edwards, botanical and animal draughtsman, was born in Usk in 1768 (see February 8); Birth in 1837 at Merthyr Tudful of Sir William Thomas Lewis, coal magnate (see August 27); Death in 1921 of Sir David Brynmor Jones, lawyer and historian; In 1925, during the Pwllheli National Eisteddfod, Plaid Genedlaethol Cymru (The National Party of Wales) was founded; Richard Burton, actor, died in 1984; Helen Wynne Thomas was killed at Greenham Common in 1989 (see August 16)

*There are 54 Joneses in 'The Dictionary of Welsh Biography', but this is a five-finger exercise for anyone who has to locate a Jones in an average Welsh telephone directory (hence the familiar Jones the Fish, Jones the Bread and, in recent times, Jones the Spy.) The recent rise of Welsh nationalism has led some people to reverse the process; even the "ap" is returning. But the most engaging last stand was made in the 18th century by a genial bankrupt who signed himself "Siôn ap William ap Siôn ap William ap Siôn ap Dafydd ap Ithel Fychan ap Cynrig ap Robert ap Iorwerth ap Rhyrid ap Iorwerth ap Madoc ap Ednawain Bendew, called after the English fashion John Jones". -* Gwyn Alf Williams 'Where Was Wales'

*On this day...*

..................................................................................................

..................................................................................................

..................................................................................................

## August 6

*FEAST DAY OF SAINTS* EFRDDYL 5th century (also July 7) at Madley (Lann Ebrdil); and CYNDEYRN (see July 25); *TRANSFIGURATION;* Around this date, Glyndŵr's forces captured Radnor Castle in 1401; In 1713, the death of Thomas Jones of Tre'r-Ddol, near Corwen, the compiler of the first Welsh almanacs; Death in 1843 of David Johns of Llanina, the Madagascar missionary and translator; Death in 1922 of Dr Thomas John Price Jenkins, the rugby international three-quarter who founded the London Welsh Rugby Club; Billy Boston, the Wigan rugby league winger, was born in Cardiff in 1934

*'The Welsh are extremely selfish, and if it is at all possible to cheat and in any way to take in a stranger they will. If one settles amongst them as farmer or otherwise, every way is used to injure him, they hamstring his cattle, open his gates and break his enclosures, in short everything possible by which they can annoy him they do, but in some degree, this may be accounted for, they are uncommonly Methodists and consequently Devils. The women are of a most disagreeable disposition, one moment all good humour and affability, the next all sulking and apparently without any cause whatsoever. They are continually knitting, both walking and sitting in their Religious Bawling Houses.' -* Sir Robert Kerr Porter, on his 1799 'Tour'

*On this day...*

..................................................................................................

..................................................................................................

..................................................................................................

## August 7

FEAST DAY OF SAINT TYDECHO (see December 17) 1st Sunday after Lammas. Henry Tudor landed at Dale near Milford Haven in 1485, with an army of 2000, on his way to take the English crown; In 1740 Jane Brereton (Melissa) died, aged 55 at Wrexham; Birth in 1759 of William Owen Pughe, poet, lexicographer, antiquarian, grammarian and editor (see June 4); Death in 1789, aged 90 of William Edwards of Eglwysilan, the builder of Pontypridd, Usk, Pontardawe, Betws, Dolau-Hirion, Wychtree and Aberavon bridges. His sons built Newport Bridge, and others at Bedwas, Llandilo and Edwinsford (see February 8); Birth in 1835 of Griffith Evans, microscopist, bacteriologist and pioneer of protozoon pathology, at Towyn, Merioneth (see December 7);

'One of the castles of Wales would contain all the castles... of Scotland' - Samuel Johnson, speaking of Caernarfon; 'That most magnificent badge of our subjection' - Thomas Pennant, also referring to Caernarfon

*On this day...*

..................................................................................................................

..................................................................................................................

..................................................................................................................

## August 8

FEAST DAY OF SAINTS CLAUDIA (GWLADYS) 1st-2nd century in Rome; CRALLO 6th century at Llangrallo (Coychurch); ELID at St Helen's (Scillies); HYCHAN 5th-6th century (also October 1, 12) at Llanhychan ; ILLOG (also October 18, 30) at Hirnant; CYNLLO (see July 16); and FFAGAN (see February 10). In 1485 Henry VII began his march across Wales which lasted until August 14; The will was proved in 1574 of Hugh Price (Hugh ap Rhys ap Rhys), founder and first benefactor of Jesus College, Oxford; In 1811, Welsh Methodists broke with the Anglican Church; Esther Williams, 'the Hollywood Mermaid' born in 1922; Terry Nation, writer and Dalek creator, was born in Cardiff in 1930; In 1948, Tom Richards of Risca won the Marathon silver medal in the London Olympics; Construction began on the new Royal Mint, at Llantrisant in 1967

'To begin at the beginning:
It is spring, moonless night in the small town, starless and bible-black, the cobblestreets silent and the hunched, courters'-and-rabbits' wood limping invisible down the sloelack, slow, black, crowblack fishingboat-bobbing sea. The houses are blind as moles (though moles see fine tonight in the snouting, velvet dingles) or blind as Captain Cat there in the muffled middle by the pump and the town-clock, the shops in mourning, the Welfare hall in widows' weeds. And all the people of the lulled and dumbfounded town are sleeping now.' - the opening lines of 'Under Milk Wood' by Dylan Thomas

*On this day...*

..................................................................................................................

..................................................................................................................

..................................................................................................................

# August 9

Holy Day of Augustine Baker, priest (1641); In 1211 William de Braos died in France, having left his wife and son to starve to death in captivity in Windsor Castle. William had previously murdered at a banquet in Abergafenni Castle Seisyll ap Dyfnallt and other Welsh lords, to gain their lands; Around this time in 1294, Welsh soldiers refused to embark for France, sparking the rebellion of Madog ap Llywelyn, who assumed the title of Prince of Wales. Edward I brought an army of 35,000 men into Wales; The singing star Donald Peers, 'The Cavalier of Song', died in 1973, aged 65 (see July 10); In 1973, Alan Lloyd Roberts became the second person to win both the Chair and the Crown, at the Ruthin National Eisteddfod; Dylan Douglas, son of Michael Douglas and Catherine Zeta Jones, born in 2000

*'At Pembroke in the evening we had the most elegant congregation I have seen since we came into Wales. Some of them came in dancing and laughing as into a theatre, but their mood was quickly changed and in a few minutes they were as serious as my subject - Death'* - John Wesley (1703-1791), 'Journal'

*On this day...*

# August 10

*FEAST DAY OF SAINT LLAWDDOG* (see January 15) at Cilgerran (Old Style); Henry IV gathers forces at Worcester in 1405, to invade Wales again and kill Glyndŵr; John, 2nd Marquess of Bute, 'the creator of modern Cardiff' was born in 1793 (see March 18); Dai'r Cantwr, Rebecca Rioter, died in a fire in Ross, 1874 (see September 24 and December 22); Birth in 1879 of the pioneer of thoracic surgery Hugh Morriston Davies, the first person to diagnose a lung tumour by x-ray (see February 4); Irene Steer, 1912 Olympic swimming gold medallist, was born in Cardiff in 1889; In 1929, this was the last day of the last National Eisteddfod to be held in England (at Liverpool); In 1940, German bombs killed 13 people in Manselton, Swansea

*Edward the King, the English King,*
*Astride his tawny steed -*
*'Now I will see if Wales,' said he,*
*'Accepts my rule indeed.*

*Are streams and mountains fair to see?*
*Are meadow pastures good?*
*Do wheat-fields bear a crop more pure*
*Since washed with rebels' blood?'*

- opening verses of the Hungarian poem 'The Bards of Wales' by Janos Arany (1817-1882)

*On this day...*

...............................................................................................................................

...............................................................................................................................

...............................................................................................................................

## August 11

*FEAST DAY OF SAINT* LLWNI (also September 16) at Llanllwni. Birth in 1809 of Robert Thomas (Ap Vychan) at Llanuwchllyn in 1809, cleric and man of letters who won 'the Chair' twice (see April 23); In 1849, 52 miners were killed at Llety Shenkin Colliery, Aberdare; Griffith James Powell, aviation pioneer and holder of the transatlantic flight record, was born in Cardiff in 1907; The composer Alun Hoddinott was born in Bargoed in 1929; J.C. (Johnnie) Clay, the Glamorgan cricketer, died in Cardiff in 1973; St David's Hall opened in Cardiff in 1982

*'The Welsh population of Merthyr is gathered in large part from the mountains and wildish valleys hereabouts, and includes some specimens of the race who (as the saying goes) have no English, with a very large number of specimens who have but little and utter it brokenly. Those of the lower class who can read - and almost all Welshmen, however poor or primitive, can read - generally read Welsh only; and in that respect, as indeed in most respects, are far in advance of Englishmen of the same state in life, who often can read nothing. To hear a poor and grimy Welshman, who looks as if he might not have a thought above bread and beer, talk about the poets and poetry of his native land, ancient and modern, is an experience which, when first encountered, gives the stranger quite a shock of agreeable surprise.'* - Wirt Sikes, 'Rambles and Studies in Old South Wales', 1881

*On this day...*

...............................................................................................................................

...............................................................................................................................

...............................................................................................................................

## August 12

*FEAST DAY OF SAINT* ELLI 6th century (also August 1 and January 23) at Llanelli; Holy Day of Ann Griffiths*, poet (1805), buried on this day in Llanfihangel-yng-Yngwynfa. In 1198 there was a disastrous battle in the valley of the Machafwy in Elfael, when the Prince of Powys Gwenwynwyn's forces were defeated by the Normans; In August and September 1409 there was the *'Last Ride'* - a massive raid led by Owain Glyndŵr, who had lost his family, assisted by

Scots and French contingents, attacking the English in North-East Wales, Cheshire and Shropshire. Welshpool and the stronghold of Shrewsbury were sacked. It seems that Glyndŵr was seeking death in battle. He virtually disappeared after this revenge attack for the capture of his family, athough Bala held out for Glyndŵr until 1414 (see March 10), and his ambassadors are still trying to influence the French Court in 1415 and 1418; Death in 1860 of the Reverend John Parker of Llanmerewig and then Llanyblodwel, author of 'Tour of Wales and its Churches'; 58 miners killed at Great Western Pit, Rhondda, in 1892; In 1935, Gareth Jones was murdered by Mongolian bandits (see August 13)

*'I am reverently ashamed and I rejoice in astonishment to think that He who has to lower Himself even to look at things in Heaven, has yet given Himself as an object of love to so poor a creature as myself ... It amazes me to think who it was on the cross ... My mind drowns in too much astonishment to be able to say anything more.' - lines from a letter by Ann Griffiths

*On this day...*

...................................................................................................

...................................................................................................

...................................................................................................

## August 13

Holy Day of Bishop Jeremy Taylor (1667). DIC PENDERYN DAY – execution of Richard Lewis in 1831 - a plaque was unveiled outside Cardiff market on this day in 1994 - he was wrongfully hung in Cardiff Gaol after the Merthyr Riots; The first Welsh Quaker settlers, promised the 'Welsh Tract'*, arrived in Pennsylvania in 1682; The sculptor John Gibson died at Lucca in 1851; Death in 1911 of the boxer Thomas Thomas (see April 5); Birth in Barri in 1905 of Gareth Richard Vaughan Jones, linguist and journalist (see August 12); In 1925, William Randolph Hearst ('Citizen Kane') bought St Donat's Castle

*William Penn had promised 'independence' to the Welsh Quakers who settled in 'The Welsh Tract', and they wrote bitterly: 'We the inhabitants of the Welsh Tract ... are the descendants of the ancient Britons ... always in the land of our Nativity, under the Crown of England, have enjoyed the liberty and privilege as to have our bounds and limits to ourselves, within the which all causes, Quarrels, Crimes and Titles were tried and wholly determined by officers, magistrates, juries of our own Language, which were our Equals ... because it was promised unto us before we came that these ancient privileges would still be ours in the New World.'

*On this day...*

...................................................................................................

...................................................................................................

...................................................................................................

## August 14

*FEAST DAY OF SAINTS* MWYNEN/MORWENNA 6th century (also July 5) at Morwenstow, Marhamchurch; OWAIN 10th century at Ystradowen; NYFAIN (see 15); and IESTYN (see April 12) in the West Country. Harlech Castle surrendered to Yorkists in the Wars of the Roses in 1468; T.E. Lawrence (of Arabia) born at Tremadoc in 1888; Sir David Treharne Evans died in 1907 (see April 21); Bala Lake Railway opened in 1972; In 1979, the longest-lasting rainbow was recorded, off the coast between Clwyd and Gwynedd, lasting over 3 hours

*'He who denies his father or his mother or his country or his language will never be a man of civilisation and virtue'* - 'Dosbarth Byrr ar y Rhan Gyntaf of Ramadeg Gymraeg', Gruffydd Robert c. 1560

*On this day...*

..............................................................................................................................

..............................................................................................................................

..............................................................................................................................

## August 15

*FEAST DAY OF SAINTS* NYFAIN 5th - 6th century (also 13, 14 and March 24) at Nefyn, Crick, Llanfair yn Nefyn; and March 24); and TWROG (see June 26); FEAST OF THE ASSUMPTION -The Catholic feast of the Virgin Mary's reception into heaven. Henry Tudor's forces advanced into England in 1485; Between 14th and 16th of August 1531, Sir Mathew Cradock (born c.1468) died and was buried at Swansea; The 'Earl of Moira' sank in the Dee Estuary in 1821, 80 people drowning; Lewis John Wynford Vaughan-Thomas born in Swansea in 1908 - 'Wynford' was a distinguished war correspondent, writer, TV director and TV personality (see February 4); Death when mountaineering in Italy of the chemist and climber Humphrey Owen Jones, aged 24 (see February 20); VJ Day - Victory over Japan was celebrated across Wales, ending the Second World War in 1945; BBC's Wenvoe television transmitter opened in 1952, the first in Wales

*'Man is a social being. It is only in his social role that he attains dignity. Only in a community can he achieve contentment. The sum total of his achievements, the masterpieces of the mind and the imagination, in utterance, in colour and image, in architecture, was at all times arrived at by co-operation and joint invention with his neighbours and fellows. He is obliged to associate and be social. He is compelled to love his community.'* - Saunders Lewis, Y Ddraig Goch newspaper, 1926

*On this day...*

..............................................................................................................................

..............................................................................................................................

..............................................................................................................................

## August 16

*FEAST DAY OF SAINT* ARMEL (ARTHMAEL) d.570 (also 14, 15, 17, June 13 and July 27, and August 4 in Brittany) at St Armel, Ergue-Armel, Plou-arzel, Ile d'Arz, Plouermel, Stratton and St Erme (Cornwall), Westminster. Ben Bowen of Treorchy (born 1878), Welsh poet, died tragically young at Ton Pentre in 1903; Death when serving with the South Wales Borderers in 1916 of Charles Meyrick Pritchard, Newport and Wales rugby forward; Major Tasker Watkins of the Welch Regiment won the Victoria Cross in Normandy in 1944; Last County Cricket match at the Arms Park before Glamorgan moved to Sophia Gardens in 1966; Helen Wynne Thomas, Greenham Martyr, born in 1966 at Newcastle Emlyn (see August 5)

*'The stories about the baboon of Maesllwch Castle grow more and more extraordinary. It is said that when visitors come to the Castle the creature descends upon their heads, clambering down the balusters of the staircase. He put Baskerville and Apperley to flight, routed them horse and foot, so that they clapped spurs to their horses and galloped away in mortal fear, the baboon racing after them. He carries the cats up to the top of the highest Castle Tower, and drops them over into space, and it is believed that the baboon seeks an opportunity to carry the young heir up to the top of the Tower and serve him in the same way.'* - Kilvert's Diary, this day in 1872

**On this day...**

...............................................................................................................................

...............................................................................................................................

...............................................................................................................................

## August 17

*FEAST DAY OF SAINT* DUNWYD d. 876 (also 22, April 17) at St Donat's, Welsh St Donat's. Rhuddlan's Dominican monks (the Black Friars) handed over their monastery to the Crown for Dissolution in 1538; John Humphrys, radio interviewer and reporter, born in 1942 in Cardiff

*'Son of a father executed by the King of England, Owen of Wales (Owain Llawgoch) had been brought up in the court of Philip VI of France. Descrbed as high-spirited, bold and bellicose, he had fought at Poitiers, in the Lombard Wars of the 1360's, for and against the Dukes of Bar in Lorraine, as a free-lance in Spain, and with Du Guesclin in the campaigns of the 1370's, in which he had returned from leading a naval raid on the Channel Islands to capture the Captal de Buch. In 1375 Owen was fresh from action at the successful siege of St Sauveur-le-Vicomte on the coast of Normandy, where for the first time cannon had been used with notable effect. Forty "engines" great and small, projecting balls of iron and leather as well as stone, failed to bring the walls down but so harassed the defenders that they could not continue resistance. "They were so covered by the engines that they did not dare go into the town or outside the castle but stayed in the towers." Even there one ball penetrated a room where an English captain*

*lay sick in bed and rolled around the walls several times "as if the thunder itself had entered his chamber", convincing him his last hour had come, before it crashed through the floor to the room below."* - Barbara Tuchman, 'A Distant Mirror - the Calamitous 14th Century', 1979

*On this day...*

...................................................................................................
...................................................................................................
...................................................................................................

# August 18

FEAST DAY OF SAINTS DOCHDWY; and ELEN d. c. 330 (also May 21 with Constantine) in Rome. Denbigh's White Friars surrendered their Monastery in 1538; In 1573 Maurice Wynn, the third husband of Catrin o'r Berain, died; Meriwether Lewis, explorer of America and leader of the Lewis and Clark Expedition, born in 1774; The Rothesay Castle sank in Conwy Bay in 1831, with 150 passengers drowning; In 1899, 19 miners died at Llest Colliery, Garw Valley

*'Hell! Hell! Hell! Torn flesh, shattered bones. Halt, O God, the mad fever, halt the spitting of the demented dogs!'* - Lewis Valentine, written durng the 3rd Battle of Ypres in 1917

*On this day...*

...................................................................................................
...................................................................................................
...................................................................................................

# August 19

FEAST DAY OF SAINTS CLEER 5th - 6th century (also October 23, November 3 and 4) at St Clear's, Clether; KING CLYDOG (CLINTANC) 5th century (also November 3) at Brecon, Clodock; and LLAWDDOG (see January 15). In 1399, Richard II was captured by Bolingbroke's men and taken to Flint Castle, indirectly leading to Glyndŵr's War in 1400; In 1538, Bangor's Dominicans and the Franciscans of Llanfaes surrendered their monasteries; The Marquis of Worcester at last surrendered Raglan Castle to Roundheads in 1646, after which it was slighted; Death of Robert Ellis (Cynddelw) at Gartheryr in 1875 (see February 3); Riots in 1911 at Llanelli, with 6 men killed; In 1919, Lloyd George announced that the coal-mines would not be nationalised, rejecting the recommendations of the Sankey Commission; In 1940, Gerrnan bombers started a fire at Pembroke Dock's fuel stores which lasted for 17 days; Death in 1969 of the archiect Sir Percy Thomas in Cardiff (see September 13)

'Languages are possibly the most complicated structures the human mind has ever invented but, tragically, our species' most impressive creations are dying. According to the British linguist David Crystal, an indigenous language currently dies every two weeks. By the end of the century, it is projected, 5,500 of the current 6,000 languages now spoken will join Latin and Greek as "dead languages". Those, of course, were once two of the world's top languages. "Sic transit", as they used to say. What we are witnessing is linguicide. A language massacre. There are no zoos, museums or cemeteries for dead languages. It's technically possible to record them for posterity, in some skeletal form, before the last speakers go to their final reward. One can create sound archives, compile dictionaries, store video footage and catalogue written material. You will lose everything that represents the life of a language: the idiolects (individual styles and quirks of speech), the subgroup dialects, the literary and expressive richness of a living tongue, its infinite capacity to reflect distinct modes of thought. There's nothing more corpse-like than a dead language. They never come back to life. And, the brute fact is that no government is going to put taxpayers' money into any such project. Save the whale, yes. But save, say, Manx (the last native speaker on the Isle of Man died in 1974) - forget it. There's no mystery about the root cause of the linguistic holocaust that we're living through... The spread of English is the product of naked linguistic superpower... How did this happen? How did a dialect, spoken by a backward, semi-literate tribe in the south-eastern corner of a small island in the North Sea, spread, like some malign pandemic virus, across the globe? Should we feel guilty that our way of speaking is obliterating so many other tongues? Is it not a more sinister form of colonialism than that which we practised a hundred years ago? Once we took just their raw materials. Now we invade their minds, by changing the primary tool by which they think: "their" language.' - John Sutherland, 'The Independent on Sunday', March 10th 2002, reviewing John McWhorter's 'The Power of Babel: A Natural History of Language'.

The author's mother grew up in the Welsh-speaking community of Trefeglwys, Montgomeryshire, where English immigration has altered the character of the village, and a Welsh friend who moved into a North Pembrokeshire village a few years ago followed ten successive English retirement couples in settling there. Upon the same day in March 2002 that Rhyl was reported to be a top 5 UK crime blackspot because of people 'on the social' moving in from Liverpool, Manchester, Crewe, Stoke and Birmingham, the author travelled from Aberystwyth to Cardiff. Stopping at Rhayader, a person from the south-east of England shouted to another English friend across the road. The person manning the tourist office was English, and the antique shop was owned by an Englishman who was speaking to an English customer. Stopping in Builth Wells, two English people came out of an estate agent's, a knot of people talking in the car-park were English and the person manning the tourist information office was also English. This was on a rainy day, well outside the tourist season, and to hear over a dozen successive English accents is either a statistical freak or yet more apocryphal evidence about an overwhelming Welsh problem. In both towns in the heart of Wales, in brief stops, I heard no-one who was Welsh speaking either English or Welsh. Politicians are afraid of accepting the fact that Welsh communities are dying out rapidly, because of the malign influence of 'political correctness'. The scathing treatment of Seimon Glyn as a 'pariah' by the media and politicians, for saying that there was a problem with massive inward migration of two groups - retirement couples, and unemployed people who are 'social problems' in England - is extremely saddening. As ever, the bearer of bad tidings is shot, while those in power will not step outside their comfort zones.

*On this day...*

..................................................................................................................................................
..................................................................................................................................................
..................................................................................................................................................

## August 20

*FEAST DAY OF SAINT* LLAWDDOG (See January 15). In 1404, Henry Dwn took Cydweli, and Glyndŵr's men also took Haverfordwest, and at Craig-y-Dorth, the English army was beaten and its survivors chased back to Monmouth Castle; Birth of Thomas Johnes in 1748, who built 'Hafod' near Cwmystwyth (see April 23); Birth in 1809 of the cleric and man of letters Morris Williams (Nicander) at Caernarfon (see January 3); Birth in Anglesey in 1824 of Hugh Hughes ('Hughes Cadfan'), one of the Welsh pioneers in Patagonia (died in the colony on March 7, 1898); Birth in 1833 of Sir James Hills-Johnes, VC, general and hero of the Indian Mutiny (see January 3); Wales' worst rail disaster in 1868, with 33 dying in a collision at Abergele; Henry Richard, *'the Prophet of Peace'* and *'the Member for Wales'*, died in 1888 at Treborth; The start of the strike in 1900 on the Taff Vale Railway, which eventually led to increased legal rights for trade unions across Britain; William John Trew, the Swansea and Wales rugby three-quarter, died at Swansea in 1926; Colin Jackson of Cardiff set the 110m hurdles world record, becoming World Athletics Champion in Stuttgart in 1993

*'The sudden decline of the national minstrelsy and customs of Wales is in a great degree to be attributed to the fanatick impostors, or illiterate plebeian preachers, who have too often been suffered to over-run the country, misleading the greater part of the common people from their lawful church, and dissuading them from their innocent amusements, such as singing, dancing and other rural sports, with which they had been accustomed to delight in from the earliest times. The consequence is, Wales, which was formerly one of the merriest and happiest countries in the world, is now become one of the dullest' -* 'The Bardic Museum', Edward Jones (1752-1824)

*On this day...*

..................................................................................................................................................
..................................................................................................................................................
..................................................................................................................................................

# August 21

The Western Mail and South Wales Echo were bought from Merthy Tudful's 'press magnate' Lord Kemsley, by the Canadian Roy Thomson in 1959; Colour TV broadcasts started in Wales in 1967, on BBC2 only; The writer Rhys Davies died in 1978

Richmond: 'The weary sun hath made a golden set,
And, by the bright track of his fiery car,
Gives token of a goodly day tomorrow.
Sir William Brandon, you shall bear my standard.
Give me some ink and paper in my tent:
I'll draw the form and model of our battle,
Limit each leader to his several charge,
And part in just proportion our small power.
My Lord of Oxford, you, Sir William Brandon,
And you, Sir Walter Herbert, stay with me.
The Earl of Pembroke keeps his regiment:
Good Captain Blunt, bear my goodnight to him,
And by the second hour of the morning
Desire the earl to see me in my tent.
Yet one thing more, good captain, do for me:
Where is Lord Stanley quarter'd, do you know?'
Blunt: 'Unless I have mista'en his colours much, -
Which, well I am assur'd, I have not done, -
His regiment lies half a mile at least
South from the mighty power of the king.'
Richmond: 'If without peril it be possible,
Good Captain Blunt, bear my good-night to him,
And give him from me this most needed note.' - lines in Shakespeare's 'Richard III' from Henry Tudor, Earl of Richmond, on the eve of the Battle of Bosworth. He needed the support of the army of Lord Stanley, a kinsman, but Richard III held Stanley's son hostage.

*On this day...*

........................................................................................................................................

........................................................................................................................................

........................................................................................................................................

# August 22

FEAST DAY OF SAINTS GWYDDELAN/LORCAN at Llanwyddelan, Dolwyddelan, Llanllugan; JOHN KEMBLE d.1679 at Pembridge Castle, Llwyn - hung, drawn and quartered at Hereford; and DUNWYD (see 17); The Battle of Bosworth Field* in 1485, where Henry VII's Welsh army defeated Richard III and established the Tudor dynasty; The Royalist cleric Christopher Love of Cardiff was executed in 1651 for corresponding with Charles II in exile; Birth in 1766 of Ezekiel Hughes, early settler at Cincinnati (see September 2); In 1943 the great Celtic treasure hoard of weapons, trumpets and cauldrons was discovered in Llyn Cerrig-Bach, Anglesey, possibly dating from the Roman invasion in AD61, when Suetonius Paulinus crossed the Menai Straits to wipe out the centre of European druidism

*'More than I have said, loving countrymen,
The leisure and enforcement of the time
Forbids to dwell on: yet remember this,
God and our good cause fight on our side;
The prayers of holy saints and wronged souls,
Like high-rear'd bulwarks, stand before our faces:
Richard except, those who we fight against
Had rather have us win than him they follow.
For what is he they follow? Truly, gentlemen;
One that made mean to come by what he hath,
And slaughter'd those that were the means to help him:
A base foul stone, made precious by the foil
Of England's chair, where he is falsely set;
One that hath ever been God's enemy.
Then, if you fight against God's enemy,
God will in justice, ward you as his soldiers:
If you do sweat to put a tyrant down,
You sleep in peace, the tyrant being slain;
If you do fight against your country's foes,
Your country's fat shall pay your pains the hire:
If you do fight in the safeguard of your wives,
Your wives shall welcome home the conquerors;
If you do free your children from the sword,
Your children's children quit it in your age.
Then, in the name of God and all these rights,
Advance your standards, draw your willing swords.
For me, the ransom of my bold attempt
Shall be this cold corse on the earth's cold face;
But if I thrive, the gain of my attempt
The least of you shall share his part thereof.
Sound drums and trumpets, boldly and cheerfully;
God and Saint George! Richmond and victory!' - Henry VII's oration to his troops, as the Earl of Richmond, before Bosworth, in Shakespeare's 'Richard III'

**On this day...**

22

...............................................................................................................................................

...............................................................................................................................................

...............................................................................................................................................

## August 23

FEAST DAY OF SAINTS EURYN 6th-7th century at Ynys Enlli; TUDFUL d.480 (also Mabsant at Easter, and Fair on September 24) at Merthyr Tydfil, Llysworney; and JUSTINIAN (see December 5). In 1170 Richard de Clare, Strongbow, invaded Ireland from Pembroke - recently blamed by an Irish MP for the Northern Ireland troubles of today; Birth in 1765 of James Davies, 'the schoolmaster of Devauden' at Blaen Trothy near Grosmont (see October 2); Birth in 1834 of Hugh Owen Thomas* at Bodedern, the world-famous orthopaedic surgeon and inventor of the 'Thomas Calliper'; The 'Tithe War' began at Llanarmon in 1886; William John (Gareth) Hughes 'The Desert Padre' was born in Llanelli in 1894, and became a Hollywood film star and priest to Nevada's Paiute Indians

*In the 18th century a Spanish-speaking boy was the only survivor of a ship which floundered off Llanfairynghornwy in Anglesey, and he was adopted by a childless couple names Thomas who farmed Maes, between the church and the sea. The boy took their name, married a local girl, and became the ancestor of a line of meddygon esgryn (bonesetters). The reputation of Evan Thomas (1735-1814), across North Wales and the Borders, was such that Viscount Bulkeley paid for a memorial tablet in the church. Evan's son Richard ap Evan of Llanfaethlu carried on the expertise, and his son Evan Thomas developed an extensive practice from Liverpool. Hugh Owen Thomas was Evan's son, and handled more fractures than any other surgeon in Britain. Hugh's nephew Sir Robert Jones (see June 28), whom he trained, carried on with his work, and the Thomas Calliper saved thousands of limbs in the Great War and is still used across the world.

*On this day...*

..................................................................................................................................

..................................................................................................................................

..................................................................................................................................

## August 24

FEAST DAY OF SAINT BARTHOLOMEW 1st century. Chirk Castle surrendered in 1659, with the collapse of 'Booth's Revolt'; In 1848, 178 Welsh emigrants died in a fire on the 'Ocean Monarch' off Colwyn Bay; Death in 1882 of John Dillwyn-Llywelyn (see January 13); In 1890 Ella Gwendolen Rees Williams (Jean Rhys) was born in Dominica; The Welsh Black Cattle Society was founded in 1904; In 1925, the Ammanford and Glyn-Neath Coal Strike ended after two months - 198 miners were prosecuted and 58 imprisoned; Glamorgan won the County Cricket Championship for the first time in 1948; In 1988, Sally Hodge of Cardiff won a gold medal in the World Track Cycling Championships in Ghent

'Great are the fires of Ebbw Vale,
And all the seas and the heavens,
Great are the ships in Barry Dock
And great the golden forests,
Great are the shadows over the Rhondda
And the mansions built in the shires,
Great are the fortunes made in Gwalia
And the promontories of slag.' - Idris Davies, verse 16 of 'The Angry Summer - a
poem of 1926'

*On this day...*

..................................................................................................................................................

..................................................................................................................................................

..................................................................................................................................................

# August 25

*FEAST DAY OF SAINTS* ELEN LLUYDDOG (see May 22); MARY (MAIR)
1st century (Assumption date, her Annunciation is April 4 and her Nativity
September 18) at Nefyn – her dedications are mainly in Pembroke, as the
Normans rededicated many Welsh churches as Llanfair. Admiral Sir Henry
Morgan, the greatest buccaneer of all time, dies in Port Royal in 1688; Llandovery
College was founded in 1847; Death in 1952 near Trealaw of the poet James
Kitchener Davies (see June 16); Death in 1946 of Arthur Tudor Edwards (see
March 7); In 1964, the last cargo of coal left Cardiff Docks;

In 1996, Jeremy Clarkson wrote in 'The Sunday Times' - '*I have just come back
from a holiday in France - a pretty country spoilt, like Wales, by the people who live
there*'

*On this day...*

..................................................................................................................................................

..................................................................................................................................................

..................................................................................................................................................

# August 26

*FEAST DAY OF SAINT* NINIAN d. 432 at Whithorn. 5000 Welsh archers won
the Battle of Crecy in 1346 - this appears to have been the first time an army wore
a uniform in Europe, with the Welsh wearing green and white tabards; The
antiquarian and historian George Owen died in 1613; In 1688 Admiral Sir Henry
Morgan, who sacked Panama in 1671, was buried at Port Royal, Jamaica; Death in
1838 at Merthyr Mawr of Sir John Nicholl (see March 16); Birth in 1887 at Neath
of Edward Hugh John Neale Dalton, Baron Dalton, economist and Chancellor of

the Exchequer (see February 13); 112 colliers died at Parc-Slip, near Bridgend in 1892; Death in 1960 of the rugby player Dr T.E. Jones-Davies (see March 4)

*'Geology, n. The science of the earth's crust - to which, doubtless, will be added that of its interior whenever a man shall come up garrulous out of a well. The geological formations of the globe aready noted are catalogued thus: The Primary or lower one, consists of rocks, bones of mired mules, gas-pipes, miners' tools, antique statues minus the nose, Spanish doubloons and ancestors. The Secondary is largely made up of red worms and moles. The Tertiary comprises railway tracks, patent pavements, grass, snakes, mouldy boots, beer bottles, tomato cans, intoxicated citizens, garbage, anarchists, snap-dogs and fools.'* - Ambrose Gwinnett Bierce, 'The Devil's Dictionary, 1911

*On this day...*

.......................................................................................................................

.......................................................................................................................

.......................................................................................................................

# August 27

FEAST DAY OF SAINTS DEGEMAN 7th-8th century (also 30) at Llandegeman, Rhoscrowther, Watchet: DAVID LEWIS d.1679 Cwm in Monmouth - hung, drawn and quartered in Usk; MEDDWID 6th century at Clocaenog; CAENOG 6th century at Clocaenog; and ROGER CADWALADR d.1610 - Executed at Leominster. Catrin o'r Berain, *'the Mother of Wales'* died in 1591; Mary Ann Evans of Tongwynlais married the future Prime Minister, Benjamin Disraeli in 1839; Charles Stewart Rolls, youngest son of Lord Llangattock, born at the Hendre, outside Monmouth, the first Briton to fly the Channel and the founder of the car company (see July 12); In 1881, there was Royal Assent for the first Parliamentary Act since the 17th century that dealt solely with Wales - the Sunday Closing Act; The painter J.D. Innes died of consumption in 1914, aged just 27 (see February 27); Death in 1914 of the coal magnate Sir William Thomas Lewis (see August 5); In 1921, Cardiff City had their first match in football's First Division, now the Premiership. In the same decade they appeared in two FA Cup Finals; In 1948 Charles Evans Hughes died, Chief Justice of the Suprmen Court, who almost became President of the USA; 1981 saw Ann Pettit of Llanpumsiant lead the Women's Peace March from City Hall Cardiff to Greenham Common, where Welsh women set up the first anti-nuclear Peace Camps; Allan Jones, singer-actor, died in New York in 1992, aged 84

*'Three things without which there can be nothing good:*
*Truth, Peace, and Generosity'* - from the Welsh Triads of Virtues

*On this day...*

.......................................................................................................................

.......................................................................................................................

.......................................................................................................................

## August 28

FEAST DAY OF SAINT MELORUS d.411; LAMMAS QUARTERDAY in SCOTLAND. The Black Friars (Dominicans) surrendered Brecon to the commissioners of the Dissolution of the Monasteries in 1538; Sir Richard Bulkeley Williams Bulkeley died in 1875 (born September 23, 1801); Death in a climbing accident in 1899 of Owen Glynne Jones (see November 2); Hugh Cudlipp, journalist and press baron, born in Cardiff in 1913; The actor Windsor Davies born in 1930; Death of Sir Edgeworth David of St Ffagans in 1934, the leader of the first expedition to reach the Magnetic South Pole (see January 28); 14 people drowned at Rhosneigr Beach, Anglesey, trying to save a Polish plane which crashed in the sea in 1941

'26% of Welshmen unemployed. Bread is dearer. England spends £1,500 million on War.' - Welsh Literary Journal, 1937. 'Unemployment was the evil that drove nearly half-a-million of our people from Wales between the two wars. It is the evil that breaks up our homes and our Welsh communities and destroys our culture and our sense of nationhood.' - S.O. Davies, MP for Merthyr, in 1949. Plus ça change..........

*On this day...*

..................................................................................................................
..................................................................................................................
..................................................................................................................

## August 29

FEAST DAY OF SAINT IEUAN GWAS PADRIG at Cinmeirch, Cerrig-y-Druidion, Llantrisant (Anglesey). Dafydd ap Llywelyn ap Iorwerth, Prince of Wales, was forced by King Henry to agree a peace at Gwern Eigron near St Asaf in 1241, surrendering some territories to England; Death of Robert Davies, musician, in a quarry rockfall in 1858 (see June 29); In Hywel Dda's Laws, 'pannage' was allowed in the woods from this day, when pigs were allowed to root amongst the undergrowth; The first supertanker discharged oil at BP's Milford Haven terminal in 1960; 1977 saw the closure of the Taff Vale, the last pub in Wales' premier shopping street, Queen Street in Cardiff

'A storm of protest broke yesterday after Italy's highest court ruled that a woman cannot be raped if she is wearing tight denim jeans, since she would have to co-operate in removing them.' 'The Times' February 12, 1999. In 950, the Laws of Hywel Dda, based upon the old Welsh-Celtic laws of hundreds of years previously, ruled that in any case of rape, the woman's word was to be preferred to the man's.

*On this day...*

..................................................................................................................
..................................................................................................................
..................................................................................................................

## August 30

FEAST DAY OF SAINT DEGEMAN (see 27) in Norwich and Cornwall. In 1536 The Grey Friars (Franciscans) surrendered their monastery at Carmarthen; A patent is taken out for a *'flying machine'* by Bill Frost of Saundersfoot in 1875, which flies in the summer of 1876, 7 years before the Wright Brothers' plane; Admiral Sir Hugh Evan-Thomas died in 1928 (see October 27); Death in 1932 of the great rugby player John Conway Rees (see January 13); In 1937, Tommy Farr narrowly lost to Joe Louis for the World Heavyweight Championship in New York (see March 1 and March 12). Most ringside observers thought he had won; In 1940, 8 people died in German air-raids at Gresford, near Wrexham

*'Hay Flower Show, the first they have had, a very successful one. A nice large tent, the poles prettily wreathed with hop vine, and the flowers fruit and vegetables prettily arranged. There was an excursion train from Builth to Hay for the occasion. The town was hung with flags. The whole country was there. A row of pretty girls, Bevans and Thomases, were sitting on a form (bench) which broke down and left the whole row sprawling on their backs, with their heels in the air. Fanny Thomas was the only one who had any presence of mind about ankles. It was quite a case of being "on view" and "open to the public" and "no reserve". Twice round the tent was enough and as Trotter of the bank and I were shaking hands with impressive cordiality our enthusiasm was so great that we tore off the top of an Osmunda (fern) frond'.* - Kilvert's Diary, this day in 1870

*On this day...*

...................................................................................................................................

...................................................................................................................................

...................................................................................................................................

## August 31

FEAST DAY OF SAINT GARMON of MAN (see July 31) in Caernarfonshire; Holy Day of Bishop Aidan (651); Owain Llawgoch*, Prince of Wales, assassinated on the orders of the English Crown at the siege of Mortagne-sur-Gironde, outside Bordeaux in 1378. His memorial will stand in the village, from the 625th anniversary in 2003; Death of the great poet Huw Morys (*Eos Ceiriog*) of Llangollen in 1709, buried in Llansilin; Birth in 1875 of the clergyman and historian Arthur Wade-Evans at Fishguard (see January 4); In 1881, the opening day of the first National Eisteddfod to be held under the auspices of the National Eisteddfod Association, the Court; Birth in 1881 of Robert Thomas Jenkins, historian, and editor of the Dictionary of Welsh Biography (see November 11); 1940 saw 10 people killed by German air-raids in Rhos and Penycae, Clwyd; Death in 1956 of Winifred Margaret Coombe Tennant (*Mam o Nedd*), suffragette and representative to the League of Nations; Death in 1960 of the author Edith Picton-Turbervill, worker for women's causes; Gary Sobers hit six sixes off an over by Malcolm Nash at Swansea in 1968; The economist Professor Brinley

Thomas died in Cardiff in 1994; Companies House in Cardiff received the remaining records from London's Companies House in 1999

*'At this time Coucy had just lost in shocking circumstances his companion from the Swiss campaign, Owen of Wales. While Coucy was in Normandy, Owen was conducting the siege of Mortagne on the Atlantic coast at the mouth of the Gironde. Arising early on a clear and lovely morning, he sat on a stump in his shirt and cloak, as was his habit, while having his hair combed by his Welsh (-a mistake, actually Scottish) squire James Lambe. This man had recently been taken into his service as a compatriot who brought him tidings of his native land and told him "how all the country of Wales would gladly have him to be their lord." Standing behind his master on the still morning before others were abroad, James Lambe plunged a Spanish dagger into Owen's body, "stabbing him clean through so that he fell down stark dead." The assassin's hand was certainly hired by the English (-there is a record of payment for the killing in the Rolls of the Exchequer), possibly to remove a focus of agitation on the Welsh border, or, as contemporaries believed, in reprisal for the miserable death in prison of the Captal de Buch, originally captured by Owen. (The French king refused to allow the Captal's ransom). If so, it was a surprisingly dishonourable blow upon an unarmed man, as recognised by the English captain inside besieged Mortagne to whom Lambe reported his deed. "He shook his head and beheld him right felly and said, 'Ah, thou has murdered him... Although this deed is for our profit... we shall have blame thereby rather than praise'." On the French side, Charles V, though terribly angered, did not altogether regret the removal of Owen, a freebooter not guiltless of nefarious deeds of his own. His murder reflected a new kind of animosity growing out of the war. Suborned assassination within the brotherhood of knights was an innovation of the 14th century.' - Barbara Tuchman, 'A Distant Mirror - the Calamitous 14th Century', 1979

**On this day...**

31

..........................................................................................................

..........................................................................................................

..........................................................................................................

# SEPTEMBER - MEDI
### Gwengolo (Breton), Gwengala (Cornish)

## September 1

FEAST DAY OF SAINTS ELIDON (also June 16) at St Lythan's; SULIEN d.1091 at Llanbadarn, Letterston; and SENWYR at Llansannor. Death at Wexford in 1176 of Maurice Fitzgerald, son of Gerald of Windsor and Princess Nest; Death in 1685 of the lawyer and diplomat Sir Leoline Jenkins of Llantrisant, the 'second founder' of Jesus College; In 1878 62 miners died at Abercarn; Gwynfor Evans born in Barri in 1912; The first football match at Ninian Park, between Cardiff and Aston Villa in 1919; W.J. Parry, leader of the North Wales quarrymen, died in 1927; A German air-raid in Swansea killed 33 people in 1940; Evan Evans Bevan Brewery of Neath was taken over by Whitbread in 1967, and on 31 May, 1972 was closed with the loss of 140 jobs; In 1985 Saunders Lewis*, nationalist, writer and one of the 'Penyberth Three', died in Cardiff, aged 93 (see January 9, September 5 and October 15)

*'That investiture, amid the cheers of the Welsh and the grovelling of archbishops and bishops and the leaders of all the Welsh denominations, was the darkest hour of the sixties.' - Saunders Lewis, on the investiture of Charles Saxe-Coburg-Gotha-Sonderburg-Glucksberg-Schleswig-Holstein as Prince of Wales in 1969

*On this day...*

..................................................................................................................................

..................................................................................................................................

..................................................................................................................................

## September 2

FEAST DAY OF SAINT SULIEN 6th century (also October 1, May 13, December 17) at    Gwernogle, Llansilin*, Corwen, Wrexham, Silian, Luxulyan. Henry IV's armies crossed the border into Wales in 1402 to fight Glyndŵr; David Charles of Llanfihangel died in 1834 and was buried at Llangynnor (see October 11); Death in 1849 of the American settler Ezekiel Hughes, a life-long friend of the Welsh-American President Harrison (see August 22); Rhos Male Voice Choir formed in 1891; Birth of Victor Spinetti, actor, at Cwm, Ebbw Vale in 1932; In 1940, 33 people died in Swansea during German air-raids (30 had been killed previously, in July and August, and another 350 were to die during the course of the war)

*'St Silin's feast-day, wine being served, a dinner of rabbits, sugar and swans'* William Cynwal (d.1588), written of Moelyrch, near Llansilin

*On this day...*

..................................................................................................................................

..................................................................................................................................

..................................................................................................................................

## September 3

FEAST DAY OF SAINTS TUDWAL (see December 1); and GWYDDELAN (see August 22). Glyndŵr's men raided Herefordshire in 1403; The White Monks, the Cistercians, surrendered Tintern Abbey in 1538; Oliver Cromwell (a.k.a. Williams) died in 1648, and this day is remembered by the Houses of Parliament as 'Cromwell's Day'; Owen Jones (Owen Myfyr) was born at Llanfihangel Glyn Myfyr, Denbighshire in 1741, and working as a skinner in London, became one of the chief benefactors of Welsh scholarship (see September 26); Coleg Harlech, the first adult education college in Wales, opened in 1927; The Welsh Guards liberated Brussels in 1944; In 1952, there was the last hanging in Cardiff Prison, but the conviction of Mahmoud Mattan was set aside in 1998; Death in 1988 of Cardiff's Hollywood Film Director, Richard Marquand

*'A nation, tied together by its language, its land, its traditions and its history forms a world, an incomparable microcosm which, if you lose it through violence or through letting it die, cannot be restored by anything on earth. Only once does God create a nation.'* - translation of lines from 'Ac Onide' (But If Not) by J.R. Jones, 1970

*On this day...*

## September 4

FEAST DAY OF SAINTS MARCELLINUS d.166 at Trier, Martletwy; and RHUDDLAD at Rhuddlad. Charles Ashton, Welsh bibliogapher and literary historian, born at Ty'nsarn, Llawr-y-Glyn, Montgomeryshire in 1848; In 1851, 14 miners died in a shaft accident at Werfa Colliery, Aberdare; Freddie Welsh (Frederick Hall Thomas), won the World Light-Heavyweight Title in 1916 - there were only 7 world titles at this time, all at different weights, with one recognising authority. Today because of the plethora of weights and authorities, over 80 people can claim to be world boxing champion at any one time; Ronnie James of Cardiff lost the World Lightweight Title in Wales' first world title fight, at Cardiff in 1946

*'Just look at the breweries South Wales has lost over the years... There were the Taff Vale and Giles & Harrap which kept the Merthyr Tydfil areas bubbling. Over the mountain the Black Lion slaked the thirsts of Aberdare. Then we had Evan Evans Bevan rolling out the barrels at Neath and in Mid-Glamorgan the Bridgend Brewery was kept busy keeping everyone's pints foaming. Also in a glass of their own at Cardiff were the redoubtable Hancock's and Ely breweries. Sparkling up at Aberbeeg were Webbs, while Phillips and Lloyd & Yorath of Newport kept a cool head in South Gwent. Now, Brains of Cardiff, Felinfoel Ales and Buckleys of Llanelli are the sole remaining independent brews left in South Wales.'* - 'The South Wales Echo', 1977 (Now only Brains, Felinfoel and the redoubtable and new Tomos Watkins are left in Wales).

Whitbread was the most voracious of the English brewers to monopolise and monotonise Welsh brewing, closely followed by Bass-Charrington, which took over the superb Hancocks Brewery, and turned the famous Hancocks HB into a tasteless concoction now brewed in England. Their equally awful Worthington is now 'the official drink of the Millennium Stadium', the only beer available there except Guinness. Hancock itself had taken over the following breweries: 1883 North & Low, Bute Dock Brewery, Cardiff; 1884 Edwin Hibbard, Newport's Anchor brewery; 1888 Dowson Brothers, Cardiff's Phoenix Brewery; 1889 Biggs & Williams, Cardiff's South Wales Brewery; 1890 Ackland & Thomas, Swansea's High Street Brewery; 1894 F.S. Lock, Cardiff's County Brewery; 1895 Henry Anthony, Cardiff's Castle Brewery; 1901 Swansea's Glamorgan Brewery; 1902 Cross & Matthews' Risca Brewery; 1904 John Biggs' Canton Cross Brewery in Cardiff; 1914 Caerleon's Hanbury Brewery; 1915 Vale of Glamorgan Brewery at Cowbridge; 1917 David Jarvis's Singleton Brewery at Swansea; 1924 John Rees' Abernant Brewery at Cwmgorse; 1927 Swansea Old Brewery; 1936 Giles & Harrap's Merthyr Brewery; and 1960 David Robers & Sons' Brewery at Aberystwyth. A revival of local brewing, as pioneered by Tomos Watkins, also offering Welsh food and entertainment, should be encouraged.

*On this day...*

..................................................................................................
..................................................................................................
..................................................................................................

## September 5

*FEAST DAY OF SAINTS* MARCHELL (also October 7) at Llanfarchell; and CORENTIN (see November 2). Dryslwyn Castle was lost to Normans in 1287 by Rhys ap Maredudd (see June 8 and January 20); Death of the Parliamentarian Philip Jones at Fonmon Castle in 1674; Birth of Evan Jones (Ieuan Gwynedd) near Dolgellau in 1820, independent minister, Welsh language supporter and journalist (see February 23); Thomas Parry Williams won the Chair on this day in 1912. After being awarded the Crown the day before, he became the first person to win both major prizes at the national Eisteddfod; An unbeaten Glamorgan team won the county cricket championship, for the second time, in 1969; In 1981 the Cardiff marchers reach Greenham Common and start the peace camps; Latin Requiem Mass in 1985 for Saunders Lewis in St David's Cathedral, Cardiff; Death of Cardiff's Clem Thomas, Swansea and Wales' rugby player and writer in 1996;

'The day was lovely and I went to Newchurch. A solitary fern cutter was at work on the Vicar's hill mowing the fern with a harsh ripping sound. From the Little Mountain the view was superb and the air exquisitively clear. The Clee Hills seemed marvellously near. The land glittered, variegated with colours and gleams of wheat, stubble and blue

*hill. The yellow potentilla jewelled the turf with its tiny gems of gold and the frail harebell trembled blue among the fern, tipped here and there with autumn yellow. The little lonely tree bowed on the mountain brow, and below lay the tiny village deep in the valley among the trees embosoming the little church with its blue spire and Emmeline's grave.'*
- Kilvert's Diary, this day in 1871

*On this day...*

## September 6

FEAST DAY OF SAINTS DUNAWD FAWR 6th century at Bangor-is-Coed (Bangor-on-Dee) - he founded this great monastery, destroyed by pagans; and IDLOES 6th - 7th century at Llanidloes. Cardiff Black Friars (Dominican) and Grey Friars (Franciscan) monasteries were surrendered to Henry VIII's men on this day in 1538, as all the great Cistercian (White Monks) abbeys across Wales were also dismantled in the Dissolution; Birth in 1882 of Thomas Henry Vile at Newport, the Newport and British Lions scrum-half who captained Wales when aged 37 (see November 30); The composer Sir Henry Walford Davies was born at Oswestry in 1869 (see March 11); Death in 1897 of Thomas Rees Morgan in Ohio - he solved the problem of 'shaping' armour plate for American warships (see March 31); In 1917, Hedd Wynn was postumously awarded the Chair at the National Eisteddfod in Birkenhead (see January 13, July 31); Jack Howells of Abertysswg, Hollywood Oscar-winning film director and cameraman, died in 1990 in Penarth, aged 77; In 1992, Mervyn Johns, actor, died, aged 93 (see February 18)

*'The language of the conqueror in the mouth of the conquered is forever the language of the slave.'* Winston Spencer Churchill

*On this day...*

## September 7

FEAST DAY OF SAINTS NINIAN (see August 26); and GARMON of MAN (see July 31, first Sunday after August 31 in Caernarfonshire). A great storm hits Henry IV's army in Wales, while Glyndŵr leads an invasion of Herefordshire in 1402; Elizabeth Tudor was born in 1533; The arson attack on the Pen-y-Berth bombing range in 1936 by Saunders Lewis, Lewis Valentine* and D.J. Williams;

*'Beth þe gwyddai mamau Cymru, a mamau pob gwlad yn wir, fel y dirdynnir ac y rhwygir eu plant! A'r Duw mawr, I beth!' - What if the mothers of Wales, and indeed the mothers of every country, knew how their children are tortured and torn to pieces? And, great God, for what purpose!' - from Lewis Valentine's diary, kept in the Flanders trenches

On this day...

.........................................................................................................................................

.........................................................................................................................................

.........................................................................................................................................


## September 8

FEAST DAY OF SAINTS CYNFARCH 6th century at Duffryn, Clwyd; and NEFYDD 5th - 6th century at Lanefydd; NATIVITY OF THE VIRGIN MARY at Llanfair, and a two-week long fair began at Cardiff; GWYL FAIR A MEDI was St Mary's Feast in reaping-time; the traditional date when swallows left Wales. Caernarfon was given a Royal Charter in 1284; In 1468, William ap William, Lord Herbert of Raglan, was given the Earldom of Pembroke, but was killed in the following year at Edgecote; The Austin Friars of Newport surrendered to Parliamentary Commissioners in 1538; Sir John Glynne, MP for Caernarfon, was expelled from the House of Commons and committed to the Tower of London, on a charge of treason in 1647 (see November 2); Robert Shields of Cardiff won Wales' first Victoria Cross in 1856, in the Crimean War; Sir Harry Secombe, singer-comedian, was born in 1921; The first Severn Bridge opened in 1966

The Constable of Chester wrote to Henry IV in 1403: 'Robert Parys, the Deputy Constable of Caernarvon Castle, has informed us through a woman, for neither man nor woman would dare carry letters on account of the rebels of Wales, whom Owain Glyndŵr, with the French and all his other power, is raising up to assault the town and castle of Caernarvon... And in the castle there are not more than 28 fighting men which is too small a force, for 11 of the abler men, who were there at the last siege of the place are dead...'

On this day...

.........................................................................................................................................

.........................................................................................................................................

.........................................................................................................................................


## September 9

FEAST DAY OF SAINTS AELRHIW 6th century at Rhiw; and THEGONNEC (see 11). The beginning of the revolt by Madog ap Llywelyn against Edward I, in

1294; Alun Pask, rugby player, born at Pontllanfraith in 1937

*'The bird swerved dapple-white in the blue sky, paused, and then swam into the commotion of rays between the sun and the lake.*
*The sleek wings vibrating in the still air stirred a venture in the heart, and yielding to the brightness, every fear fled with the wonder of the flight'* - Euros Bowen - 'Winged in Gold'

**On this day...**

......................................................................................................................................

......................................................................................................................................

......................................................................................................................................

## September 10

*FEAST DAY OF SAINTS* DEINIOL WYN 6th century (also September 11, 21, 22, November 21, December 10) at Bangor, Marchwiel, Llanwchllyn, Llanfair, Itton, St Deiniol's Ash, Llanddeiniol, Hawarden, Worthenbury, St Daniel's, Brittany; and BARLOC at Chester; Holy Day of William Salesbury, translator (1584) and Bishop William Morgan, translator (1604). Bishop William Morgan died on this day in 1604. Henry IV invades Wales again in 1405, relieving the siege of Coity Castle in Glamorgan; Sir John Lynn-Thomas, pioneer surgeon, born near Llandysul; The rugby player Rowe Harding born at Swansea in 1901; 12 miners died at Llanbradach Colliery in 1901

*'The Welsh language is a vast drawback to Wales, and a manifold barrier to the moral progress and commercial prosperity of the people. It is not easy to over estimate its evil effects'* - 1847 Report on the State of Education in Wales, the infamous 'Treachery of the Blue Books'

**On this day...**

......................................................................................................................................

......................................................................................................................................

......................................................................................................................................

## September 11

*FEAST DAY OF SAINTS* DEINIOL (see 10); and THEGONNEC 6th century (all through September 8-14) at St Thegonnec. Death of the historian Theophilus Evans, who discovered the healing powers of Llanwrtyd Wells water, in 1767 (see February 21) In 1878, 268 men and children were killed at the Prince of Wales Colliery, Abercarn; First Concert at Cardiff's St David's Hall in 1982

*'Llandrindod Wells. The Famous Spa of Central Wales. The splendid, bracing air, and the saline, sulpur, magnesium and chalybeate waters are very efficacious in the treatment of gout, rheumatism, anaemia, neurasthenia, dyspepsia, diabetes and liver affections. Complete system of baths; dowsing radiant heat bath; massage and nauheim treatment'* - 18th century Llandrindod Wells advertisement

*On this day...*

....................................................................................................................................
....................................................................................................................................
....................................................................................................................................

## September 12

*FEAST DAY OF SAINTS* AILBE (ELFYW) d.527 or 531 (also 13, Feb 27) at St Elvis, Emly; and THEGONNEC (see 11). Newport Transporter Bridge opened in 1906, one of only 3 remaining in the world; The actor Desmond Wilkinson Llywelyn* ('Q' in the James Bond movies) was born in 1914 (see December 19); The foundation stone of St David's College, Lampeter, was laid in 1922; Ray Gravell, Llanelli and Wales rugby centre and broadcaster, born in 1951

**'Pay attention, Bond'* - 'Q'

*On this day...*

....................................................................................................................................
....................................................................................................................................
....................................................................................................................................

## September 13

*FEAST DAY OF SAINT* AILBE (see 12). William Cecil (Lord Burghley) born in 1520; Birth in 1883 of Sir Percy Edward Thomas, architect and President of RIBA (see August 19); Sir Eugene Cross (d.1981), who left school at 11 and became manager of the Ebbw Vale Steel Works and a local benefactor, was born in Ebbw Vale in 1896; Roald Dahl, children's author was born in Cardiff on this day, and christened in the Docks' Norwegian Church in 1916; Death in 1930 of Jehoiada Hodges of Newport and Wales, a superb rugby forward. In 1903 against England, the Welsh wing Pearson retired injured and Hodges left the scrum to replace him, there being no substitutes allowed. Hodges promptly scored three tries

*'Hay Fair. Roads lively with men, horses and sheep. We were busy all day dressing the Church or preparing decorations. Mrs Price and Miss Elcox had got a quantity of wild hops from their fields and were arranging bright red apples for ornament. Also they had boughs loaded with rosy apples and quantities of bright yellow Siberian crabs. At school*

*the children were busy teasing out corn from a loose heap on the floor, sitting among the straw and tying up wheat, barley and oats in small sheaves and bundles. Gipsy Lizzie was amongst them, up to her beautiful eyes in corn and straw. The schoolmaster, the boys and I gathering stringed ivy from the trees in the Castle Clump.'* - Kilvert's Diary, this day in 1870

**On this day...**

...................................................................................................................................

...................................................................................................................................

...................................................................................................................................

## September 14

*FEAST DAY OF SAINT* DWYWAU 6th century at Llanddwywau; FFINAN 6th century (also possibly January 14) at Llanffinan, Lumphanan, Llancarfan; *HOLY CROSS DAY - When the Holy Cross appeared to Constantine before battle.* Birth in 1603 of Sir John Vaughan of Trawsgoed. In 1668 as Judge of Common Pleas, he made the first ruling that juries could not be fined, for returning a verdict against the direction of the judge (see December 10); William Fuller of Swansea won the VC in the Great War in 1914; The Labour politician Cledwyn Hughes born at Holyhead in 1916; The death in 1977 of Jim Sullivan of Cardiff, possibly the greatest rugby league player of all time

*'Following are sample definitions from an unpublished dictionary for which (in behalf of the author) I am ready to receive subscriptions: "Love, the folly of thinking much of another before one knows anything of oneself." "Courtship, the timid sipping of two thirsty souls from a goblet which both can easily drain but none replenish." "Marriage, a feminine device for imposing silence, whereby one woman is made to guard the good name of a dozen more." "Divorce, a resumption of diplomatic relations and rectification of boundaries".'* - Ambrose Gwinnett Bierce, in his San Francisco Evening Post column, this day in 1878

**On this day...**

...................................................................................................................................

...................................................................................................................................

...................................................................................................................................

## September 15

*FEAST DAY OF SAINT* TEGWYN 6th century at Llandecwyn (1st Sunday after Holy Cross Day, see September 14). Beaumaris given its charter in 1291; Henry IV's army leaves Hereford, and moves to Carmarthen, to attack Glyndŵr's forces in 1402; Bridgend Rugby Club founded in 1878; Aneurin Bevan born, September 15, 1897; W.J. (Billy) Cleaver, rugby star, born at Treorchy in 1921; Death of

Rhys Gabe in Cardiff in 1967 - it was said that the three-quarter line of Gabe, Gwyn Nicholls, ET Morgan and Willie Llewellyn was Wales' finest ever

*'No amount of cajolery, and no attempts at ethical and social seduction, can eradicate from my heart a deep burning hatred for the Tory Party ..........So far as I am concerned they are lower than vermin'* – Aneurin Bevan, October 3rd, 1957

**On this day...**

..................................................................................................................................

..................................................................................................................................

..................................................................................................................................

## September 16

Glyndŵr Day - It is celebrated at the site of his mansion at Glyndŵrfyrdwy - Owain Glyndŵr was invested as Prince of Wales by the nobility in 1400, when he raised the Red Dragon of Cadwaladr to reclaim Welsh nationhood; Henry V* (Harry of Monmouth) born at Monmouth in 1387*; Death in 1697 of Sion ap Sion of Ruabon, Quaker pioneer in Wales; Birth in 1882 of Mary Myfanwy Wood, missionary to China (see January 26)

*Fluellen: *'I do believe your majesty takes no scorn to wear the leek upon St Tavy's Day'.*
King Henry: *'I wear it for a memorable honour; For I am Welsh, you know, good countryman.'*
- Shakespeare's 'King Henry V', Act IV, Scene 7

**On this day...**

..................................................................................................................................

..................................................................................................................................

..................................................................................................................................

## September 17

FEAST DAY OF SAINTS SOCRATES AND STEPHANUS d.c. 603 at Monmouth. At the Battle of Montgomery in 1644, Robert Broughton of Marchwiel was captured by Parliamentarians; Cardiff Castle and town surrendered to the Parliamentarians in 1645, and the city walls were slighted; Peregrine Phillips, the Puritan 'Apostle of Pembrokeshire' died in 1691 near Haverfordwest; Birth in Gwaelod-y-Garth of Henry Seymour Berry, industrialist who became a director of 66 companies and 1st Baron Buckland of Bwlch (see May 23 and May 2)

*In September take three draughts of milk in the morning daily. After this you may take what you wish, for vegetables and fruit are now ripe, though bread is apt to be mouldy.*

*Whosoever is bled on September 17th, will not be attacked by colic, ague nor cough that year'* - 13th century 'Meddygon Myddfai

*On this day...*

........................

## September 18

THE NATIVITY OF MAIR (see August 21). In 1400, Owain Glyndŵr attacked Reginald Grey's township of Ruthin, beginning a war of independence that was not to end until 1421. The September Rampage and the Gwynedd Rising lasted until September 23; In 1644, Roundheads overcame Cavaliers at the Battle of Montgomery, with about 400 Royalists killed; Death in 1667 of Rowland Vaughan of Caer-gai, Royalist, poet and translator; The Welsh Church Act, to establish the Church in Wales, was passed in 1914; Death in Dieppe in 1939 of the artist Gwen John (see June 22); Atlantic College opened at St Donat's in 1961; In 1997, in the referendum on devolution, the Welsh capital Cardiff voted 'no' to a National Assembly

From the diary of Lady Eleanor Butler, one of the 'Ladies of Llangollen' on this day in 1785: *'Rose at 7. Soft morning inclines to rain. Went the rounds after Breakfast. Our shoes from Chirk. Vile. Scolded Thomas for growing fat. From 10 to 1 writing and reading ('La Rivalite') to my beloved. She drawing, spent half an hour in the shrubbery. Mild, grey day. From half past 1 till 3 reading. From 4 to 7 read to my Sally. Finished 'La Rivalite', began 'Warton on Milton'. In the shrubbery till 8. Powell returned from Wrexham. No letters. 8 till 9 read 'L'Esprit des Croisades'. Papered our Hair. An uninterrupted delightful day.'*

*On this day...*

........................

## September 19

FEAST DAY OF SAINT SETNA (see August 3) in Brittany; GWENFREWI (WINIFRED) 7th century (also September 20, November 3 and 4, June 22) at Holywell, Shrewsbury, St Winifred's Well, Gwytherin. Around this time in 1402, Caerffili, Newport, Caerleon and Usk are taken by Glyndŵr's forces; Dowlais Iron Works began operations in 1759; Rydal School, Colwyn Bay, opened in 1885; David Lord of Wrexham won the VC at Arnhem in 1944; Johnny Owen lost his 1980 World Bantamweight Title fight at Los Angeles, and later died in a coma on November 4

'*Arrogance is the façade of the charlatan*' - 'The Path to Inexperience', T.D. Breverton 2002

*On this day...*

..............................................................................................................................................

..............................................................................................................................................

..............................................................................................................................................

## September 20

FEAST DAY OF SAINTS EIGION (1st Sunday after September 20) at Llaneigion; and GWENFREWI (see 19). Probable death date of Owain Glyndŵr, at Monnington Court, Herefordshire in 1415 or 1416; Prince Arthur Tudor was born in 1486; In 1856, 13 miners drowned in Brynally Colliery, Pentre Broughton, Clwyd; Rachel Roberts born in 1927 in Llanelli (see November 29)

'*Light breaks where no sun shines;*
*Where no sea runs, the waters of the heart*
*Push in their tides;*
*And, broken ghosts with glow-worms in their heads,*
*The things of light*
*File through the flesh where no flesh decks the bones.*' - Dylan Thomas, first verse of 'Light Breaks Where No Sun Shines'

*On this day...*

..............................................................................................................................................

..............................................................................................................................................

..............................................................................................................................................

## September 21

FEAST DAY OF SAINTS MATTHEW 1st century; and MABON 6th century at Llanfabon, Gileston; The Nights Grow Longer than the days - a significant date in the Celtic Calendar. Thomas Salusbury was executed at Shrewsbury for alleged complicity in the Babington Plot in 1586; Edward Jones of Plas Cadwgan, Denbigh, was executed on Tower Hill in 1586 for his part in the Babington Plot

'*From this high quarried ledge I see*
*The place for which the Quakers once*
*Collected clothes, my fathers' home,*
*Our stubborn bankrupt village sprawled*
*In jaded dusk beneath its nameless hills;*
*The drab streets strung across the cwm,*

*Derelict workings, tips of slag*
*The gospellers and gamblers use*
*And children scrutting for the coal*
*That winter dole cannot purvey;*
*Allotments where the collier digs*
*While engines hack the coal within his brain;'*
Lines from 'The Mountain over Aberdare' by Alun Lewis (1915-1944)

*On this day...*

## September 22

*FEAST DAY OF SAINT* DEINIOL (See September 10). Henry IV's great army retreats to England in 1402, leaving Glyndŵr in control of most of Wales; Thomas Charles Edwards, first Principal of the University College of Wales at Aberystwyth, and second Principal of Bala College, was born in 1837; Birth in 1841, at Llanelly, Breconshire, of Lewis Probert, preacher and theologian; Cardiff Rugby Club was formed in 1876; Death in 1879 of 84 miners at Waunllwyd, Ebbw Vale; Dannie Abse, poet, born in Cardiff in 1923; In 1934, 265 men were killed at the Gresford Colliery, outside Wrexham; The Brecon Beacons* were designated as a National Park in 1955; Brian Curvis of Swansea lost a World Welterweight title fight in London in 1964

*Brecon and the Border Counties used to be strong-holds of cider-making, which should be resurrected: 'These Brecon farm-houses were unlike any I had seen in Wales. They were large as mansions, with spacious beamed rooms, huge fireplaces, and often with staircases of real splendour. At the very first one we visited no one was about. Andy stumped through the door into the great kitchen, which was deserted, then through the chain of big rooms which was the ground floor. I followed more slowly, admiring the magnificent furniture, collectors' pieces put to the daily work for which they were intended. The oak of Brecon is different from that of the North. It is not the black bog-oak, but a dark golden wood glowing with light from within, in all cases that I saw, gleaming with a mirror-finish of a surface polishing which must have been inherited from several generations of female arms.*
*Still no one appeared at this first place of call despite Andy's shouts and stamps. Whereupon he withdrew me from contemplation of an ancient dresser, laden with pewter and willow-pattern plates, and whisked me through the farmyard to an open shed in which stood two cider-barrels, with a capacity that I should judge of 72 gallons apiece. Andy told me the far one was empty and directed me to take the much-thumbed glass from the top of the other, and fill it. This I did. "It'll blow the top of your head off," Andy remarked. Metaphorically, he was right. I handed him the glass, speechlessly. "It's the one drink I can't touch," he said in smug refusal. "Bad for my head. You have another." I did so, and clambered back into the car in a state of near-paralysis. I was*

*well used to Devon cider, but it had no more fitted me to encounter this Brecon brand than an aptitude on a donkey fits a man to win the Grand National'* - Thomas Firbank 'A Country of Memorable Honour', 1953

*On this day...*

# September 23

*FEAST DAY OF SAINTS* POPE LINUS d. 76 (also November 26) at Rome; TEGLA 1st century (also 24, 25, 27, 28) at Rome, Llandegley?; and PADARN (see April 15). In 1796 John Evans of Waunfawr reached the Mandan Indians (the 'lost Welsh tribe') on the Upper Missouri. Later, the Welsh-American explorer Meriwether Lewis would winter with them; David Davies (Dai'r Cantwr), Rebecca Rioter, was arrested at the Plough and Harrow Inn at Pum Heol near Llanelli in 1843, and taken to Carmarthen Gaol; The miners' leader and MP William Brace was born at Risca in 1865 (see October 12); Death in 1988 of the composer and conductor Arwel Hughes, in Cardiff

*'Soul, since I was made in necessity blameless*
*True it is, woe is me that thou shouldst have come to my design,*
*Neither for my own sake, nor for death, nor for end, nor for beginning.*
*It as with seven faculties that I was thus blessed,*
*With seven created beings I was placed for purification;*
*I was gleaming fire when I was ceased to exist;*
*I was dust of the earth, and grief could not reach me;*
*I was a high wind, being less evil than good;*
*I was a mist on a mountain seeking supplies of stags;*
*I was blossoms of trees on the face of the earth.*
*If the Lord had blessed me, He would have placed me on matter....'*
From 'The Soul', in 'The Black Book of Carmarthen', 12th century

*On this day...*

# September 24

*FEAST DAY OF SAINTS* MEUGAN 6th century (also 25, 26, February 14, April 24, November 15) at Mawgan, Llanfeugan, Capel Meugan, Ruthin,

Trevigan, St Maughan's, Llanrhydd; and TUDFUL (see August 23) - Apple and Pear Fair at Merthyr Tydfil. In 1245, one of Henry III's supply ships was looted and its crew killed at Conwy Morfa; In 1400, Owain Glyndŵr's forces attacked and took Denbigh, Flint, Hawarden and Rhudlan castles; In 1403, Henry IV's fourth royal expedition to Wales reached Carmarthen, with troops from 35 English shires, but soon returned to England; Colonel John Jones fought with distinction, leading the Parliamentarian infantry in the Battle of Rowton Heath, 1645; James Davies (born 1648), copyist of Welsh literature, died at Llanllawddog in 1722; Samuel (S.R.) Roberts, the publisher and social activist, died at Conwy in 1885 (see March 6); Death in 1942 of David Walters (see May 27)

*'Incorporation, n. The act of uniting several persons into one fiction called a corporation, in order that they may be no longer responsible for their actions. A, B and C are a corporation. A robs, B steals and C (it is necessary that there be one gentleman in the concern) cheats. It is a plundering, thieving, swindling coroporation. But A, B and C, who have jointly determined and severally executed every crime of the corporation, are blameless. It is wrong to mention them by name when censuring their acts as a corporation, but right when praising. Incorporation is somewhat like the ring of Gyges: it bestows the blessing of invisibility - comforable to knaves. The scoundrel who invented incorporation is dead - he has disincorporated.'* - Ambrose Gwinnett Bierce, 'The Devil's Dictionary, 1911

**On this day...**

## September 25
FEAST DAY OF SAINTS CAIAN 5th-6th century (also November 1, 15) at Tregaian; MARCELLUS 4th century at Llanddeusant; LLEONFELL at Llanlleonfel; CADOG (see February 24); TEYRNOG (see April 4) and MEUGAN (see 24); HOLY ROOD DAY, OLD STYLE. By the Treaty of Montgomery, Henry III recognised Llywelyn ap Gruffydd as Prince of Wales, the first such recognition of a Welsh ruler by an English-French king; In 1400, Henry IV tortured and dismembered Goronwy ap Tudor at Shrewsbury, sending his quarters to the towns of Chester, Hereford, Ludlow and Bristol, as a warning to the Welsh not to support Owain Glyndŵr; In 1793, Felicia Hemans was born; John 'Ceiriog' Hughes, poet, was born at Llanarmon in 1832 (see April 23); William Morris (Billy) Hughes was born in 1862, and became Prime Minister of Australia from 1915-1922; Tracy Edwards, round-the-world yachtswoman, born in 1962; The actor-writer Emlyn Williams died in 1987, aged 86 (see November 26); Catherine Zeta Jones was born in Swansea in 1969; R.S. Thomas, Wales' leading poet, *'the Solzhenitsyn of Wales'* died in 2000

*'Lo here I sit in Holyhead*

*With muddy ale and mouldy bread*
*All Christian victuals stink of fish*
*I'm where my enemies would wish*
*Convict of lies is every sign*
*The inn has not one drop of wine*
*I'm fasten'd by both wind and tide*
*I see the ship at anchor ride*
*The captain swears the sea's too rough*
*He has not passengers enough...'*
Lines from 'Holyhead, September 25, 1727' by a disgruntled Jonathan Swift

*On this day...*

## September 26

*FEAST DAY OF SAINTS* BARUC (BARRI) 6th century (also 27, November 29) at Barri, Penmark, Bedwas; ELFAN 2nd century at Glastonbury, Aberdare; and MEUGAN (see 24); HOLY ROOD DAY; Ffair Gwyl y Grog, Cardigan; Holy Day of Bishop Lancelot Andrewes. Birth in 1742 in Radnorshire of Thomas Jones, landscape painter and pupil of Richard Wilson; Death, aged 91, in 1754 of Henry John of Blaenau Gwent, Baptist evangelist and hymn-writer; Death of Owain Myfyr in 1814, a guiding force in Welsh learning, buried in Allhallows, London (see September 3); Birth in 1842 of William John Parry, who became President of the North Wales Quarrymen's Union; Death of David Charles Davies in 1891 at Bangor, lecturer and preacher (see May 11); In 1915, Keir Hardie*, MP for Merthyr Tudful, died; In 1919, Dame Adelina Patti died at Craig-y-Nos Castle; Death of the poet W.H. Davies in 1940, aged 69 (see July 3)

*\*'All Celtic people are, at heart, Communists.'* - Keir Hardie

*On this day...*

## September 27

*FEAST DAY OF SAINT* BARUC (see 26). Around this time in 1408, Aberystwyth Castle fell to the English, and effectively the tide turned against Glyndŵr after 8 years of war; Samuel Adams, *'the father of the American Revolution'* was born in 1722 (see October 2); Death of Lucy Thomas, who sold Welsh coal to London, *'the mother of the Welsh coal trade'* in 1847; Birth in 1870 of Thomas Jones, author, editor of the Gregynog Press and principal founder of Coleg Harlech (see October 15)

*'The Welsh do not sing their traditional songs in unison, but in many parts, and in many modes and modulations. So that in a choir of singers - a customary thing among these people - you will hear as many different parts and voices as you see heads: but in the end they all join together in a smooth and sweet B-flat resonance and melodic harmony'* - Giraldus Cambrensis, 1188

**On this day...**

..........................................................................................................................................................
..........................................................................................................................................................
..........................................................................................................................................................

# September 28

*FEAST DAY OF SAINTS* CYNWYD 6th century (also October 15)
Llangynwyd Fawr - At Christmas and New Year, the Celtic custom of the 'Mari Llwyd' and wassail has still not died out in this village; and FAUSTUS (see January 13). On this day in 1400, Henry IV led his army of 13,000 men into Wales, having executed 8 alleged traitors at Shrewsbury - this was the first of 5 unsuccessful invasions over 10 years; W.J. Parry, North Wales quarrymen's leader, born in 1842; Death of Thomas Gee, publisher of Y Gwyddoniadur, the 10-volume Welsh encyclopaedia, in 1898, aged 83 (see January 24); In 1937 Captain Grffith James Powell of Cardiff piloted the flying boat Cambria from Newfoundland to Ireland, setting a transatlantic crossing record

*'While I gaze upon a scene such as this, my soul overflows with meditation. I recall past ages of the Christian Church and strive to separate their Godliness from their superstition. Amidst all that labyrinth of perplexing error I recognize the forbearance of God, the corruptions of the present age differ more in their nature than in their extent from those of earlier times, and where an apostolic church like ours has either been neglected or insulted, it is folly to sing the praises of our modern Christianity. From the 5th to the 15th century this Cathedral enjoyed a high degree of scholastic and religious welfare. For at least a thousand years it retained the light of learning'* - Written this day in 1836 by John Parker in St David's Cathedral in his 'Tour of Wales and its Churches.' In the 13th century, Pope Callixtus decreed that two visits to this ancient home of Christianity were the equivalent of one to Rome

**On this day...**

..........................................................................................................................................................
..........................................................................................................................................................
..........................................................................................................................................................

# September 29

FEAST DAY OF SAINT MIHANGEL, MICHAEL - patron saint of the sea, boats and horses, remembered at St Michael's Mount in Cornwall and Mont St Michel in Brittany; *MICHAELMAS QUARTERDAY* - Traditionally the luckiest day of the year, only bettered by February 29. The Treaty of Montgomery in 1267 gave lands to Llywelyn the Great; Cydweli was taken by Glyndŵr's forces in 1403, despite the fact that Henry IV's great fourth invasion force was just 7 miles away in Carmarthen; Rhodri Morgan, MP and First Secretary of the British (National) Assembly was born in Cardiff in 1939; Death in 1954 of William John Griffith, scholar (see February 14); Death of the Olympic triple gold-medallist swimmer, Paulo Radmilovich, in 1968

*'Three godly deeds in a man:*
*To forgive the wrongs done to him,*
*To amend everything he can,*
*And to refrain from injustice.'* - from the Welsh Triads of Virtues

*On this day...*

.......................................................................................................................

.......................................................................................................................

.......................................................................................................................

# September 30

*FEAST DAY OF SAINT NIDAN* 6th century (November 3 in Scotland) at Llanidan, Bryn Siencyn; ANNE D'AURAY, mother of Mary, said to have retired to the province of Cornouaille in Brittany, where Jesus came to visit with the tin traders. Henry IV's three armies retreat to England in 1401, having failed to subdue Owain Glyndŵr; Evan James, writer of the words of the National Anthem, died in 1878; The 11-month lock-out at Penrhyn Colliery began in 1896; Daniel Davies, cashier at the Ocean Collieries, Ystrad, Glamorgan - schoolmaster, writer and benefactor - died in Treorchy in 1916; Llanrhaiadr-yn-Mochnant water pipeline explosion in 1967, attributed to the Free Wales Army

*'O Lord God, save us from tinned donkey,*
*From Soviet scientific magazines,*
*From the Scottish Sabbath, from American war films,*
*From the demagogues of Aberdare and Abadan,*
*And, above all, O Lord God, save us from the Pentecostals'* - from 'Come to Our Revival Meeting' by the truly great Idris Davies

*On this day...*

.......................................................................................................................

.......................................................................................................................

.......................................................................................................................

# OCTOBER - HYDREF
### Here (Breton); Hedra (Cornish)

## October 1

FEAST DAY OF SAINTS MEILYR 6th century at Mylor, Amesbury Abbey; SULIEN (See September 2); HYCHAN (See August 8); TYSILIO (See November 8); and GARMON of MAN (see July 31). Denbigh received its borough charter in 1285; In 1401, Henry IV brings forces from Worcester on a second invasion of Wales, looting, raping and summarily executing Welsh people through Brecon, Llandovery, Carmarthen, Cardigan, Aberystwyth and Painscastle and desecrating Strata Florida Abbey; Henry IV returns to Worcester in 1405, his fifth invasion having failed, and Glyndŵr returns to Harlech; In 1648, Royalists are defeated at the Battle of Red Hill, Beaumaris; Arthur Blayney (see February 11), benefactor-landlord, died and was buried at Tregynog on October 6. (Blayney comes from 'blaenau' and the family claimed descent from Brochwel Ysgythrog ('the fanged'); William Davies, musician, born at Rhosllanerchrugog in 1859 (d. Jan.30, 1907); The Tal-y-Llyn Railway opened in 1866; The football star Trevor Ford was born in Swansea in 1923; Gareth Hughes, Hollywood film star, died in 1965 in Reno, Nevada (see August 23);The first match at the Millennium Stadium in the 1999 Rugby World Cup saw Wales beat Argentina in their group

*'I find even amongst intelligent and enlightened English people a great ignorance. Can any English author imagine getting up in the morning to sit at a desk for eight hours to write in a language which has no official status in its own country? Can any English author imagine writing in a language which might quite easily die and disappear as a living tongue in the first few decades of the next century? This is why I have begun to feel recently that writing in Welsh is a classic 20th-century experience. You are writing on the edge of a catastrophe.'* -the novelist William Owen Roberts, c.1993

*On this day...*

........................................................................................................................

........................................................................................................................

........................................................................................................................

........................................................................................................................

## October 2

FEAST DAY OF SAINT ANDRAS (also October 1) at St Andrews. Mabsantau held also at St Fagans, Whitchurch, Fairwater, Michaelstone. In 1644, Parliamentarians under Myddleton captured William Herbert's Powis Castle; Birth in 1787 of Thomas Price (Carnhuanawc), historian and antiquary (see November 7); Samuel Adams died in 1803 (see September 27); Death of James Davies at Llangattock 1849 (see August 23); In 1900 at Merthyr Tudful, Keir Hardie became the first Labour MP to be elected; The writer Jan Morris was born in 1926; Neil Kinnock was elected Leader of the Labour Party in 1983

*Do you remember 1926? That summer of soups and speeches,*

The sunlight on the idle wheels and the deserted crossing,
And the laughter and the cursing in the moonlit streets?
Do you remember 1926? The slogans and the penny concerts,
The jazz-bands and the moorland picnics,
And the slanderous tongues of famous cities?
Do you remember 1926? The great dream and the swift disaster,
The fanatic and the traitor, and more than all,
The bravery of the simple, faithful folk?
'Ay, ay, we remember 1926,' said Dai and Shinkin,
As they stood on the kerb in Charing Cross Road,
'And we shall remember 1926 until our blood is dry.' - Verse VIII of 'Gwalia Deserta'
by Idris Davies

*On this day...*

............................................................................................................................................

............................................................................................................................................

............................................................................................................................................

## October 3

*FEAST DAY OF SAINTS KEA (CYNAN)* d.c.550 (also November 5) at
Landkey, Kea, St Quay, Cleder; FFRACAN 5th - 6th century at St Fragan,
Ploufragan; and TYRNOG (see July 2) In 1283, Dafydd ap Gruffudd, the last
native Prince of Wales, was hung, drawn and quartered at Shrewsbury, ending the
War which also saw his brother Llywelyn murdered; In 1448, Beaumaris Castle
surrendered for the second time to Roundheads; In 1785, the first Irish Mail
Coach left London for Holyhead; Death in 1889 of Robert John Pryse at Bethesda
(see July 4)

*'Three Just Knights were in Arthur's Court: Blaes son of the Earl of Llychlyn, and
Cadog son of Gwynlliw the Bearded, and Pedrog Splintered-Spear, son of Prince
Clement of Cornwall. The peculiarities of those were that whoever might do wrong to
the weak, they contended against him who did him wrong in the cause of justice; and
whoever might do wrong they slew, however strong he might be. For those three had
dedicated themselves to preserve justice by every Law; Blaes by earthly Law; Cadog by
the Law of the Church, and Pedrog by the Law of arms. And those were called the Just
Knights.' - Peniarth MS 127*

*On this day...*

............................................................................................................................................

............................................................................................................................................

............................................................................................................................................

# October 4

Alice Matilda Langland Wiliams (Alys Mallt), the author and Celtophile, was born at Oystermouth in 1867 (see October 28); The radical miner's leader Noah Ablett was born in Porth in 1883 (see October 31); The 3rd Marquess of Bute died in 1900

*'Logic, n. The art of thinking and reasoning in strict accordance with the limitations and incapacities of the human misunderstanding. The basic of logic is the syllogism, consisting of a major and a minor premise and a conclusion - thus:*
*Major Premise: Sixty men can do a piece of work sixty times more quickly than one man.*
*Minor Premise: One man can dig a post hole in sixty seconds, therefore -*
*Conclusion: Sixty men can dig a post hole in one second. This may be called the syllogism arithmetical, in which, by combining logic and mathematics, we obtain a double certainty and are twice blessed.'* – Ambrose Bierce.

*On this day...*

...........................................................................................................................
...........................................................................................................................
...........................................................................................................................

# October 5

*FEAST DAY OF SAINTS* TUDUR 6th century (also 7) at Mynydd Islwyn; and CYNHAFAL (7th century) at Llangunhafal; Birth in 1788 near Cardiff of the antiquary John Montgomery Traherne (see February 5); Thomas Charles (of Bala) died in 1814, and is buried at Llanycil (see October 14); Sidney Gilchrist Thomas and his cousin Percy Thomas succeeded at Blaenavon in open-hearth steel-making experiments in 1878, revolutionising the steel industry; University College Swansea opened in 1920; Glynis Johns, actress, born at Pretoria in 1923, the daughter of Mervyn Johns (see February 18)

*'There's holy holy people*
*They are in capel bach -*
*They don't like surpliced choirs,*
*They don't like Sospan Fach.*

*They don't like Sunday concerts,*
*Or women playing ball,*
*They don't like Williams Parry much*
*Or Shakespeare at all.*

*They don't like beer or bishops,*
*Or pictures without texts,*
*They don't like any other*
*Of the nonconformist sects.*

*And when they go to Heaven*
*They won't like that too well,*
*For the music will be sweeter*
*Than the music played in Hell.'* - Idris Davies 'Capel Calvin'

**On this day...**

5 .............................................................................................
.............................................................................................
.............................................................................................

## October 6

*FEAST DAY OF SAINT TYFAI (TYFEI)* (see March 27). In 1836 Anne Evans (Allen Raine) was born in Newcastle Emlyn; Dai Rees captained the winning British Ryder Cup team in 1957; In 1989 Bette Davis died; A 12-foot statue was unveiled at Llandovery in 2001 to commemorate the 600th anniversary of the torture, hanging, drawing and quartering of Llywelyn ap Gruffydd Fychan in 1401 by the usurper King Henry IV (Bolingbroke). Henry personally supervised the torture, after Llywelyn had led the king's invasion force on a wild goose chase after Owain Glyndŵr during the summer. Henry had then discovered that Llywelyn had two sons serving with Glyndŵr, and that Llywelyn had led him away from the last Welsh Prince of Wales.

*'When I see the enthusiasm these Eisteddfods can awaken in your whole people, and then think of the tastes, the literature, the amusements, of our own lower middle classes, I am filled with admiration for you. It is a consoling thought and one which history allows us to entertain, that nations disinherited of political success may yet leave their mark on the world's progress, and contribute powerfully to the civilisation of mankind ... In a certain measure the children of Taliesin and Ossian have now their opportunity for renewing the famous feat of the Greeks, and conquering their conquerors. No service England can render the Celts by giving you a share in her many good qualities can surpass what the Celts can at the moment do for England by communicating to us some of theirs.'* - Matthew Arnold, c.1865 (see quote for October 7)

**On this day...**

6 .............................................................................................
.............................................................................................
.............................................................................................

## October 7

*FEAST DAY OF SAINTS CAIN (CEINWEN, KEYNE)* 5th century (also October 8) at Llangain, St Keyne's Well, Llangeinor, Runston (St Kenya's); TUDUR (see 5); CYNOG (see 9); and MARCHELL (see September 5). Colonel

Morgan Jones, Texas rail magnate, was born in Tregynon near Newtown in 1839; Sir William Davies born in Talley in 1863, editor-in-chief of The Western Mail from 1901-1931 (see March 17); In 1883 the miners' leader Noah Ablett was born at Porth; Albert Jenkins, rugby star, died in 1953 at Llanelli (see March 11); In 1957 the Windscale (Sellafied) nuclear reactor fire sent a radioactive plume of smoke over the north of England, and milk distribution had to stop; Death in 1957 of Arthur Leach (see November 12)

'In October drink wine and eat minnows. Let your diet consist of fresh meat and wholesome vegetables' - Meddygon Myddfai, 13th century.

On this day...

........................................................................................................

........................................................................................................

........................................................................................................

## October 8

FEAST DAY OF SAINTS CAMMARCH 6th century at Llangammarch; CEINWEN 5th - 6th century at Llangeinwen, Cerrig Ceinwen; CAIN (See 7); and CYNOG (see 9). About this time Gruffudd ap Nicholas judged the poets and Dafydd ab Edmwnd awarded the Chair at the eisteddfod which revised the bardic metres and regulated the bards (at Carmarthen or Dinefwr in 1450); Death in 1849 of Admiral Sir Edward Campbell Rich Owen, the commander of the 1809 Walcheren Expedition; Birth in 1872 of John Cowper Powys*, novelist and poet (see June 17); Death at Utica in 1884 of John William Jones, editor of Y Drych (see January 11); Birth in 1932 at Tredegar of Ray Reardon, six-times World Snooker Champion; Rhoose Airport first opened as an RAF fighter station in 1941; The poet Vernon Watkins died in Seattle in 1967 (see June 27)

*'... I soon gave up trying to learn Welsh. But the idea of Wales and the idea of Welsh mythology went drumming on like an incantation through my tantalized soul.' - John Cowper Powys, 'Autobiography', 1934

On this day...

........................................................................................................

........................................................................................................

........................................................................................................

## October 9

FEAST DAY OF SAINTS CADWALADR FENDIGAID d.664 (also November 12) at Llangadwaladr, Magor, Michaelston-y-Fedw; ALMEDHA (see August 1); CYNOG AP BRYCHAN d. 492 (also 7, 8, 10, 11, Sunday after second Thursday in October, February 11, January 24 in Padstow) at Defynog, Ystradgynlais, Battle, Penderyn, Llangynog, Padstow, Merthyr Cynog, Llangunnock, Pinnick. Upon October 9th, 1401, Llywelyn ap Gruffydd Fychan of Caeo was hung, drawn and quartered in Llandovery in the presence of Henry IV (see October 6); Cardiff's Bute Dock opened in 1839; Crawshay Bailey, Nantyglo Ironmaster, died at Llanfoist House in 1872; 1873 saw Britain's first sheepdog trial at Bala, organised by R.J. Lloyd-Price, Squire of Rhiwlas, and the founder of Bala Whiskey; Death in 1900 of the 3rd Marquess of Bute (born 1847), who excavated and rebuilt much of Cardiff Castle

*'The camera zooms in*
*on punk-spikes of oiled feathers*
*and the no-understanding,*
*no-reproach, of round unblinking eyes*
*that say nothing, simply see,*
*and see now this last thing.'* - lines from 'Oil-spill, 1991' by Ruth Bidgood.

*On this day...*

........................................................................................................
........................................................................................................
........................................................................................................

## October 10

*FEAST DAY OF SAINTS* PEULIN (See March 12); MELLON c. 257 - c. 311 (also 22) at St Mellons, Rouen; TANWG 6th century at Llandanwg; and IESTYN (see April 12); OLD MICHAELMASS DAY*. William Adams, of Pen-y-Cae, Ebbw Vale was born in 1813, who later developed the Ebbw Vale Steel, Iron and Coal Company; Birth of Timothy Richard in 1845, *'one of the greatest missionaries whom any branch of the church has sent to China'*, at Ffaldybrenin, Carmarthenshire (see April 17); Birth of Thomas Gwynn Jones, poet and scholar, at Betws yn Rhos, Denbighshire in 1871 (see March 7); S.A. and J.R. Brain bought the Old Brewery in St Mary Street, Cardiff, with its own well, in 1882; Arthur Joseph ('Monkey') Gould was born at Newport in 1864, playing rugby for Newport from the age of 16, playing for Wales 27 times. He scored a record 44 tries in one season in Wales, and his playing career lasted from 1862 to 1887 (see January 2); The 'Leinster' was torpedoed in 1918 between Holyhead and Dublin, with 501 lives being lost; Talyllyn Railway Society was formed in 1950, the first such preservation society in Britain

*\*'It is an old custom in these parts for the poor people to go about round the farm-houses to beg and gather milk between and about the two Michaelmasses, that they may be able to make some puddings and pancakes against Bryngwyn and Clyro Feasts, which are on the same day, next Sunday, the Sunday after old Michaelmass Day or Hay Fair, October 10th. The old custom is still kept up in Bryngwyn and at some hill farms in Clyro, but it is honoured at comparatively few houses now, and scarcely anywhere in*

*Clyro Vale. Wern Fawr is one of the best houses to go to, a hospitable old-fashioned house where they keep up the old customs. Besides being given a gallon of milk to be carried away, the poor people are fed and refreshed to help them on their journey to the next farm, for they wander many miles for milk and it is a weary tramp before they reach home. I turned in to old Hannah's and sat with her an hour talking over old times, and listening to her reminiscences and tales of the dear old times, the simple kindly primitive times 'in the Bryngwyn' nearly 90 years ago.…Hannah living in 'the Bryngwyn' wore a tall Welsh hat until she was grown up.'* - Kilvert's Diary, October 14, 1870

**On this day...**

..............................................................................................................................

..............................................................................................................................

..............................................................................................................................

## October 11

*FEAST DAY OF SAINTS* CENNECH (CANICE) c. 525-600 at Llangennech, St Kenox, Llancarfan, Glasnevin; and LEVAN 6th century at St Levan. Llywelyn II destroyed Gilbert de Clare's Caerffili Castle in 1270; In 1555 Lewis ('Baron') Owen, sheriff of Merioneth, was ambushed by the 'Red Bandits of Mawddwy' and killed at Llidiart-y-barwn near Mallwyd; The hymn-writer David Charles, brother of Thomas Charles, was born in 1762 at Llanfihangel Abercowin (see September 2); Meriwether Lewis the American explorer died, probably murdered, in 1809; The South Wales Railway reached Carmarthen in 1852; Sir William Llywelyn Davies born near Pwllheli in 1887, chief librarian of the National Library of Wales for 22 years (see November 11); 'The Fed' (the South Wales Miners' Federation) was formed in Cardiff in 1898, with William Abraham (Mabon) as its President; Death in 1956 of David James Davies at Carmel (see June 2); Death of 'Harry Parry' in 1956 (see January 12)

*'The Welsh language is the curse of Wales… Its prevalence and the ignorance of English have excluded and even now exclude the Welsh people from civilisation, the improvement and the material prosperity of their English neighbours. Their antiquated and semi-barbarous language, in short, shrouds them in darkness… For all purposes, Welsh is a dead language… An Eisteddfod is one of the most mischievous and selfish pieces of sentimentalism which could possibly be perpetrated. It is simply a foolish interference with the natural progress of civilisation and prosperity … Not only the energy and power, but the intelligence and music of Europe have come mainly from Teutonic sources, and this glorification of everything Celtic, if it were not pedantry, would be sheer ignorance. The sooner all Welsh specialities disappear from the face of the earth the better.'* - Leader in The Times, 1865

**On this day...**

..............................................................................................................................

..............................................................................................................................

..............................................................................................................................

## October 12

*FEAST DAY OF SAINTS* HYCHAN (see August 8); and GARMON of MAN (see July 12); Columbus* Day in America; Adam, a Welshman trained in Paris, was consecrated Bishop of St Asaf in 1175; In 1645, Carmarthen surrendered to Parliamentarians; In 1867, David Llewellyn (Lyn) Harding, the premier Welsh actor of his day, was born at St Bride's, Wentloog (see December 26); Florence Soper (1861-1957) of Blaina married Bramwell Booth in 1882, and began a career in social work in the Salvation Army; Varina Banks Howell Davis, the *'First Lady of the Confederacy'* died in 1905; Kenneth Griffith, actor-writer, was born in Tenby in 1921; There was the first 'stay-down' strike in South Wales, at Nine Mile Point Colliery, Gwent, in 1935; The miners' leader William Brace died in Newport in 1947 (see September 23); The National Trust took over Penrhyn Castle, the symbol of slate-workers' oppression, in 1951; In 1978, the oil tanker Christos Bitas hit a reef off Pembrokeshire, killing thousands of seabirds and causing major pollution

*In Welsh tradition Madoc, a son of the great Owain Gwynedd, discovered America (see the Madoc1170.com website). George Borrow, in 'Wild Wales, 1862, wrote: *Madawg 'was a great sailor and the first to discover Tir y Gorllewin, or America. Not many years ago his tomb was discovered there with an inscription in old Welsh - saying who he was, and how he loved the sea. I have seen the lines which were found on the tomb'. His descendants 'are still to be found in a part of America speaking the pure Iaith Cymraeg, better Welsh than we of Wales do.'* DNA testing is progressing to try and link with the Mandan Indians, who worshipped the 'lone white man', had coracles, pale skins and many words in common with the Welsh language.

*On this day...*

## October 13

*FEAST DAY OF SAINTS* EDWARD THE CONFESSOR d. 1066 at Knighton (also January 5): and LEONORE (see February 16). In 1278 Llywelyn ap Gruffudd married Eleanor de Montfort at Worcester Cathedral. She had previously been captured, and imprisoned for three years by Edward I at Windsor, to prevent the marriage; In 1858, 20 miners died at Lower Duffryn Colliery, Mountain Ash; In 1858, 14 miners died of gas suffocation at Primrose Colliery, Ystalyfera; Charles Ashton (see September 4) committed suicide at Dinas Mawddwy, 1899; Donald Houston died in Portugal in 1991, aged 67 (see November 6)

(Because of legislation) *'the use of the coracle as a fishing craft has declined very rapidly in recent years and today coracle fishing is limited to three rivers only, the Teifi, Towy and Taf in west Wales. In the 1920's and 1930's, coracles were to be found on many other rivers such as the Dee, the Eastern Cleddau in Pembrokeshire, Monmow and the Severn, while in the late 19th century other rivers such as the Wye, Usk, Conway, Dyfi, Nevern and Loughor had coracle fishermen. Each river had its own specific type of craft, but many examples have disappeared without a record being made of them... A coracle was last used for angling on the Usk around 1930, but undoubtedly coracle fishing was well known on the river and its tributaries as well as on Llangors Lake (Llyn Safaddan) until the late 19th century. In Camden's '"Brittania" of 1586, "Llyn Savaddan... In English, 'tis called Brecknockmore... well stored with otters and also Perches, Tenches and Eels, which the Fishermen take in their Coracles".'*

*On this day...*

## October 14

FEAST DAY OF SAINTS BROTHEN 6th - 7th century (also 15 and 18) at Llanfrothen, Dwygyfylchi; SELEVAN 6th century at East Levan, Brittany; and TEWDWR (see 15). Thomas Myddleton beat Royalist forces at Montgomery in 1644; The Methodist leader Thomas Charles born at Llanfihangel Abercowin near St Clears in 1755 (see October 5); First rugby match at Cardiff's Arms Park in 1876; Birth in 1892 of Sir John Lias Cecil Cecil-Williams, solicitor and driving force behind the publication of 'The Dictionary of Welsh Biography' (see November 30); In 1907, Allan Jones, actor in Marx Bothers films, singer of 'The Donkey Serenade', and father of the crooner Jack Jones, was born in Scranton, Pennsylvania. His father was a miner from Cwmbach in the Cynon Valley; In 1913, 439 men were killed in an explosion at the Universal Colliery, Senghenydd; Harry Parr Davies of Neath, composer and revue-writer, died in Chelsea in 1955; 61,056, a record attendance for Ninian Park, watched Wales v. England in 1961; Death in 1962 at Six Bells of George Daggar (see November 6)

*'Under contract with Coucy dated October 14, 1375, the prodigious Owen of Wales was to lead 400 men at a pay of 400 francs a month plus another 100 francs for his lieutenant, Owen ap Rhys. He was to take second place to no other captain and make no other alliance until released, while Coucy in turn was to make no peace without Owen's agreement. Any town or fortress taken by Owen was to be yielded to Coucy, but he could retain booty and prisoners worth less than 200 francs in ransom. Of those worth more than that, Coucy was to receive one sixth of the value, and in the event of the Duke of Austria himself being captured, Owen was required to deliver him to Coucy in return for payment of 10,000 francs. The enterprise became a magnet for restless*

*swords, attracting from their annual Prussian sport 100 knights of the Teutonic Order ... The pointed helmets and cowl-like hoods on heavy cloaks worn against the cold were noticed by all observers. Called Gugler (from the Swiss-German for cowl or point), the hoods gave their name to what became known as the Gugler War.'* - Barbara Tuchman, 'A Distant Mirror', 1978

**On this day...**

October 15

*FEAST DAY OF SAINTS* SELEVAN (see 14); TEGLA d.750 (also 26, June 1) at Llandegley, Llandegla, St Tegla's Well, Ochanfort; TEWDWR 6th century (also 14, 16, March 13) at Darowain; CYNWYD (see September 28); and RHISIART GWYN, or RICHARD WHITE c.1536-1584 (see 17, also October 25) at Overton, Overstock - one of the *'Forty Saints'*, he was hung, drawn and quartered at Wrexham. In 1400 Henry IV returned from his first invasion of Wales against Glyndŵr, having looted Anglesey, Bangor, Harlech and Llanfaes Friary - the mission was an expensive failure; The 12 year-old Prince Henry who was born at Monmouth, son of Henry IV, was invested as Prince of Wales* in 1399; Death in 1555 of Sir John Price (Rhys ap Gwilym ap Llywelin ap Rhys Llwyd), manuscript collector and Henry VIII's secretary of the Council of Wales and the Marches; William Blethin of Shrenewton Court, Bishop of Llandaf, died in 1590 and was buried at Mathern; In 1751 David Samwell, who sailed with Captain Cook, was born at Nantglyn (see November 23); The nationalist and writer Saunders Lewis was born in 1893; A National Hunger March started from Cardiff to London, protesting against unemployment in 1932; Death in 1943 at Bangor of Sir Thomas Artemus Jones, who fought for the use of Welsh in courts, and refused to imprison debtors who could not pay their debts (see February 18); Death in 1955 of Thomas Jones (see September 27); In 2001 The Times reports that Elizabeth Saxe-Coburg-Gotha (a.k.a. Windsor) is at least six times wealthier than Buckingham Palace has admitted, with personal assets of over £1 billion because of a confidential taxation-avoidance arrangement existing since 1952 - she spends £600,000 a year on horses. This amount does not include paintings or homes which belong to the state, but just personal assets. Her son Charles Saxe-Coburg-Gotha-Sonderburg-Gluckburg-Schleswig-Holstein (of Wales) is worth over a third of a billion pounds.

* *'... the ceremony ought to make every Welshman who was patriotic blush with shame. Every flunkey in Wales, Liberal and Tory alike was grovelling on his hands and knees to take part in the ceremony. Funds could be raised for that purpose with ease, but when there was money wanted to help workers to gain even a living wage, it could only*

*be found with difficulty.'* - Keir Hardie's speech in 1911 to the May Day Labour Rally in Tonypandy, referring to the coronation of Edward as Prince of Wales in that year. Edward VIII later gave up the throne for a strange-looking divorcee, and led a life of utter, shiftless, tax-paid, treacherous futility. Hardie had written previously in 'The Merthyr Pioneer': *'Wales is to have an "Investiture" as a reminder that an English king and his robber barons strove for ages to destroy the Welsh people and finally succeeded in robbing them of their lands ... and then had the insolence to have his son "invested" in their midst.'*

**On this day...**

..................................................................................................................................

..................................................................................................................................

..................................................................................................................................

## October 16

*FEAST DAY OF SAINT* TEWDWR (see 15); Holy Day of Daniel Rowland, priest and preacher (1790). Death of Thomas Davis, Bishop of St Asaf in 1573; Rowland Ellis, of Bryn Mawr near Dolgellau, led 100 Quakers to Pennsylvania in 1686 to escape persecution. They sailed from Miford Haven, and settled at Bryn Mawr, now Lower Merion in Pennsylvania. The famous Bryn Mawr College in America remembers his birth-place; Daniel Rowland, Methodist leader, died at Llangeithio in 1790; Birth in 1834 of Sir Pryce Pryce-Jones at Newtown, the pioneer of mail-order (see January 11); In 1872 Aberystwyth College opened, the precursor of the University of Wales, funded by David Davies and thousands of the Welsh people; Maudie Edwards, the actress, was born in Neath in 1906; Ivor Allchurch, the great Welsh footballer, was born at Llanelli in 1937; In 1991, aged under 18, Ryan Giggs of Manchester United was the youngest footballer to be capped by Wales

*'Many, multifarious birds and many-coloured foods,*
*A myriad vegetables in Dafydd's court.*
*It was full of oranges, of drink from young vines,*
*It was a rare place, all colours of wines.'* - Tudur Aled (fl.1480-1526)

**On this day...**

..................................................................................................................................

..................................................................................................................................

..................................................................................................................................

## October 17

*FEAST DAY OF SAINT* ABBOT CYNOG (Sunday after 2nd Thursday of October, see 9); RHISIART GWYN (alternative date for his execution at

Wrexham in 1584, the first Welsh Catholic Martyr). In 1660 the regicide John Jones of Maes-y-Garnedd, Meriioneth was executed at Covent Garden; An explosion in 1863 killed 39 miners at Morfa Colliery, Port Talbot; Swansea Rugby Club was formed in 1874; Death of the Chartist Morgan Willams at Merthyr in 1883; Sir John Morris-Jones, grammarian and poet, was born at Trefor, Anglesey in 1886; First 'Welsh Day' debate in the House of Commons in 1944; James Griffiths bcame the first Secretary of State for Wales in 1964; Rugby's short-lived 'National Stadium', which replaced the Arms Park, opened in 1970 (Cardiff RFC has retained the Arms Park name for its own adjacent ground); Gus Risman of Barri, rugby league star, died in 1994

*Bob Jones had been born in Glamorgan. Almost alone among his classmates he had turned from the broad-trodden track to the pits, continued to educate himself, and taken to printing. Except for three or four of them, those school friends of his were dead. "Old at thirty was a man in the mines," Bob said. "I used to meet my old school-fellows sometimes, and one after another I'd see the lung-disease had got them. They'd come home from the pits played out. You'd see them walking up a bit of a hill, or up the stairs in the house. They'd take it slow, not wanting anyone to notice, like a man on a mountain stops to look at the view, or tie a bootlace, when he's pretending he's not tired. Hard it was to get the compensation. The doctors would say it was T.B., and the man had had it before ever he began in the pits."*
*Bob looked at me to see how strong my stomach was before he went on. "The women would stand by the bed of a dying man. Often with his last breath he'd cough up not blood, but a hard black plug that was a bit of his brittle lung, and that was the proof he'd died of silicosis." -* Thomas Firbank, 'A Country of Memorable Honour', 1953

*On this day...*

## October 18

FEAST DAY OF SAINTS CADWALADR 6th century at St Segal near Chateaulin; GWEN OF CORNWALL d. 544 at St Wenn, Gwennap; GWEN (GWENLLIAN) d. 492 at Talgarth, Llanwensan; ILLOG (see August 8); and SAINT LUKE *1st century* - this date was called St Luke's Little Summer in England, and St Michael's Little Summer in Wales - *HAF BACH MIHANGEL.* On the Welsh borders, until late in the 19th century, congregations were allowed to pelt their preachers with crab-apples on this day. Richard 'Beau' Nash was born in Swansea in 1674 (see February 3); Birth in 1759 at Brecon of Theophilus Jones, 'the historian of Brecknock'; Hugh Pugh's flat (boat) 'Ann' was wrecked on the St Tudwal Islands in 1858, remembered in the song *'Fflat Huw Puw'**; University College Bangor opened in 1884; Death in 1948 of the poet I.D. Hooson (see May 2); The office of Secretary of State for Wales was created in

1964; Lyn 'The Leap' Davies won the long-jump gold medal at the Tokyo Olympics; Trawsfynydd Nuclear Power Station, Britain's only inland generator, opened in 1968 in an area of outstanding national beauty. It has been 'mothballed' for years because of the horrendous costs of decommissioning, and lies in an area subject to ground faults and earthquake activity

*'Mae swn ym Mhortinllaen, swn hwyliau'n codi:*
*Blocie'I gyd yn gwichian, Dafydd Jones yn gweiddi:*
*Ni fedra'I aros gartre yn fy myw;*
*Rhaid I mi fod yn llongwr iawn ar Fflat Huw Puw.*
*Fflat Huw Puw yn hwylio heno, swn codi angor;*
*Mi fynna'I fynd I forio:*
*Mi wisga'I gap pig gloew tra bydda'I byw,*
*Os ca'I fynd yn llongwr ar Fflat Huw Puw.'*
(There's a sound in Portinllaen of sails being hoisted. The blocks creak, Dafydd Jones shouts 'I can't stay at home, upon my life. I must go as a proper sailor on Huw Puw's flat. Huw Puw's flat's sailing tonight. The sound of an anchor being pulled. I'll wear a bright peaked cap as long as I live, if I can go as a proper sailor on Huw Puw's flat.')

*On this day...*

..................................................................................................................
..................................................................................................................
..................................................................................................................
..................................................................................................................

## October 19

*FEAST DAY OF SAINTS* MADRUN (with Anhun) (see April 9) at Trawsfynydd (with Anhun), Tintagel, Minster; and ETHBIN 6th century; Holy Day of Henry Martyn, pastor, translator and missionary. 1238 saw the voluntary unification of Wales at Ystrad Fflur (Strata Florida Abbey), when the princes of Wales swore allegiance to Llywelyn the Great and his son Dafydd; In 1401, John Charlton, Lord of Powys, was killed in a skirmish with Glyndŵr's men; In 1831 the Calvinistic Methodist Association decided at Tredegar that no trade unionist could be admitted to church membership; Death in 1874 of the political agitator Hugh Williams, at Ferryside; Fred Keenor of Cardiff, captain of Cardiff's FA Cup-winnning team, died in 1972; In 1964, housing, local government and roads were given to the new Welsh Office to administer; In 1982, Dr Iorwerth Peate, inspiration and first Curator of the superb Welsh Folk Museum at St Ffagans, died

*'This afternoon on the edge of autumn*
*Our laughter feathers the quiet air*
*Over tombs of princes. We idle*
*In an old nave, lightly approach*
*Old altars. Our eyes, our hands*

*Know fragments only; from these*
*The Abbey climbs and arches into the past.*
*We look up and find*
*Only our own late August sky.*
*Ystrad Fflur, your shadows fall*
*Benevolently still on your ancient lands*
*And on us too, who touch your stones*
*Not without homage. Take our laughter*
*On your consenting altars,*
*And the the centuries borne up*
*By your broken pillars, add*
*The light weight of an hour*
*At the end of summer.'*
'At Strata Florida' by Ruth Bidgood

**On this day...**

..................................................................................................................................................
..................................................................................................................................................
..................................................................................................................................................

## October 20
*FEAST DAY OF SAINT* CAMMARCH (see 8). The Methodist leader Thomas Charles died in Bala in 1814; The novelist Daniel Owen was born at Mold in 1836 (see October 22); The Liverpool and Wales football star Ian Rush was born at St Asaf in 1961

*'It is to this day the fashion among the Britons to reckon the faith and religion of Englishmen as naught and to hold no more converse with them than with the heathen'* - The Venerable Bede (c.673-735), who hated the fact that the Welsh Church was the oldest established Christian religion in the world, compared to the new Roman version that the Saxon barbarians adopted.

**On this day...**

..................................................................................................................................................
..................................................................................................................................................
..................................................................................................................................................

## October 21
*FEAST DAY OF SAINTS* LLEUCI 5th century (also December 13) at Bettws Leici, Abernant; LLYR FORWYN 5th century? at Llanyre, Llanllyr; URSULA d.453 at Cologne; GWRW (also November 3) at Eglwyswrw; and TUDWEN (see 27). In 1965, the official opening of the hated Trywerin Reservoir was marred by protests; 1966 - the Aberfan Disaster* - a terrifying day for Wales still

imprinted on the national psyche, for whom no-one was held responsible. 116 children and 28 adults were smothered by slag. Those who admired and eulogised the sainted George Thomas should examine the relevant Cabinet Papers which were released under the 30-Year Rule.

*'Before this we stand breathless. Our eyes speak, our thoughts rage, but our tongues have momentarily given up the ghost of immemorial grievance. No touch of the whip has hurt like this.' - Gwyn Thomas, 1966

**On this day...**

............................................................................................................................

............................................................................................................................

............................................................................................................................

## October 22

FEAST DAY OF SAINTS CORDULA 5th century; MELLON (see 11); MAELOG (see 22); IA (see February 3); and GWYNNO and NOETHON (see 23); THE EARTH'S BIRTHDAY - In Jewish folklore, God created the Earth on this day in 4004 BC. The novelist Daniel Owen died in 1895 (see October 20); In 1942 the Welsh Courts Act allowed evidence to be given in Welsh

'Thee was not an orange, not a pear,
Not any fruit off any tree,
Not the freshly-gathered fruit of any orchard,
Not nuts from any wood that I could not a portion have.' - Guto'r Glyn (c.1494—1493), writing of Dinas Mawddwy in Meirionyddd

**On this day...**

............................................................................................................................

............................................................................................................................

............................................................................................................................

## October 23

FEAST DAY OF SAINTS GWYNNO and NOETHON 6th century at Llancarfan (also October 22, 24); and CLEER (see August 19). In 1400, Henry IV in Shrewsbury, issued a pardon to all Welshmen except Glyndŵr and the Tudor brothers. Glyndŵr's son Gruffudd accepted the pardon, ensuring that the line would not die out; William Herbert, MP for Cardiff, died at the Battle of Edgehill, with thousands of other Welsh followers of Charles I in 1642; Cardiff was granted City status in 1905; William Lewis of Milford Haven won the Victoria Cross with the Welch Regiment at Salonika (Thessaloniki) in 1916; Swansea's Guildhall opened in 1934; Claerwen Dam opened in 1952

It is well worth quoting parts of 'De Excidio' to show the feeling with which Gildas wrote of his times. Interestingly he calls Vortigern 'unlucky' in the first extract

(from Chapters 23 and 24), when he invited the Saxons into Kent to act as mercenaries, against the constant attacks from Ireland and Scotland. In the second extract, from Chapter 25, we can see his great admiration for Emrys Wledig, Ambrosius Aurelianus, who pushed back the ravaging Saxons for a time.
'They first landed on the eastern side of the island, by the invitation of the unlucky king, and there fixed their sharp talons, apparently to fight in favour of the island, but alas ! more truly against it. Their mother-land, finding her first brood thus successful, sends forth a larger company of her wolfish offspring, which sailing over, join themselves to their bastard-born comrades. From that time the germ of iniquity and the root of contention planted their poison amongst us, as we deserved, and shot forth into leaves and branches'.............. 'For the fire of vengeance, justly kindled by former crimes,spread from sea to sea, fed by the hands of our foes in the east, and did not cease, until, destroying the neighbouring towns and lands, it reached the other side of the island, and dipped its red and savage tongue in the western ocean.............. So that all the columns were levelled with the ground by the frequent strokes of the battering-ram, all the husbandmen routed, together with their bishops, priests and people, while the sword gleamed, and the flames crackled around them on every side. Lamentable to behold, in the midst of the streets lay the tops of lofty towers, tumbled to the ground, stones of high walls, holy altars, fragments of human bodies, covered with livid clots of coagulated blood, looking as if they had been squeezed together in a press; and with no chance of being buried, save in the ruins of the houses, or in the ravening bellies of wild beasts and birds; with reverence be it spoken for their blessed souls, if, indeed, there were so many found who were carried, at that time, into the high heaven by the holy angels. So entirely had the vintage, once so fine, degenerated and become bitter, that, in the words of the prophet, there was hardly a grape or ear of corn to be seen where the husbandman had turned his back.'
'Some, therefore, of the miserable remnant, being taken in the mountains, were murdered in great numbers; others, contrained by fammine, came and yielded themselves to be slaves for ever to their foes, running the risk of being instantly slain, which truly was the greatest favour which could be offered them; some others passed beyond the seas with loud lamentations instead of the voice of exhortation. "Thou hast given us as sheep to be slaughtered, and among the Gentiles hast thou dispersed us." Others, committing the safeguard of their lives, which were in continual jeopardy, to the mountains, precipices, thickly wooded forests, and to the rocks of the seas (albeit with trembling hearts), remained still in the country. But in the meanwhile, an opportunity happening, when these most cruel robbers were returned home, the poor remnants of our nation (to whom flocked from divers places round about our miserable countrymen as fast as bees to their hives, for fear of an ensuing storm), being strengthened by God, calling upon him with all their hearts, as the poet says, - "With their unnumbered vows they burden Heaven," that they might not be brought to utter destruction, took arms under the conduct of Ambrosius Aurelianus, a modest man, who of all the Roman nation was then alone in the confusion of this troubled period left alive. His parents, who for their merit were adorned with the purple, had been slain in these same broils, and now his progeny in these our days, although shamefully degenerated from the worthiness of our ancestors, provoke to battle their cruel conquerors, and by the goodness of our Lord obtain the victory.' It is hardly surprising from this contemporary writing, that the Celtic Church refused to evangelise the Saxons in later years, incurring the wrath of Bede. (Extract from the entry on St Gildas (c.498-570) in 'The Book of Welsh Saints' by T.D.Breverton)

*23*

## October 24

*FEAST DAY OF SAINTS* CADFARCH mid 6th century at Penegos, Abererch; MAGLORIUS d. 575 (also 22, July 24) at Dol, Sark, Dinan, St Jacques in Paris; and GWYNNO and NOETHON (NWYTHON) (see 23); *UNITED NATIONS DAY.* University College Cardiff opened in 1883; Newport RFC beat South Africa 9-3 in 1912; Phil Bennett, fly-half for Wales and the Lions was born at Felinfoel in 1948; The novelist T. Rowland Hughes died at Cardiff in 1949; Jonathan Davies, the rugby union and league fly-half was born at Trimsaran in 1962

Geofrey of Monmouth wrote of a grim future for *'the people of Britain'*, the Welsh, in this passage upon Vortigern. He used the metaphor of the Red Dragon of Cadwaladr and Wales and the White Dragon of Wessex and England: *"While Vortigern, King of the Britons, was still sitting on the flank of the pool which had drained of its water, there emerged two dragons, one white, one red. As soon as they were near enough to each other, they fought bitterly, breathing out fire as they panted. The white dragon began to have the upper hand and to force the red one back to the pool. The red dragon bewailed the fact that it was being driven out and then turned upon the white one and forced it backwards in its turn. As they struggled on in this way, the King ordered Ambrosius Merlin to explain just what this battle of the dragons meant. Merlin immediately burst into tears. He went into a prophetic trance and then spoke as follows: 'Alas for the red dragon, for its end is near. Its cavernous den shall be occupied by the white dragon, which stands for the Saxons whom you have invited over. The red dragon represents the people of Britain, who will be overrun by the white one: for Britain's mountains and valleys shall be levelled, and the streams in its valleys shall run with blood.'"*

*24*

## October 25

*FEAST DAY OF SAINTS* CANNA 6th century at Llangan (Pontcanna and Trecanna, Canna's Town which became Canton in Cardiff, remember this saint); GWYDDNO 6th century at Leon, Lan-Gouezenou, Saint Houdon; WINNOW 6th century (also May 31) at St Winnow, St Twinnell's?; and SADWRN (see November 29); Holy Day of Bishop Lewis Bayley, writer; THE FORTY MARTYRS OF ENGLAND AND WALES including PHILIP EVANS (July 22,

1679), RICHARD GWYN (October 15, 1584), JOHN JONES (July 12, 1598, JOHN KEMBLE (August 22, 1679), DAVID LEWIS (August 27, 1679), NICHOLAS OWEN (February 2, 1606) and JOHN ROBERTS (December 10, 1610). These were Catholics, executed between 1535 and 1679, canonised by the Pope on this day in 1970. In 1415, Welsh archers won the Battle of Agincourt for Henry V, and Dafydd Gam, previously captured in 1412 and ransomed by Glyndŵr, died on the battlefield. Henry's Welsh longbowmen first gave the two-finger sign; Rex Willis of Cardiff RFC and Wales was born in 1924

'In 1970,Richard Gwyn of Llanidloes, a Catholic schoolmaster, was canonised. Four hundred years earlier, he had refused to take the Oath of Supremacy, and to attend church. He was severely tortured during four years in gaol. At his trial he was heavily fined and asked how he would pay. He smiled and said '*I have something towards it – six pence.*' The response of the judge to this jest was a sentence that Gwyn be '*drawn on a hurdle to the place of execution where he shall hang half-dead, and so be cut down alive, his members cast into the fire, his belly ripped open unto the breast, his head cut off, his bowels, liver, lungs, heart thrown likewise into the fire.*' Gwyn exclaimed '*What is all this ? Is it any more than one death ?*' The execution took place in 1584. (From 'The Book of Welsh Saints', 2000, by T.D.Breverton)

*On this day...*

..................................................................................................................

..................................................................................................................

..................................................................................................................

## October 26

*FEAST DAY OF SAINTS GWYNNO* b. 487 or 507 (also 22,23,24, April 13, December 26) at Llanwnog, Llanwynno, Llantrisant, St Gwynno's Forest; and ANEIRIN GWAWDRYDD 6th century. Gruffudd ap Nicholas and his sons were granted pardons during the Wars of the Roses in 1456; In 1859, the 'Royal Charter' sank off the Anglesey coast in a gale, drowning 483 people; Birth in 1875 of Sir Lewis Casson, actor, unionist and producer (see May 16); Llanwern Steelworks opened in 1962 - closure announced in 2001; Death in 1963 of Baron Evans (see January 1)

'*This gem of Gothic woodwork is as nearly perfect is design as anything that we know of. It would be difficult for us to suggest any alterations that would not be injurious. Never have we met with the variety, lightness, elegance and regularity so successfully combined as in this beautiful screen. It is a remarkably fine specimen of Gothic woodwork in a style very different from what is met elsewhere*' - The Rev. John Parker describing the chancel screen at St Gwynog's Church, Llanwnog, in 1828

*On this day...*

..................................................................................................................

..................................................................................................................

..................................................................................................................

## October 27

FEAST DAY OF SAINTS TUDWEN 6th century (also 21) at Llandudwen; LLYR FORWYN (see 21); and IA (see February 3). Vavasor Powell, Puritan divine, died in 1670 and was buried in Bunhill Fields (see December 18); Lewis Edwards, theologian, preacher and for 50 years Principal of Bala College, was born in Pen-llwyn, Ceredigion in 1809 (see July 19); Death in 1853 of Michael Jones, first principal of Bala Independent College; Edward Latham Bevan, first Bishop of Swansea and Brecon, was born in 1861; Admiral Sir Hugh Evan-Thomas was born at Llwyn-madoc, Brecon, in 1862, and served at Jutland (see August 30); Death of Richard Davies, Liberal MP for Anglesey, at Treborth in 1896; James J. Davies, the 'Iron Puddler' was born in Tredegar in 1863 - he became an American Senator and Cabinet Member (see November 22); Dylan Marlais Thomas*, poet, was born in Swansea in 1914 (see November 9)

*'Now as I was young and easy under the apple boughs
About the lilting house and happy as the grass was green,
The night above the dingle starry,
Time let me hail and climb
Golden in the heydays of his eyes,
And honoured among wagons I was prince of the apple towns
And once below a time I lordly had the trees and leaves
Trail with daisies and barley
Down the rivers of the windfall light'
'Fern Hill' (first verse) by Dylan Thomas

*On this day...*

..................................................................................................................
..................................................................................................................
..................................................................................................................

## October 28

FEAST DAY OF SIMON ZELOTES 1st century (also July 1). The first English tax on Wales was imposed in 1291; Denbigh Castle was captured by Parliamentarians in 1644; William Bulkeley, the diarist, died in 1691 (see November 4) ; John Dyer*, the famous poet and cleric, of Aberglasney, near Llangathen, was christened at Llanfynydd in 1701 (see December 15); Death in 1761 of the eccentric Sir John Pryce, who used to sleep with the embalmed corpses of his first two wives; In 1789 Mary Evans (Y Fantell Wen, Whitemantle) was buried at Llanfihangel-y-traethau, the 'immortal' leader of a sect around Harlech and Penmachno; 'Y Fonesig Alys Mallt' died at St Dogmael's in 1950 (see October 4); 'Billy' Hughes, Welsh-born Prime Minister of Australia, died in 1952; In 1957 the 'Save Trywerin' campaign began with an 'all-Wales conference' at Cardiff - the less said about Trywerin the better, because it demonstrates that democracy has never been granted to the Welsh nation - COFIWCH TRYWERIN

*'Tis now the raven's bleak abode;
'Tis now th'apartment of the toad;
And there the fox securely breeds;
And there the poisonous adder breeds,
- John Dyer, 'Grongar Hill'

*Conceal'd in ruins, moss and weeds;
While ever and anon there falls
Huge heaps of hoary, moulder'd walls...'*

**On this day...**

..............................................................................................................................

..............................................................................................................................

..............................................................................................................................

## October 29
Mutton Davies, Royalist soldier of Gwysaney and Llannerch Park, Sheriff and MP for Flint, died in 1684, aged 50; In 1909, 26 miners died at Darren Colliery, New Tredegar; Cardiff City Hall opened in 1906; Death in 1907 of Megan Watts Hughes, vocalist and orphanage-founder (see February 12); Last race at Tenby race-course in 1936

*'Three antagonists of goodness:*
*Pride, Passion And Covetousness.'* - from the Welsh Triads of Virtues

**On this day...**

..............................................................................................................................

..............................................................................................................................

..............................................................................................................................

## October 30
*FEAST DAY OF SAINTS* ISSUI at Patrishow; ILLOG 6th century (see August 8); and ARILD (see July 20); Holy Day of Richard Hooker, priest and teacher. Henry Tudor's coronation, where he created the Welsh Yeomen of the Guard, the first permanent armed body in Britain; In 1698 Bridget Vaughan (Madam Bevan) was christened; John Adams, Welsh-American President, was born in 1735; In 1894 the archdruid David Griffith (Clwydfardd) died; The rugby second-row Brian Price was born at Bargoed in 1937; Newport beat New Zealand 3-0 in 1963

According to Iolo Morgannwg's 'Genealogy of Iestyn ap Gwrgan', *'Caradog built a palace, after the manner of the Romans, at Abergwerydwyr, called now Llandunwyd Major, or St Donat's. His daughter, Eurgain, married a Roman chieftain, who accompanied her to Cambria. This chieftain had been converted to Christianity, as well as his wife Eurgain, who first introduced the faith among the Cambro-Britons, and sent for Ilid (a native of the land of Israel) from Rome to Britain. This Ilid is called, in the service of commemoration, St Joseph of Arimathea. He became principal teacher of Christianity to the Cambro-Britons, and introduced good order into the côr of Eurgain, which she had established for twelve saints near the place now called Llantwit; but which was burnt in the time of King Edgar. After this arrangement, Ilid went to Ynys Afallen in Gwlad yr Haf, where he died and was buried.'* Côr Eurgain, or Côr Worgorn, appears to be the great Romano-Celtic villa outside Llanilltud Fawr. Whether Iolo knew it existed, as it was covered by grass, is open to doubt. (Entry upon St Eurgain, 1st-2nd century, in 'The Book of Welsh Saints', T.D.Breverton

**On this day...**

## October 31

*FEAST DAY OF SAINTS* DOGMAEL 5th-6th century (also June 14 as TEGWEL) at St Dogmael's, Dogwel, Brittany; HYWEL FARCHOG 6th century at Llanhowell, Llanllywel, Crickhowell; and ERTH 6th century at Slane; *EVE OF SAMHAIN, OMEN EVE - For the Celts, the spirits of the dead roamed the* night. CALAN GAEAF - *the First Day of Winter in Wales;* This was the Celtic 'Old Year Night'; VIGIL OF ALL SAINTS; *HALLOWE'EN.* Birth in 1841 of Timothy Richards Lewis at Llangan, surgeon, pathologist and tropical medicine pioneer (see May 7); First day of a 4-month lock-out at Dinorwic Quarry in 1885; The miners' leader Noah Ablett died at Merthyr Tudful in 1935 (see October 4); The noted painter and Bohemian Augustus John died in 1961; Llanelli beat new Zealand 9-3 in 1972

*There is something wrong about growing animals*
*They jump and leap just like your child*
*They gambol, roll and run wild*
*There is something wrong about growing animals*
*They're frightened but want to know what's round the bend*
*They're happy and loving and in the end*
*There's something wrong about growing animals*
*To eat them*
- 'Skinning Up' from 'The Path to Inexperience', T.D. Breverton

**On this day...**

# NOVEMBER - TACHWEDD
## (Remnant)
### Mis Du (Black Month, Breton), Mis Du (Cornish)

## November 1

*FEAST DAY OF SAINTS* AELHAIARN 6th-7th century at Llanaelhaiarn, Guilsfield (Cegidfa); BIGAL (BIGEL) at Llanfigel, Ynys Bigel (West Mouse Island), Begelly; CADFAN 5th century at Llangadfan, Tywyn, Ynys Enlli; CAFFO 6th century at Llangaffo; CALLWEN 5th century at Capel Callwen, Cellan; CEDOL at Llangedol; CLYDAU 5th century at Clydai; CLYDWYN 5th century at Llanglydwyn; CYNFELIN 6th century at Llangynfelin, Trallwng (Welshpool); DWNA 6th - 7th century at Llanddona; GWENFYL 5th century (also 2, July 6 with Callwen) at Defynog, Gwynfil; GWENRHIW 5th - 6th century at Kerry (Gwenrhiw); GWYNLLEU 5th - 6th century at Nantgwnlle; GWRIN 6th century (see May 1) at Llanwrin; GWRYD 11th - 12th century - a Welsh friar canonised by the Catholic church; GWYDDIN at Gwythian; GWYNNORO 6th century at Llanpumsaint; MORHAEARN at Trewalchmai; RHWYDRYS at Llanrhwydrys; and many other Welsh saints were comemorated upon this day; this was the traditional start of the Welsh Year, *CALAN GAEAF*, the Old New Year's Day. In 1536, the Act of Union between England and Wales came into effect; in1775 a tidal wave (tsunami) from the earthquake which destroyed central Lisbon, affected all the South Wales coastline; On this day in 1800, John Adams became the first resident of The White House in Washington; Alfred George Edwards, the first Archbishop of Wales, was born at Llan-ym-Mawddwy rectory in Merioneth in 1848 (see June 1 and July 22); The poet-painter David Jones was born in 1895, said by T.S. Eliot to be on a par with Pound, Joyce and himself among 20th century writers; The last turnpike toll-gates in Britain were removed in Anglesey in 1895; The composer William Mathias was born at Whitland in 1934; In 1982, S4C, the Welsh language TV channel, was launched

*'Libraries gave us power*
*Then work came and made us free*
*What price now*
*For a shallow piece of dignity'* - Nicky Wire, Manic Street Preachers

*On this day...*

...................................................................................................................

...................................................................................................................

...................................................................................................................

## November 2

*FEAST DAY OF SAINTS* CORENTIN* 5th century (also May 1, September 5, December 11, 12) - a Founder Saint of Brittany remembered at Quimper, Cury; ERNIN 6th century at Locarn; LLECHID 6th - 7th century (also December 1) at Llanllechid; CELYNIN 7th century (also 20) at Llangelynin, Caernarfon; and GWENFYL (see November 1); *ALL SOULS* - Souling Day involved Souling Songs and Soul-Caking. Owain Glyndŵr unfurled his new banner, the golden lion of Uther Pendragon, before attacking the town and castle of Caernarfon in 1401. The Welsh won the Battle of Tuthill, but the English retained the castle; In 1839, a Chartist meeting at the Coach and Horses Inn, Blackwood, decided to hold a massive demonstration in Newport on the next day; Birth in 1867 of Owen Glynne Jones, mountaineer and pioneer rock climber (see August 28); Isaac Foulkes died near Ruthin in 1904, aged 67 (see November 9, May 22)

*'Eight sorts of mead for the table,*
*Eight dishes in twofold adorning it.*
*Eight sorts of sauces - eight piping hot -*
*Eight sorts of wines and delicacies'* - Guto'r Glyn, 15th century

*On this day...*

## November 3

*FEAST DAY OF SAINTS* CAEMEN 6th - 7th century at Eglwys Gymmun, Antrim; CRISTIOLUS 6th century at Eglwyswrw, Penrydd, Llangristiolus; GWENFOE at Wenvoe; GWYDDFACH d. 610 near Meifod; GWENFREWI (Feast of her Death, see September 10) at Holywell; GWRW (see November 3); and CLYDOG (see August 19). Death at Carmarthen in 1456 of Edmund Tudor, Earl of Richmond and (posthumous) father of Henry VII; In 1503, 1500 Roman Catholics gathered to bathe at Holywell, and in 1593 Father Gerard bathed there; In 1666 James Howell of Llangamarch, author, traveller, secret agent and historiographer to Charles I, was buried in London's Temple church; Birth in 1794 near Cadoxton-juxta-Neath of David Thomas, pioneer of the American iron industry (see June 20); Chartists, led by John Frost, Zephania Williams and William Jones surround Newport's Westgate Hotel in 1839 and a riot ensues; Death in 1857 of Admiral William Fitzwilliam Owen, hydrographer who also served throughout the Napoleonic Wars; The Cymruphile Prince Louis-Lucien Buonaparte died in 1891, aged 78; In 1926, 97% of South Wales miners were still on strike, although the TUC had called off the General Strike on May 12; Death in 1931 of A.J. Cook, South Wales' miners leader; In 1982, only Ceredigion and Dwyfor voted to stay 'dry' on Sundays

'On this side Wales - Wales, where the past still lives. Where every place has its tradition, every name its poetry, and where the people, the genuine people, still knows this past, this tradition, this poetry, and lives with it, and clings to it; while, alas, the prosperous Saxon on the other side, the invader from Liverpool and Birkenhead, has long forgotten his.' - 'On the Study of Celtic Literature', Matthew Arnold (1822-1888)

*On this day...*

.....................................................................................................................
.....................................................................................................................
.....................................................................................................................
.....................................................................................................................

## November 4

FEAST DAY OF SAINTS DYFRIG (see May 29); CLEER (see August 19); CLYDOG (see August 19); GWENFAEN (see 5); RHWYDRYS (1st Sunday in November); Llanrhwydrys; and GWENFREWI (see September 19). Between the 3rd and 6th of this month in 1282, Archbishop Pecham of Canterbury was with Llywelyn ap Gruffudd at Abergwyngeryn, trying to end the war with Edward I; In 1461, the hero of Mortimer's Cross, William ap William ap Thomas, becomes Lord Herbert of Raglan; The first lighthouse on the Skerries, off Anglesey, was built in 1673; William Bulkeley born at Llanfechell, Anglesey in 1691 (see October 28); Richard Price of Tynton, Llangeinor, gives a speech to Parliament on the anniversary of Cromwell's death, in 1789; Death in 1799 of the cleric and great economist Josiah Tucker of Laugharne; In 1910, the Cardiff airship pioneer Ernest Thompson Willows, made the first airship crossing from England to France in 'The City of Cardiff'; Death in 1962 of Sir Ifor Willams (see April 16); In 1980, the boxer Johnny Owen died in a coma, 7 weeks after his world-title bout on September 15

*'Green-coloured sauce in all the glass-partitioned*
*Manors up to Anglesey,*
*A sauce made of measures of gushing vinegar,*
*Strong chives, Pretty nancy, parsley, thyme,*
*Sorrel and dittany and raspberry leaves.'* - the gentleman-poet Ieuan ap Rhydderch (fl.1430-1470), writing of his home of Parc Rhydderch, Llanbadarn Odyn, near Tregaron. 'Pretty Nancy' is London Pride, and 'dittany' is a type of cress.

*On this day...*

.....................................................................................................................
.....................................................................................................................
.....................................................................................................................
.....................................................................................................................

# November 5

FEAST DAY OF SAINTS CYBI 6th century (also November 6, 7 and 8) at Llangybi, Holy Island (Ynys Gybi), Llangibby, Tredunnock, Cornwall; GWENFAEN (also 4) at Rhoscolyn; KEA (see October 3); IAGO (see July 24); and GWETHENOC (see July 24). On either this day or November 6, Anna Harriet Leonowens, tutor to the King of Siam's children, was born in 1831; In 1975, the following areas voted to stay 'dry' on Sundays: Anglesey, Arfon, Carmarthen, Ceredigion (Cardigan), Dwyfor and Meirionydd; Death in 1962 of the editor and journalist Percy Cudlipp, born in Cardiff on November 10, 1905 (the brother of the national editors Hugh and Reginald Cudlipp)

*'Rarebit, n. A Welsh rabbit, in the speech of the humourless, who point out that it is not a rabbit. To whom it may be solemnly explained that the comestible known as toad-in-the-hole is really not a toad, and that riz-de-veau a la financière is not the smile of a calf prepared after the recipe of a she-banker'* - Ambrose Gwinnett Bierce, 'The Devil's Dictionary', 1911

*On this day...*

## November 6

FEAST DAY OF SAINTS CEIDIO AB YNYR GWENT 6th century (also November 3) at Ceidio; EDWEN 7th century at Llanedwen, Eglwys Fach; GWYNDAF HEN 6th century (also April 21) at Llanwnda (Pembs), Llanwnda (Caerns); MELAINE d.c.535 at Mullion, St Mellyan, Rennes; WINNOC d.717 at St Winnow, St Winoc; ILLTUD (see February 7); and LEONORE 6th century at Limoges, France, Italy, Bavaria. In 1282, Luke de Tany's army was destroyed on the Menai Straits after breaking his truce with Llywelyn II; Birth in 1840 at Gwynfe of Sir John Williams, Court physician and principal founder of the National Library of Wales (see May 24); Birth at Cwmbran in 1879 of the unionist and MP George Daggar (see October 14); Evan Roberts leads Wales' last great religious revival, beginning at Blaenannerch, Dyfed on this day in 1904; Death in 1913 of Sir William Henry Preece (see February 15); Donald Houston, actor, was born in Tonypandy in 1923 (see October 13); The great scrum-half Onllwyn Brace was born in 1932; In 1966, the following counties voted to stay 'dry' on Sundays: Anglesey, Caernarfon, Cardigan, Carmarthen and Merioneth; In 1988 Steve Jones becomes the first Briton to win the New York Marathon

*'Such a happy day. Thank God for such a happy day. I have seen my love, my own, I have seen Daisy. She was so lovely and sweet and kind and the old beautiful love is as fresh and strong as ever. I never saw her more happy and affectionate and her lovely Welsh eyes grew radiant whenever they met mine. She was looking prettier than ever*

*and the East wind had freshened her pretty colour and her lovely hair was shining like gold. She wore a brown stuff dress and white ribbons in her hat. I wonder if Daisy and I will ever read these pages together. I think we shall. As I went to Llan Thomas this afternoon I met the Tregoyd travelling carriage with imperials on the roof dashing along the road to Hay and round the turn by Victoria Cottage. Lady Hereford and De Bohun Devereux (my old St Leonard's pupil at Thatch Cottage) were inside and on their way to Whitfield.'* - Kilvert's Diary, this day in 1871

*On this day...*

...........................................................................................................................

...........................................................................................................................

...........................................................................................................................

# November 7

*FEAST DAY OF SAINTS* CYNGAR (DOCHAU) 5th century (also November 27, March 7, May 12) at Llangefni, Langar, Llanwngar, Llandough-juxta-Cardiff, Llandough-juxta-Cowbridge; IAGO (see July 24); and ILLTUD (see February 7). Holy Day of Bishop Richard Davies (the son of Dafydd ap Gronw) of St Davids in 1581, the translator of the Prayer Book and New Testament of 1567 (with William Salesbury). Death in 1848 of Thomas Price (Carnhuanawc) in Llanfihangel Cwm-du (see October 2); Death in 1877 of Richard Calvert Jones (see December 4); In 1910, riots begin in Tonypandy; Elaine Morgan, evolutionist and author was born in 1920 in Pontypridd; In 1937 Dame Gwyneth Jones, the soprano, was born at Pontnewydd, near Pontypool

*'For Cowbridge hath no sober man*
*Or none of milk sop thinkers*
*And no philosophical fools*
*But great and glorious drinkers'* - Iolo Morganwg. In 1851, Cowbridge had 23 taverns and coaching inns, nearly all brewing their own beer, for an adult male population of 274. There were still 21 pubs in 1914. The last brewery in Cowbridge made its last brew on May 15, 1955

*On this day...*

...........................................................................................................................

...........................................................................................................................

...........................................................................................................................

# November 8

*HOLY DAY OF THE SAINTS OF WALES*
*FEAST DAY OF SAINTS* EDI at Llanedy?; TYSILIO d. 640 (also November 12, and October 1 in Brittany) at Meifod, Llandysilio, Llanfair P.G., Bryn Eglwys,

Cammarch, Shrewsbury, Chirk, Llanllugan, Guilsfield, Welshpool, Pleyben, Plomodiern, Sizun; CYBI d. c. 554 (also 5, 6, 7, August 13, last Sunday before July 25) at Holy Island, Holyhead, Llangyby, Llangibby; and NOE (see April 27); In the 9 days from Hallowe'en to the Eve of the Feast of St Martin, sheep were brought down from the hills, and farm workers were discharged. Owain Glyndŵr's* estates were siezed by the crown and granted to John Beaufort, Earl of Somerset, in 1400, beginning a twenty-year war; Birth in 1802 of Benjamin Hall, Lord Llanover, after whom 'Big Ben' is named (see April 27); Birth in 1802 of Wiliam Rees (Gwilym Hiraethog), cleric, writer, editor, radical, nationalist and politician, at Llansannan. Founder of 'Yr Amserau', he also died on this day, in 1883; In 1867, 178 men and children were killed at the Ferndale Colliery in the Rhondda; In 1884, 14 miners died at Pochin Colliery, Tredegar; The naturalist Ronald Lockley was born in Cardiff in 1903; In 1910, over 60 shops were attacked by starving workers at Tonypandy and a miner was killed by police. The Home Secretary, Winston Churchill, sent London policemen, then troops, to restore order; In 1961, the following counties voted to stay 'dry' on Sundays: Anglesey, Cardigan, Caernarfon, Carmarthen, Denbigh, Merioneth, Mortgomery and Pembroke; Death in 1965 of Viscount Hall (see December 31); In 1989, only Dwyfor voted to remain dry on Sundays

*'Owen de Glendour, a Welshman who had been squire to the Earl of Arundel, came to Parliament complaining that Lord de Grey Ruthin had usurped certain lands of his in Wales, but no argument helped against Lord de Grey. The Bishop of St Asaph gave counsel in Parliament that they should not entirely despise Owen, as the Welsh might revolt. But those in Parliament said they cared nothing for the bare-footed clowns' - from a contemporary monastic chronicle, The Eulogium

*On this day...*

...........................................................................................................................

...........................................................................................................................

...........................................................................................................................

# November 9

FEAST DAY OF SAINTS CYNON 6th century at Capel Cynon, Tregynon, Llangynwyd; and PABO d. 530 at Llanbabo, Llanerchymedd. The Treaty of Aberconwy in 1277 was imposed upon Llywelyn II, confining his authority to Gwynedd Uwch Conwy; Anglesey was lost by Glyndŵr's supporters in 1406, although some fighting continued until 1407; John Glynne MP, of Glynllifon, Caernarfon, matriculated at Oxford on this day in 1621 and later bought Hawarden Castle and Manor (see September 8, November 15); Isaac Foulkes, founder, owner and editor of 'Y Cymro' was born at Llanfwrog in 1836 (see November 2, May 22); The writer Rhys Davies born in Blaenclydach, Rhondda in 1903; The first hunger march from the Rhondda started in 1927; Dylan

Thomas* died in New York in 1953 (see October 27); The painter Ceri Richards died in 1971; 3 men killed at Corus (formerly British Steel) plant at Port Talbot in 2001 - workers complained that the furnace had been extended beyond its natural life-span in the interests of accountants

*Years and years and years ago,
when I was a boy, when there
were wolves in Wales, and birds
the colour of red-flannel
petticoats whisked past the harp-
shaped hills, when we sang and
wallowed all night and day in
caves that smelt like Sunday
afternoons in damp front
farmhouse parlours and we
chased, with the jawbones of
deacons, the English and the
bears, before the motor-car,
before the wheel, before the
duchess-faced horse, when we
rode the daft and happy hills
bareback, it snowed and it
snowed. But here a small boy says:
'It snowed last year, too.
I made a snowman and my
brother knocked it down and I
knocked my brother down and
then we had tea.' - lines from 'A Child's Christmas in Wales' by Dylan Thomas

*On this day...*

..............................................................................................................................................................................

..............................................................................................................................................................................

..............................................................................................................................................................................

## November 10

FEAST DAY OF SAINTS CYNFARWY (also November 7, 8 and 11) at Llechgynfarwy; and ELAITH 6th century at Amlwch. The radical and poet John Jones (Jac Glan-y-Gors) was born at Cerrig-y-Druidion in 1766 (see May 21); H.M. Stanley uttered 'Dr Livingstone, I presume' at Ujiji, Lake Tanganyika in 1871; Death in 1883 of Maria Jane Williams (Llinos), musician, at Aberpergwm; Richard Burton born at Pontrhydyfen in 1925; The Daughters of the American Revolution erected a plaque to Prince Madoc at Mobile, Alabama in 1953

'There is the same oppressive atmosphere (in the Rhondda) that one experienced in the *streets of Odessa and Sepastopol during the unrest in Russia in the winter of 1904. It is extraordinary to find it here in the British Isles'* - 'The Times' correspondent, from Tonypandy, 1910

**On this day...**

.....................................................................................................................................

.....................................................................................................................................

.....................................................................................................................................

# November 11

FEAST DAY OF SAINT CYNDDILIG 6th century (also November 1) at Llanrhystud; EDEYRN 5th-6th century (also November 23) at Llanedeyrn; MARTIN 4th century (also 12, July 4) at St Martin's; and RHEDYW (GREDFYW) see July 6 at Llanllyfni: MARTINMAS. At Martinmas Fairs, servants were hired. St Martin's Day replaced the day of the Graeco-Roman god of wine and parties, Bacchus. No wheels were allowed to turn on Martin's Day. In 1282, Llywelyn ap Gruffudd refused the offer of exile to high office in England in return for submitting to Edward I; In 1865 Mary Edwards Walker was given the American Congressional Medal of Honor; Llanelli rugby club was formed in 1875; The Great War ended in 1918, with over 30,000 Welshmen dead; Roy Jenkins, politician, born in 1920; Death in 1952 of Sir William Davies, at Aberystwyth (see October 11); Death in 1969 of Robert Thomas Jenkins (see August 31)

*'Mr George Venables sent me a brace of Llysdinam pheasants and a rabbit. Baskerville shot 3 woodcocks this afternoon near the Llainau. This morning Catherine Price of the New Inn was married to Davies, a young Painscastle blacksmith, before the Hay registrar. What I call a gipsy "jump the broom" marriage. The wedding feast was at the New Inn which is now shut up as an inn and abolished. As I passed the house I heard music and dancing, the people dancing at the wedding. They were dancing in an upper room, unfurnished, tramp, tramp, tramp, to the jingling of a concertina, the stamping was tremendous. I thought they would have brought the floor down. They seemed to be jumping round and round. When I came back the dance seemed to have degenerated into a romp and the girls were squealing, as if they were being kissed or tickled and not against their will.* - Kilvert's Diary, this day in 1871

**On this day...**

.....................................................................................................................................

.....................................................................................................................................

.....................................................................................................................................

# November 12

FEAST DAY OF SAINTS CYNFRAN 6th century (also November 11) at Llysfaen; FFRAID LEIAN 6th century at Llansanffraid Glyn Conwy, St David's; MADOG AP GILDAS 6th century at Llanmadog, Nolton; WULVELLA 7th - 8th century at Gulval; KING CADWALADR (see October 9); GWRDAF (see December 5) and MARTIN (see 11); OLD ALL SAINTS DAY. Birth in Tenby in 1869 of Arthur Leonard Leach, archaeologist, historian and geologist (see October 7); Sir Lewis Morris, poet and educationist, died in 1907; Bryn Meredith, Newport, Wales and Lions hooker, born in 1930 at Cwmbran; Newport beat South Africa 11-6 in 1969, the only club to have beaten the Springboks twice

'The hand that signed the paper felled a city;
Five sovereign fingers taxed the breath,
Doubled the globe of death and halved a country;
These five kings did a king to death.' – Dylan Thomas 'The Hand That Signed The Paper'

*On this day...*

...............................................................................................................................
...............................................................................................................................
...............................................................................................................................

# November 13

FEAST DAY OF SAINTS BRICE at Eglwys Brewys; MAELOG (also 12, 14); and GREDIFAEL (see 30); Holy Day of Charles Simeon, priest and teacher (1836); Birth in 1819 at Carmarthen of Henry Brinley Richards, pianist, harpist and composer of 'God Bless the Prince of Wales' (see May 2); Sir Evan Vincent Evans died in 1934 (see November 18 and 25); Some pubs opened in areas in Wales on Sunday in 1961, for the first time since the 1881 Sunday Closing Act; BBC Wales was formed in 1978

'a powerful detergent, repelling, bracing, cicatrising, anti-scorbutic and deobstruent medicine, as hath appeared by the notable cures they have effected... in inveterate ulcers, the itch, mange, scab, tetterous eruptions, dysentries, internal haemorrages, in gleets, the flor albus, and diorhea, in the worms, agues, dropsies and jaundice' - Dr John Butty in 1760 describing the medicinal uses of the water drawn from the Parys 'Copper-Mountain' in Anglesey

*On this day...*

...............................................................................................................................
...............................................................................................................................
...............................................................................................................................

## November 14

FEAST DAY OF SAINTS DYFRIG (see May 29); MALO d. c. 621 (also November 15) at St Malo, Saintes, Archingeay – One of the Seven Founders of the Breton Church; and MAELOG (see 13). Field Marshall Sir Stapleton Cotton, 1st Viscount Combermere, born in 1773 at Llewenni; Birth at Barri in 1884 of Sir Robert John Webber, managing director of the Western Mail & Echo group (see December 18); Construction started upon David Davies' Barri Docks in 1884

*(The rescue bucket's) 'slow descent was followed by a parched groan from thousands of parched throats. The groan became a mass moan which kept time with the motion of the bucket and its human cargo as it slithered out of sight, leaving nothing but the snaky rope to mark its existence. Imperceptibly the moan took shape, was given form. Deeper than the sea, it nestled a path through the voids in the thunder. Sometimes it was subdued by fiercely crashing roars, but it always returned to ride their crests, until at last it swept a clear road of domination above the storm. At once a prayer and a challenge, the old Welsh hymn burned its fiery way into the hearts of the grieving men and women on the pit-head, melting their sobs into music which mastered the tempest and rang down the valley of doom. Mournfully the cadences of the hymn, harmonised in the common agony, broke the air with emotional vibrations.*
*Beth sydd ymi yn y byd*
*Ond Gorthrymderau mawr o byd.*
*(What in this world for me*
*But great grief and agony.)*
*The pit had become in one night a crematorium surrounded by thousands of mourning people.'* - from 'Cwmardy' by Lewis Jones, 1937

*On this day...*

..................................................................................................................

..................................................................................................................

..................................................................................................................

## November 15

FEAST DAY OF SAINTS CAIAN (see September 25); CYNFAB at Capel Cynfab; MALO (see 14); and MEUGAN (see September 24). Llywelyn the Great's forces took Usk and Abergafenni castles in 1233; John Glynne MP died in in 1666 in London (see November 9); Death in 1722 of the reformer John Vaughan of Derllys Court, the father of Bridget Bevan; In 1753, 69 people drowned when the 'William and Mary' was wrecked on Pembrey Sands; Death in 1845 of Rear-Admiral Sir Salusbury Pryce Humphreys of Montgomery, the captain who seized the American warship Chesapeake in 1807; Aneurin Bevan MP, founder of the National Health Service, was born in Tredegar in 1897 (see July 6); Petula Sally Olwen Clark was born in 1932

'The English fight for power, the Welsh for liberty; the one to procure gain, the other to avoid loss; the English hirelings for money; the Welsh patriots for their country.' - 'The Description of Wales' by Giraldus Cambrensis (c.1146-1223)

*On this day...*

## November 16
FEAST DAY OF SAINT AFAN BUALLT fl.500-542 (also November 17, December 16, 17) at Llantrisant in Anglesey, Llanafan Fawr, Llanafan Trawsgoed, Lanavan. In 1326, Edward II was captured and taken to Llantrisant Castle, before being murdered at Berkeley Castle; The golfer Dai Rees died in 1983; The Gwyn Nicholls Memorial Gates, after removal for the building of the Millennium Stadium and restoration, were resited at Cardiff RFC's Arms Park in 2001

'Seven minutes to go ... and seventy times seven times to
the minute
this drumming of the diaphragm.
Every one of these, stood, separate, upright, above ground,
Blinked to the broad light
Risen dry mouthed from the chalk...
But sweet sister death has gone debauched today and stalks
On this high ground with strumpet confidence...
By one and one the line gaps, where her fancy will...'
Lines from 'In Parenthesis', by David Jones, the greatest poem about World War I

*On this day...*

## November 17
FEAST DAY OF SAINT AFAN see November 16. Llywelyn the Great defeated Henry III at Grosmont in 1233, and forced his army back to Hereford; Edward I attainted Llywelyn ap Gruffydd as a rebel in 1276; Mary Tudor died in 1558; Robert Owen, 'the first Socialist of the modern world' died in 1858 (see May 14); The Welsh formed a second Welsh settlement in Patagonia, inland at Cwm Hyfryd in 1888; Explosion at Cardiff's Temple of Peace in 1967, attributed to the Free Wales Army; Naunton Wayne, actor, died in 1970, aged 69 (see June 22);

'The New Scientist' (November 17, 2001) announced that Amersham plc of Cardiff is Britain's second greatest radioactive polluter after Sellafield, with carcinogenic tritium being released into the air

On this day in 1877, Ambrose Gwinnett Bierce wrote in his column in the San Francisco Evening Post: 'The following definitions are from the Idiot's Unabridged Dictionary, in use at the office of the Evening Post: 'Creditor': n. A miscreant who would be benefited by the resumption of debt payments. Debtor n. A worthy person, in whose interest the national finances should be so managed as to depreciate the national currency.'

*On this day...*

..................................................................................................................
..................................................................................................................
..................................................................................................................

# November 18

*FEAST DAY OF SAINTS* CEIDIO AP CAW 6th century at Rhodwydd Geidio; MABYN 6th century (also February 15) at St Mabyn; MAWES 5th century at St Mawes, Ile Modez, Quimper, Treguier, Lesneven, St Modez; and PIRAN (see March 5) at St Piran's Chapel, Cardiff; In 1406, Glyndŵr led his men across North-East Wales, following their successful raid in October; In 1646, Parliamentary forces took Conwy Castle and town; In 1840, the paddle steamer 'City of Bristol' sank off Llangennith, killing 30 passengers; Sir Evan Vincent Evans, eisteddfodwr and secretary of the Honourable Society of Cymmrodorion, was born near Llangelynnin in 1851 (or possibly November 25, 1852 - see November 13); Henry Richard became the first radical MP to be elected in Wales, in 1868 at Merthyr Tudful

*'Tri peth y dylem eu caru - aroglau meillionen, blas llaeth a chan adar y coed' - 'Three things we ought to love - the fragrance of clover, the taste of milk and the song of woodland birds.'*

*On this day...*

..................................................................................................................
..................................................................................................................
..................................................................................................................

# November 19

*FEAST DAY OF SAINTS* LLWYDIAN; and CORBRE (see 22). In 1926, with 86% of South Wales miners still on strike, the proposal is made to return to work. For an extra hour a day's work, from now on they received less than half the pay that they did in 1921- poverty was terrible; Jack Kelsey, the Arsenal and Wales goal-keeper, was born in 1929 at Llansamlet; Gwent beat the Springboks 14-8 at Ebbw Vale in 1969

In 1997, Simon Heffer writes on this day in 'The Daily Mail' *'Calling Wales is a nation is rather like describing William Hague as a formidable world statesman...the Welsh language is like so many minority tongues everyone pretends to cherish but nobody speaks... it was lucky for the Welsh that they had the English to civilise them, an experiment they happily conducted with varying degrees of success over the next 7 centuries'*

*On this day...*

...........................................................................................................................................

...........................................................................................................................................

...........................................................................................................................................

# November 20

*FEAST DAY OF SAINTS* COLMAN 7th century (also June 7) at Fishguard, Llangolman, Capel Golman, Dromore; EDMUND IRONSIDE 9th century at Crickhowell; UFELWY 6th century at St George-super-Ely (Lanufelwyn), St Eval, Withiel, Lancillo, Bolgros; and CELYNIN (see 2) at Llangelynin (Merioneth), Trywerin, Capel Celyn*. Death in 1712 of Bishop Humphrey of Bangor (see November 24); The educationist Sir Hugh Owen died in 1881; In 1893 the charter of the University of Wales received Royal Assent; Charles Rolls of Monmouth and Henry Royce founded Rolls-Royce in 1906; Sir David Davies was born in Beaufort, Monmouthshire in 1909 - after leaving school at 14, he became General Secretary of the Iron and Steel Trades Confederation, and first Chairman of the Welsh Development Agency (on November 18, 1975); Wilfred Wooller, rugby and cricket star, born at Rhos-on-Sea in 1912; Snowdonia was designated a National Park in 1951

*'Come, David, with your stone from the river,*
*And God behind your sling,*
*To keep the hymns of Capel Celyn*
*... from the murderous waters of the devil's dam.*
*Capel Celyn will not have an empty graveyard,*
*Nor will home and crops and song and harp*
*Be buried under the dam of the uncircumcised giant.'*
- translation of lines from 'Cwm Trywerin' in Gwenallt's 'Gwreiddiau' (Roots) 1959, protesting about the drowning of the village of Capel Celyn under the waters of Trywerin Reservoir

*On this day...*

...........................................................................................................................................

...........................................................................................................................................

...........................................................................................................................................

# November 21

FEAST DAY OF SAINTS KING DIGAIN 5th century at Llangernyw; CYNWYL (see January 5) at Aberporth; and DEINIOL (see September 10). Cardiff beat the All-Blacks 8-3 in 1953; Wales won the Golf World Cup in Hawaii in 1987

*'Twenty-four years remind the tears of my eyes.*
*(Bury the dead for fear that they walk to the grave in labour.)*
*In the groin of the natural doorway I crouched like a tailor*
*Sewing a shroud for a journey*
*By the light of the meat-eating sun.*
*Dressed to die, the sensual strut begun,*
*With my red veins full of money,*
*In the final direction of the elementary town*
*I advance for as long as forever is.'* - Dylan Thomas, 'Twenty-four Years'

*On this day...*

# November 22

FEAST DAY OF SAINTS CORBRE 6th century (also November 19) at Hen Eglwys; PEULIN (see March 12); GREDIFAEL (see 30); and DEINIOLEN (see 22). The Cistercian Abbey at Margam was founded in 1147; Mary Ann Evans (George Eliot*) was born in 1819; John Hughes, the composer of 'Cwm Rhondda', was born in 1873 (see May 14); The 'Great Strike' at Penrhyn slate quarries began in 1900 and lasted until 1903 - poor Welsh-speaking radical chapel-goers were pitted against an arrogant English Anglican Tory castle-builder, when 'cynffonwyr' (blacklegs) were thrown out of the Bethesda community. The strike lasted 3 years, one of the longest recorded; Death in America of James J. Davies, the Iron Puddler in 1947 (see October 27); Rupert Davies, the actor who played 'Maigret', died of cancer in 1976, aged 59; Tommy Evans of Badfinger committed suicide in 1983, eight years after the suicide of his co-writer, Pete Ham (see April 23 and 27)

**'A woman dictates before marriage in order that she may have an appetite for submission afterwards'* – George Eliot, 'Middlemarch', 1872.

*On this day...*

209

# November 23

*FEAST DAY OF SAINTS* CLEMENT 1st century at Tenby; DEINIOLEN 6th century (also November 22) at Bangor, Llanddeiniolen Fab; MINVER (see February 23); and EDEYRN (see November 11). The 6th century foundation of Dyfrig (Dubricius) at Llandaff was first consecrated as a cathedral in 1266; In 1407, the assassinantion of the Duke of Orleans in Paris, possibly on English orders, removed Glyndŵr's main supporter from the French Court (see December 7); Death in 1798 of David Samwell, naval surgeon and poet (see November 2); Birth in 1884 of the author and playwright Jack Jones at Merthyr (see May 7); Birth in Cardiff in 1953 of Griffith (Griff) Rhys Jones, comedian; Death in 1965 in Chicago of Llywelyn Morris Humphries, a.k.a. Murray the Camel, Murray the Hump, and a former Public Enemy No. 1

*'Three things a man experiences through litigation: expense, care and trouble'* 'The Welsh Triads' c.900

*On this day...*

.....................................................................................................................
.....................................................................................................................
.....................................................................................................................

# November 24

*FEAST DAY OF SAINTS* BUDOC d. 560 at Beuzy, Castanec; CLEMENT d. 100 (see 23); MINVER (see February 23); CYNGAR (see November 7); and CYNIN (see January 18). Birth in 1648 of Bishop Humphrey Humphreys of Bangor, antiquary and historian (see November 20); Death in 1904 of Lewis Jones of Caernarfon, leader of the Patagonian colonists for 35 years; Alun Davies Owen, radio and TV playwright, born in 1925 at Menai Bridge (see December 6); The great Pontypool, Wales and Lions prop-forward Graham Price, one-third of the famed 'Pontypool Front Row', was born in Egypt in 1951; On November 24, 2001, the Irish Government took out full-page advertisements in the UK press, protesting about the Sellafield Nuclear Processing Centre, because of the terrorist threat and radioactive waste disposal affecting the Irish Sea between Wales and Ireland. This was formerly called Windscale, but shamelessly 'rebranded' in the years following the 1957 reactor fire and consequent 33-35 deaths, and other spillages and disasters. It is reminiscent of the War Office now being named the Ministry of Defence, as a small country still attempts to be in the 'top four' league of arms spending, and its standards of living plummet relatively to those countries which use their scarce resources more wisely. Annual 'Defence' Spending: Britain £24billion (=c£500 p.a. for every man, woman and child); France £16billion; Germany £14billion

*'Lle bo eglwys gan Dduw bydd capel gan y diafol'* - *'Where God has a church, the devil will have a chapel'*

# November 25

*FEAST DAY OF SAINTS CATHERINE* 4th century at Worcester; and TYFANOG at Ramsey Island (Ynys Dyfanog). Prince Henry assembles an army at Hereford in 1404 to attack Glyndŵr; Chirk Aqueduct opened in 1801; Sir Evan Vincent Evans, eisteddfodwr, born in Llangelynnin in 1851 (see November 13); The actor-writer Emlyn Williams was born at Mostyn in 1905; The author Fanny Mary Katherine Bulkeley-Owen (born 1845) died in 1927 at Shrewsbury; Joe Erskine won the Empire heavyweight title in 1957; In 2001, hidden away in the Sunday newspapers, is the fact the the British Government has agreed to spend £35billion of taxpayers' money to clean up Sellafield's previous contamination, thus allowing it to be sold to a private company to carry on contaminating the world

*'There in the mountain dusk the dream was born,*
*The spirit fired, and the calm disturbed*
*By the just anger of the blood.*
*Wilder than the politician's yellow tongue*
*And stronger than the demagogue's thunder,*
*The insistent language and the dream would ring*
*Through the dear and secret places of the soul.*
*And fresher than the April torrent, the words of indignation*
*Would clothe themselves with beauty and be heard*
*Among the far undying echoes of the world.*

*And slowly the west would lose its crimson curves,*
*The larks descend, the hidden plovers cry,*
*And the vast night would darken all the hills.'* - from Verse XXIX of 'Gwalia Deserta' by Idris Davies

## 25

# November 26

*FEAST DAY OF SAINTS* EDREN at St Edren's; TEILO (see February 9); and POPE LINUS (see September 23). The Pontcysyllte Aqueduct opened in 1805;

Ernest Willows' first airship flew in Cardiff in 1909; Dr Mary Edwards Walker, the only woman to have been awarded the Congressional Medal of Honour, was born in 1832; In 1852 the industrialist Sir Josiah John Guest died and was buried at Dowlais, where he had been born on February 2, 1785; The actor-playwright George Emlyn Williams was born in Mostyn, Flint in 1905 (see September 25); Rachel Roberts, the actress, committed suicide in Beverley Hills in 1980 (see September 20)

'Their objective this time was the Abbey of Fraubrunnen, where no less an enemy than Owen of Wales was quartered with a large company. Carrying the banner of the Bear, the citizens (of Berne) marched though the night of November 26th (1375) in intense cold, and surrounded the abbey before dawn. With loud yells and flaming torches they fired the buildings and fell upon the sleeping "English", killing many before they woke. The rest sprang to their weapons in a desperate defence: cloisters once accustomed to ceremonial silence rang with the shouts and clang of battle, the contenders fought "stab for stab and blow for blow", smoke and flames filled every building of the abbey. Owen swung his sword "with savage rage", the Bernese leader, Hannes Rieder, was killed, but his men forced the Guglers to flight. "And those who fled were slain and those who stayed were burned up". Owen escaped, leaving 800 of his men dead. The Swiss too suffered heavy losses, but the survivors carried glory back to Berne ... Ballads told how the "Knight of Cussin set out to seize castle and town", with "forty thousand lances in those pointed hats"; how he "thought the land was all his and brought his kinsmen of England to help him with body and goods"; how "Duke Yfo (Owain) of Wales came with his golden helm"; how the Bishop of Basle treacherously promised to serve the Gugler, and how at last when Duke Yfo came to Fraubrunnen, "The bear roared You shall not escape me! I will slay, stab and burn you!" - Barbara Tuchman, 'A Distant Mirror', 1978

*On this day...*

...................................................................................................................................

...................................................................................................................................

...................................................................................................................................

# November 27

FEAST DAY OF SAINTS ALLGO 6th century (also 1st Sunday in May) at Llanallgo; and CYNGAR (see 7). The hated Reginald de Grey of Ruthin was released by Owain Glyndŵr in 1402, on payment of 10,000 marks (£6666), which helped Glyndŵr finance his war; Mary Darby Robinson (Perdita) was born in 1758; Death of Thomas John of Cilgerran, the Calvinistic Methodist minister, in 1862*; Birth in 1877 at Holt of Leigh Richmond Roose, goalkeeper for Stoke, Glasgow Rangers, Everton, Sunderland and Wales (missing in action in France, 1917); The last Welsh settlers arrived in Chubut, Patagonia in 1911; The rugby star Gareth Griffiths was born at Penygraig in 1931

*'He was a celebrated preacher in his day. His bony, emaciated body, his pallid countenance, and his dramatic and bodeful manner when preaching inspired his congregation with something akin to terror.' - The Dictionary of Welsh Biography to 1940

*On this day...*

..............................................................................................................................
..............................................................................................................................
..............................................................................................................................

## November 28

FEAST DAY OF SAINT JUTHWARA (see December 23); Death of the heroic Prince Owain ap Gruffudd ap Cynan, 'Owain Gwynedd' in 1170; In 1760, 90 drowned when the 'Caesar' capsized off Gower's Pwll Du Head; Death in 1894 of the industrialist and metallurgical patentee Henry Hussey Vivian (see July 6); Death of Reginald Arthur Gibbs in 1938 (b. 1872), Cardiff shipowner, who played rugby for Wales 16 times, scoring a try in the first match at Twickenham against England in 1910, and who was in the team that beat the South Africans in 1906; In 2000, in a Sunday Times poll of the *'most significant figures of the last millennium'*, 100 world leaders, scientists and artists voted Elizabeth Tudor 4th and Owain Glyndŵr 7th (Gutenberg was 1st)

*'Three things which evil cannot be:*
*Conformity to Law,*
*Knowledge and Love.'* - from the Welsh Triads of Virtues

*On this day...*

..............................................................................................................................
..............................................................................................................................
..............................................................................................................................

## November 29

FEAST DAY OF SAINTS SADWRN 6th century (also October 25) at Llansadwrn, Henllan; SADYRNIN d. 832 at St David's; and BARUC (see September 26). Birth at Llanfair Caereinion in 1837 of John Griffiths, artist and recorder of Indian art (see December 1); Birth in 1876 of Joseph Edward Davies, international lawyer and American Ambassador to Russia (1936-38), Belgium (1938), Russia again (1943-45) and Britain (1945 (see May 9); The novelist Kate Roberts was born at Blaenau Ffestiniog in 1881; Ryan Giggs was born in Cardiff in 1973 - his father Danny Wilson played rugby for Cardiff before playing rugby league 'up North'; WRU Centenary match in 1980 at the Arms Park

*'The hand that signed the treaty bred a fever,*
*And famine grew, and locusts came;*
*Great is the hand that holds dominion over*
*Man by a scribbled name.'* Dylan Thomas 1914-1953

*On this day...*

November 30

FEAST DAY OF SAINTS ANDREW 1st century; GREDIFAL 6th century (also November 13, 14 and 22) at Penymynydd; GWENLLWYFO at Llanllwyfo; TUDNO 6th century (see June 5); and GWRST (see December 1). Catrin Glyndŵr married Edmund Mortimer in 1402. Although de Grey and Clanvowe had been ransomed, the King had not allowed Mortimer to be ransomed, because of the legal right of the Mortimers to the English Crown; The *'Copper King'*, Thomas Williams, died in Anglesey in 1802 (see May 13); The philosopher Sir Henry Jones born in 1852, the son of a Llangernyw shoemaker (see February 4); Mary Harris (Mother) Jones died in 1930, aged 100; Death in 1958 of Thomas Henry Vile at Newport in 1958 (see September 6); Death in 1964 of Sir John Cecil-Williams (see October 14); The novelist Richard Llewellyn died in 1983

*'And after the mist, everywhere was light. And when they looked in the direction where they had seen flocks and herds and dwelling places, they now saw no living thing, no house, no animal, no smoke, no fire, no man, no inhabited dwelling, only the deserted rooms of the court, without man nor beast living in them: their companions too were lost, vanished without a sign, leaving the four alone. "Oh Lord God", said Manawyddan. "Where are our retainers? And the men that were with us? Let us try and find them." They came to the great hall and found no one. They searched the rooms and the sleeping quarters and found no one. In the mead cellar and in the kitchen they looked and found only desolation.'* - lines from the Mabinogion

*On this day...*

# DECEMBER - RHAGFYR
## Kerzu, Kerdu, Keverdu, (Black Month, Breton), Cevardhu (Cornish)

## December 1

FEAST DAYS OF SAINTS GWRST 6th century (- his fair was on November 30, later December 11 and 12) at Llanrwst; BISHOP TUDWAL 5th-6th century (also November 30, December 2, September 3) St Tudwal's Island, St Tugdual's cathedral in Treguier, Chartres, Laval – One of the Breton Founding Saints; and LLECHID (See 2); Holy Day of Nicholas Ferrar, deacon (1637). Catrin Glyndŵr and her daughters were buried in St Swithin's, London in 1413, four years after their capture at Harlech; In 1468 Dafydd ab Ifan ab Einion, who defended Harlech for the Lancastrian cause from 1460-1468, was pardoned; In 1737, the first lighthouse was erected on Flat Holm; Death of Robert Davies (Bardd Nantglyn), poet and grammarian in 1835; In 1860, 176 men and children were killed at Risca Colliery, in Gwent; Birth of Frederick Charles Richards, artist, in Newport in 1878 (see March 27); Wales lost the first rugby international with South Africa, at Swansea in 1906; Death in 1918 of the artist John Griffiths (see November 29); Miners returned to work in 1926 after a 7-month strike

*'Glorious the northern lights a-stream;*
*Glorious the song, when God's the theme;*
*Glorious the thunder's roar:*
*Glorious hosanna from the den;*
*Glorious the catholic amen;*
*Glorious the martyr's gore:'* - lines from 'A Song to David' by Christopher Smart (1722-1771)

*On this day...*

## December 2

FEAST DAY OF SAINTS LLECHID 6th century (also 1) at Llanllechid; TUDWAL (See 1); GWRST (See 1); and EDERN (see January 6). Dr Martha Carey Thomas died in 1935; Michael D. Jones, advocate of Patagonia to preserve Welsh culture and language, died at Llanuwchllyn in 1898; The Tottenham and Wales centre-half, Mike England was born at Prestatyn in 1941; In 1989, Janet Ackland of Llandough won the World Singles Bowls Championship in New Zealand; A survey published this day in 2001 affirmed that 50-60% of the people in the south-east of England and south of Scotland were of Celtic origins, not

Anglo-Saxon. The greatest density of Celts in the British Isles, the original Britons, was found in Wales, at 90%.

The New Temperance Hotel opened in Tredegar on this day in 1861, as temperance surged through the valleys. 7000 had signed the pledge not to drink alcohol in Tredegar in 1859, and that summer the Rhymney Brewery's receipts dropped by £500 a month, a tremendous sum. John Jones of Rhyl had written in a temperance magazine in 1840: *'None can hardly enter the churches without being teetotallers. Yea, some churches refuse all but such, and have they not lawful grounds to stand upon for doing so? Why? Because hundreds have been misled by these cursed drinks from their profession, and have backslided across the alcoholic half pints, and have been cast like Jonah, into the sea of intemperance, but teetotalism like the whale swallows them and casts them on dry ground; blessed by God for such a glorious cause. Hallelujah!'* However, in 1861, the Star of Gwent reported *'when the first wave of teetotalism was over... the working class, after most seriously alarming the publicans, returned to their cwrw (beer) and degraded habits.'* Waves of teetotalist fervour alternated with backsliding into 'bad habits', throughout the 19th century in Wales.

*On this day...*

..................................................................................................................................
..................................................................................................................................
..................................................................................................................................

# December 3
*FEAST DAY OF SAINTS* LLEURWG (see May 26); and GWYNEN (see 13). Burial of the missionary to the Khasi Hills Daniel Jones, and his daughter, at Cherrapoonjee, India, in 1846;  In 1919 there was a national conference for Welsh Home Rule held at Shrewsbury; Tracy Edwards' all-female crew in 'Maiden' landed at Fremantle in 1989, with the best stage result by a British yacht for 12 years; In 2001, the English Government gave permision for Sellafield to operate the MOX (mixed oxide) plant, which could discharge radioactive material into the Celtic Sea, despite the protests of the Irish Government. Sellafield is Britain's worst radioactive polluter, followed by Amersham Internatonal, situated in the City of Cardiff

*'A people called Welsh, so bold and ferocious that, when unarmed, they do not fear to encounter an armed force, being ready to shed their blood in defence of their country, and to sacrifice their lives for renown'* - from a letter from Henry II, c.1165, to the Eastern Holy Roman Emperor in Byzantium

*On this day...*

..................................................................................................................................
..................................................................................................................................
..................................................................................................................................

# December 4

*FEAST DAY OF SAINT* EMERITA 2nd century. In 1378, an entry in the Exchequer Rolls details the assassination of Owain Llawgoch at Mortagne-sur-Gironde, on the orders of the English Crown: *'To John Lambe, an esquire of Scotland, because he duly killed Owynn de Gales, a rebel and enemy of the King in France... by writ of Privy seal £20'*; In 1531 Sir Rhys ap Gruffydd was executed for treason; Birth at Swansea in 1802 of the artist, priest and pioneer photographer Richard Calvert Jones (see November 7); Death in 1849 of Gwallter Mechain (see July 15), book-collector and patriot, at Llanrhaeadr-ym-Mochnant; In 1875, 22 miners died at Old Pit, Tredegar

*'In the deep vale of Ewyas, which is shut in on all sides by a circle of lofty mountains and which is no more than three arrow-shots in width, there stands the abbey church of St John the Baptist. It is roofed in with sheets of lead and built of squared stones, which are admirably suited to the nature of the place... It is a site most suited to the practice of religion and better chosen for canonical discipline than that of any of the other monasteries in the whole Island of Britain'* - Giraldus Cambrensis, writing of Llantony Abbey in 1188

*On this day...*

.............................................................................................................

.............................................................................................................

.............................................................................................................

# December 5

*FEAST DAY OF SAINTS* CAWRDAF 6th century (also November 12) at Abererch, Llangoed under Llaniestin, Miskin; JUSTINIAN 6th century (also August 23) at Ramsey Island, Llanstinan, St Stinan; and GWRDAF (also November 12) at Llanwrda (possibly the same saint as Cawrdaf). The Abermenai ferry sank near Caernarfon in 1785, with 54 drowning; Griffith Davies, the actuary who gave a scientific basis to assurance, was born in 1788 at Llandwrog (see March 25); The Tal-y-Foel ferry near Caernarfon sank in 1820, with 25 drowning; In 1875, 12 miners died in Llan Colliery, Pentyrch; Jefferson Davis, Confederate leader, died in 1889 (see June 3)

*'There was a witenagemot (Saxon parliament) in London, and Aelfgar the eorl, Leofric the eorl's son, was outlawed without any kind of guilt; and he went then to Ireland, and there procured himself a fleet, which was of eighteen ships besides his own, and they went to Wales, to King Griffin (Gruffudd ap Llywelyn ap Seisyllt), with that force, and he received them into his protection. And then with the Irishmen, and with Welshmen, they gathered a great force; and Ranulf the eorl gathered a great force on the other hand at Herefordport. And they sought them out there; but before there was any spear thrown, the English people fled, because they were on horses; and there great slaughter was made, about four or five hundred, and they made none on the other side. And they then betook themselves to the town, and that they burned; and the great minster which*

*Aethalstan the venerable bishop had before caused to be built, they plundered and bereaved of relics, and of vestments, and of all things; and slew some people, and some they led away.'* - entry in the Anglo-Saxon Chronicle for 1055, although Welsh sources such as the Gwentian Chronicle place the raid on Hereford in 1060. In 1056, Gruffudd had atacked Hereford, killing Bishop Leofgar, and in 1058 had again invaded England, this time with a Norwegian force under Macht (Magnus), son of Harald. (see the quote for December 5)

*On this day...*

## December 6

*FEAST DAY OF BISHOP NICHOLAS 6th century* - a Turkish saint, favoured by the Normans, who is now associated with Christmas. Death in 1663 of the famous judge David Jenkins of Hensol, Pendeulwyn, who had been imprisoned by Parliamentarians until the Restoration; The death of the miners' leader and radical C.B. Stanton of Aberaman, in 1946; Dai Dower won the Empire Flyweight title in 1955; Alun Owen died in 1994, aged 69 (see November 24)

*'1060 - Caradoc ap Rhydderch ap Iestyn engaged Harold (Godwinson, and his brother Tostig) to bring an army into South Wales, and there he was joined by a large army of the men of Glamorgan and Gwent. They then went against Gruffudd (ap Llywelyn ap Seisyllt), who came to meet them with a large army of the men of Gwynedd, Powys and South Wales, and a great battle ensued, where Gruffudd was killed through the treachery of Madoc Min, Bishop of Bangor, the same who had previously caused, through treachery, the death of his father, Llywelyn ap Seisyllt.'* - the Anglo-Saxon Chronicle. This event actually happened on August 5, 1063, when Gruffudd, last King of the Britons, died.

*On this day...*

## December 7

*FEAST DAY OF SAINT* EDREN (See November 26). Death of Gruffudd ap Madog of Prince of Powys and Lord of Dinas Bran* Castle in 1270; The 1407 Anglo-French Truce left Wales under Glyndŵr out of the peace settlement, because of the assassination of the Duke of Orleans (see November 23); The composer Daniel Jones was born in 1912; David Lloyd George became Prime

Minister in 1916, at the height of the Great War; The opera singer Helen Watts was born at Milford Haven in 1928; Death of Griffith Evans in 1935 (see August 7); The broadcaster John Morgan died in 1988

*George Borrow translated a 17th century englyn by the bard Roger Cyffin as:
'Gone, gone are thy gates, Dinas Bran on the height!
Thy warders are blood-crows and ravens I trow;
Now no-one will wend from the field of the fight
To the fortress on high, save the raven and crow.'

*On this day...*

..................................................................................................................................

..................................................................................................................................

..................................................................................................................................

## December 8

FEAST DAY OF SAINTS BUDOC d. 600 (also December 9) at St Budeaux, Budoc, Steynton, Plourin; and CYNIDR 6th century (see April 4). David Lloyd George became the first Welshman since the 17th century to achieve a Cabinet office, becoming President of the Board of Trade in 1905

'Brains SA - some argue that the name SA derives from the initials of founder Samuel Arthur Brain; in fact, it originally stood for Special Ale. This beer is always known simply by its initials in its home city, where it is regarded with great affection and loyalty. It is sub-titled Best Bitter, and is enjoyed as an easy-drinking beer that nonetheless has plenty of satisfying flavours. Like many Welsh beers, it is accented towards maltiness. SA has a spicy aroma; a light, faintly almondy, crystal-malt character, soft on the tongue; and finishes with a late, dry, appetite-tickling fruitiness and hoppiness. Wales' national sport is intended to be evoked by the jersey-like quartered design (on its label). - from Michael Jackson's 'Great Beer Guide' of 500 international beers. It is also known as 'Skull Attack' to Glamorgan locals, and the author deeply regrets the brewery decision to stop selling SA in 2-pint flagons of natural (non-widgeted, non-nitrogenised) beer.

*On this day...*

..................................................................................................................................

..................................................................................................................................

..................................................................................................................................

## December 9

FEAST DAY OF SAINT BUDOC (see December 8). The writer-actress Dianan Morgan died in 1996, aged 86 (see May 29); The Welch Regiment marched into Jerusalem in 1917, the first Christian force there, since Saladin retook the city in 1187

*'Here is a chant of a primordial kind.*
*Who existed before darkness or light?*
*Where are the roots of the world?*
*On what day was Adam created?*
*... Common men do not receive knowledge.*
*Sorrowful is he who by evil deeds*
*Has lost the fellowship of heaven's country.*
*... Whence comes night and day?*
*Why is the eagle grey?*
*Why is night dark?*
*Why is the linnet green?*
*Why does the sea swell?*
*Why is this not known? ...'* Taliesin, 6th century

*On this day...*

## December 10

FEAST DAY OF SAINTS DEINIOL (see September 10); JOHN ROBERTS d. 1610 from Trawsfynydd – Hung, drawn and quartered in London; ALBAN ARTHAN, in some traditions the beginning of the Welsh New Year. Sir Hugh Middleton, who gave London its fresh water supplies, died in 1631; Death of fever in 1649 of Michael Jones, commander-in-chief of Ireland for Parliament; Death in 1674 of the noted judge Sir John Vaughan (see September 14); The trial of the Newport Chartists began in 1839 at Monmouth; In 1880, 101 men and children were killed at Penygraig Naval Colliery, Rhondda; Thomas Bevan, 'Caradawc y Fenni' (born September 13, 1802) Abergafenni eisteddfodwr, died in 1882

*'Anger makes dull men witty, but it keeps them poor.'* Queen Elizabeth I, 1533-1603

*On this day...*

## December 11

FEAST DAY OF SAINTS CIAN 7th century at Llangian; GWRST (see December 1) at Llanrwst; PERIS (see July 26); FFLEWYN (see 12); and CORENTIN (see November 2), a founder saint of Brittany. LLYWELYN II KILLED BY TREACHERY* - At Cilmeri or Aberedw, near Builth. The Welsh army was slaughtered in cold blood at nearby Llanganten Wells, 1282; Bridget Bevan died in 1779, and was buried near Grifith Jones at Llanddowror; In 1863, 12 miners died at Green Pit Colliery, Rhiwabon, Clwyd; Ronald Lewis, actor and film star, born in Port Talbot in 1928 (see January 25)

'*Mine now to curse the English who robbed me,
Mine now the need to bewail his death,
Mine now to speak hardly with God, who took him
And left me without him....
Fair head of Llywelyn, it shocks the world
That an iron pole has transfixed it now.
Head of my lord, dread pain afflicts me,
Head of my soul, a head without speech,
Head, once honoured in nine-hundred lands
And praised at nine-hundred feasts.
Head of a king whose hand bore iron,
Head of a king-hawk, breaching the battle-line,
Head of a king-like wolf in battle,
May the king of heaven care for him now!
A great lord, he had a host with him
Ready to travel to Brittany.
The true royal king of Aberffraw,
May the bright land of heaven now be his home.'
From 'The Elegy for Llywelyn ap Gruffydd', by Owain ab yr Ynad Goch, 1283

**On this day...**

.................................................................................................................
.................................................................................................................
.................................................................................................................

# December 12

*FEAST DAY OF SAINTS* FFLEWYN and GREDIFAEL 6th century (also 11) at Llanfflewyn, Whitland; FFINIAN c475-550 at Clonard, Llancarfan; and GWRST (see 1). Death in 1595 of Sir Roger Williams, soldier and author, buried in St Paul's Cathedral; The travel writer Thomas Pennant died at Whitford, near Holywell, in 1798; The first rugby international ever played in Wales was won by England in 1882 at Swansea; John James Osborne, the original 'angry young man' playwright, whose father was from Newport, was born in 1929; Construction began on Llyn Brianne dam in 1968

With Llywelyn's death, gone is my mind.
Heart frozen in the breast with terror,
Desire decays like dried-up branches.
See you not the rush of wind and rain?
See you not the oaks lash each other?

*See you not the ocean scourging the shore?*
*See you not the truth is portending?*
*See you not the sun hurtling the sky?*
*See you not that the stars have fallen?*
*Have you no belief in God, foolish men?*
*See you not that the world is ending?*
*Ah, God, that the sea would cover the land!*
*What is left us that we should linger?*
*No place to flee from terror's prison,*
*No place to live; wretched is living!*
*No counsel, no clasp, no path left open*
*One way to be freed from fear's sad strife.'*
- from Joseph Clancy's translation of 'The Elegy for Llywelyn ap Gruffudd',
c.1282-1293

**On this day...**

.................................................................................................................

.................................................................................................................

.................................................................................................................

# December 13

FEAST DAY OF SAINTS COLUMB 6th century at St Columb Major;
GWYNEN 6th century (also December 3) at Llanwnen; and GWYNAU &
GWYNWS 5th - 6th century at Llanwnws; MEMORIAL SERVICE FOR
LLYWELYN II - 'Ein Lliw Olaf' is commemorated in the Ruins of Abbey
Cwmhir; This was the date of the first arson attack on a holiday home, in 1979

*'My very dear and well-beloved John Greyndor, Hoel Vaughan, and all gentlemen of*
*Radnor and Presteigne. I greet you very much and make known to you that Owain*
*Glyndŵr has raised a quarrel of which the object is, if King Richard be alive, to restore*
*him to his crown; and if not that, my honoured nephew, who is the right heir to the said*
*crown shall be king of England, and that the said Owain will assert his right in Wales.*
*And I, seeing and considering that the said quarrel is good and reasonable, have*
*consented to join in it, and to aid and maintain it, and by the grace of God to a good*
*end, Amen. I ardently hope and from my heart that you will support and enable me to*
*bring this struggle of mine to a successful issue.'* - Letter on this day in 1402, written
from Maelienydd by Edmund Mortimer, fighting for Glyndŵr, to his estate
manager, hoping that Richard II had not yet been murdered by Henry IV

**On this day...**

.................................................................................................................

.................................................................................................................

.................................................................................................................

## December 14

Probable death date of John Dee, Elizabeth I's advisor, polymath, and 'the magus of his age', in 1608; Birth at Swansea of Griffith John, missionary in China, in 1831 (see July 25); In 1850, 13 miners died at New Duffryn Colliery, Mountain Ash; Birth in 1863 of Margaret Sidney Davies, art collector and social benefactress (see March 13); Myrna Loy (née Williams) died in 1993

*'Inundation, n. A flood. The greatest inundation of which we have any account was the Noachian deluge described by Moses, Berosus and an Assyrian chronicler translated by the late Mr George Smith. Inundations are caused variously, but this one was due to a long spell of wet weather - forty days and forty nights, Moses says. So much water fell in that period that it covered every mountain on the earth, some of which - the highest being near where Noah lived - have an elevation above sea-level of 30,000 feet. Our heaviest rains are in the region of about 6 inches in 24 hours - a fall of two weeks would strangle one who should attempt to walk abroad in it. But Noah's rain fell at the rate of 750 feet per 24 hours, or 31 and a half feet an hour. It was quite a rain.'* - Ambrose Gwinnett Bierce, 'The Devil's Dictionary, 1911

*On this day...*

## December 15

*FEAST DAY OF SAINT TANGWN* 6th century at Llangoed. Birth in 1533 at Llangadwaladr of Lewis Owen, who became a confidante of the Pope and Bishop of Cassano; Death in 1560 of Sir Thomas Parry, Elizabeth I's advisor; Death of John Dyer, poet, in 1757 (see October 28); Birth in Cardiff of 'Gentleman' Jim Driscoll, boxer (see January 30); Arthur Machen died, aged 84, in 1947 (see March 3); The sculptor Goscombe John died in 1952 (see February 21); The actor Ray Smith died in Llandough Hospital of meningitis in 1991, aged just 55 (see May 1); Port Talbot's Rob Brydon won the 'best TV Comedy Actor award in 2001, following his 'best newcomer' award in 2000

*'Surely, fair gull on the tide,*
*Of the same colour as snow or the white moon,*
*Your beauty is unspotted,*
*A fragment like sun, gauntlet of the salt sea.*
*Light you are on the ocean wave,*
*Swift, proud, fish-eating bird.*
*There you'd go at anchor,*
*Hand in hand with me, sea lily.*
*Fashioned like writing paper shining in nature,*

*A nun atop the sea-tide are you'*
Lines from 'The Seagull' by Dafydd ap Gwilym (c.1320-80) trans. R.M. Loomis

*On this day...*

.................................................................................................................
.................................................................................................................
.................................................................................................................

## December 16

*FEAST DAY OF SAINTS* ISAN 6th century at Llanishen, Rhoose?; and AFAN (see November 16). In 1326 Edward II was captured at Penrhys Chapel in the Rhondda, and taken to be murdered at Berkeley Castle, despite the efforts of Rhys ap Gruffydd to free him; *'The Sons of Liberty'*, led by Samuel Adams, staged the Boston Tea Party and started the American Revolution in 1773; The travel-writer and naturalist Thomas Pennant died at Whitford, Holywell in 1798 (see June 14); Wales beat the undefeated All-Blacks in 1905; Rhymney Breweries with 730 pubs merged with Ely Breweries with 260 pubs on this day in 1959. After takeover by Whitbread, from 1969 the breweries and brands vanished; In 1987 Michael Heseltine spearheaded the revolt in the House of Commons against Poll Tax, saying that it would forever be known as 'The Tory Tax' - *'It would mean more tax collectors and more evasion, and more evasion would mean more resentment, and all would be built on a platform of crude regression which sought to make equal in the eyes of the tax collector the rich and the poor, the slum dweller and the landed aristocrat.'* Over 2,000,000 people quickly 'vanished' from tbe electoral rolls.

Spending upon 'defence' costs the United Kingdom £500 for each member of its population every year. Over the next few years, the English government is spending on its 200,000 soldiers, sailors and airmen the following, which no politician has queried: Armoured vehicles for the marines £60million; Unmanned aerial vehicles £230million; Air-to-air missiles £1.6billion; Helicopters £2billion; Nuclear submarine conversions £3billion; Transport aircraft £4billion; Frigates £4.5billion; Two aircraft-carriers £9.7billion; Eurofighters £15billion etc., etc. Of course, it is 100% certain that all these estimates will go massively over budget. At the same time the author's 82 year-old father languishes for years on a hospital waiting list while the Westminster state machine spends his 50 years of tax contributions (he left school at 14) upon war. If the country halved its defence spending, each family of 4 people would have an extra £1000 to spend each year, or the UK would have schools and hospitals to rival those in countries which spend their finances more wisely. If just a fraction of the £1500 billion (equivalent) 'defence' spending since World War II had been diverted into the UK infrastructure, many of today's social problems could have been ameliorated.

## December 17

FEAST DAY OF SAINTS BRIAC d. 570 at Bourbriac; TYDECHO 6th century at Llanymawddwy, Garthbeibio, Cemaes; and SANNAN (see March 1); SATURNALIA This Roman Feast of 7 days was the precursor of Christmas, and slaves became master for the day. *Saturn was the god of vegetation and crops, which explains the need for greenery in Christmas tree decorations. It was also the time of giving gifts.* Death in 1636 of John Jones of Llanfrynach (Leander), scholar, linguist and first President-General of the English Benedictines; Birth of Sir Guildhaume Myrddin Evans KCMG in 1894 at Aberystruth, Monmouthshire, who became President of the International Labour Organisation (see February 15); Death in 1869 of Sarah Jacob of Llanfihangel Iorath, 'the fasting girl', aged 12 (see May 12); Death in 1905 of Robert Jones Derfel (see July 24); Death in 1915 of Sir John Rhys (see June 21); A public meeting in 1956 in Liverpool approved the flooding of Trywerin - as its water is no longer required by Liverpool's vanished factories, a politician could make a case for its reinstatement as a historic valley and National Park; The Royal Mint at Llantrisant opened in 1968; Eynon Hawkins (born June 27, 1920) died in 2001. He was a miner and professional rugby league player from Llanharan, who won the Albert (now the George) Cross saving his fellow sailors when the British Dominion was sunk on January 10, 1943

A 2001 letter to the Western Mail entitled 'Heroic Past' from Adrien Jones of Cymdeithas Owain Glyndŵr reads *'May I congratulate you for the excellent series on famous Welsh heroes which has taught so many readers who had never known of them, a poor reflection on the education policies of our schools which preferred to induct their chidren with English history rather than their own? Is it any wonder we are often so apathetic to our past and lacking pride in the nation's achievements when our children are denied their inheritance? It is through examination of our predecessors' history that we learn from it, for it follows that fine words are followed by fine deeds. The ideas and knowledge we have inherited from the past have a tremendous influence on our thinking, whether we acknowledge it or not, and so by ignoring it we have a long way to go in meeting the standards and conception of our nation that so many other nations take for granted. The greatest Welshman was perhaps Owain Glyndŵr, ignored by history which was happy to leave his memory fade away, though his efforts saved the nation and gave it our identity. Which other nation would allow such a man to disappear into oblivion, unmarked, unremembered for his achievements, like his resting place forgotten?'* (Note: this author spent five years lobbying the Western Mail and varous media companies to run a series on Welsh heroes and achievements, and has just published G.J. Brough's 'Glyn Dwr's War - The Campaigns of the Last Prince of Wales.')

..................................................................................................................................

..................................................................................................................................

..................................................................................................................................

# December 18

FEAST DAY OF SAINTS TEGFEDD ferch AMWN DDU 6th century at Llanymawddwy, Garthbeibio; and MUINIS 5th century at Ardagh; THE CELTIC FEAST OF EPONA - The Celtic goddess of Horses. Around this time in 1401, Owain Glyndŵr's emissary (Dafydd ap Ieuan Goch) to Robert II of Scotland was captured and beheaded - '*A certain knight called Sir David ap Jevan Goz, of the County of Cardigan, who for full twenty years had fought against the Saracens with the King of Cyprus and other Christians, being sent by the King of France to the King of Scotland on Owen's behalf, was taken captive by English sailors and imprisoned in the Tower of London*' - Adam of Usk; Vavasor Powell denounced Cromwell in 1653, and three days later was arrested; In 1790, 110 people drowned when the 'Clermont' was wrecked off Holyhead; David Davies (Dai Top Sawyer, Davies the Ocean), industrialist and founder of Barri Docks, was born at Llandinam in 1818; Iolo Morganwg died at Trefflemin (Flemingston) in 1826 (see March 10); In 1843, the tramp-scholar and linguist Dic Aberdaron died at St Asaf; In 1876, 20 miners died at South Wales Pit, Abertillery; Death in 1962 of Sir Robert Webber (see November 14); Bobby Jones, Welsh-American golfer, died in 1971

Wales presently has 4% of the UK population and 46% of its wind turbines, all onshore, in the remaining beautiful areas which have not been compulsorily taken by the military, English water authorities or the Pine Forestry Commission. Cader Idris, our second largest mountain, could be despoiled forever. The proposal is for for 39 more huge turbines to be built at Cefn Croes, yet 56 wind stations of this capacity will be needed to replace the polluting nuclear dinosaur at Wylfa Head. A letter in the Western Mail on this day in 2001, from Gerald M. Edwards of Taffs Well, should be absorbed by all Welsh people: '*Sir, I feel totally helpless (Of course that is exactly what I am). Mr Williams, the UK Energy Minister, said this is a new age for Wales as a global leader in wind generation. We are used to listening to foolish statements from government ministers. I am not sure whether Mr Wilson is trying to hoodwink us or is just not up to his job. He should visit California. South of Los Angeles, he will find an immense windfarm (or ranch?) with thousands of turbines. So how is Wales a global leader?*

*Mr Wilson's excuse for making public statements appears to be based on ignorance. He tells us Wales is blessed with wind. Some blessing if Wales is to be burdened with many more windfarms. Strikes me as a curse. We have an Environment Minister, Sue Essex, who I gather is delighted at the prospect of having the biggest windfarm in the UK being sited in beautiful, wild countryside and visble for miles. I assume Sue Essex thinks that the environment is somewhere else. Perhaps the environment is not actually in Wales.*

*Many hillside coal tips in the Valleys have been removed but many remain. Now the replacement scars, windfarms, are starting to shoot up like weeds, providing a relatively tiny amount of electricity, whatever their claims. The turbines will be more obtrusive in the countryside than coal tips over the whole of Wales. Anyone travelling on the M4 can see the windfarm near Gilfach Goch for mile after mile and that is what is destined for the whole of Wales if the lunacy is not halted. My plea is to await sea technology, which will be far more effective than wid power and would not result in the ruination of the countryside and tourism.'*

**On this day...**

.......................................................................................................................

.......................................................................................................................

.......................................................................................................................

## December 19
FEAST DAY OF RHYSTUD 6th century at Llanrhystud (held on the Tuesday before Christmas). Edward I was in Conwy in 1294, to try to subdue the revolt of Madog ap Llywelyn, son of the last Lord of Meirionydd; In 1902, judgement was awarded for the Taff Vale Railway Company against the union, the Amalgamated Society of Railway Servants; Elizabeth Phillips Hughes, educationist, died in 1925; Wales beat the All-Blacks in 1953, thanks to a cross-kick by Clem Thomas to Ken Jones; Dr Richard Tecwyn Williams died in 1979 (see February 20); The actor Desmond Llewelyn was killed in a car-crash in 1999, aged 85 (see September 12); In 2001, Kylie Minogue was voted the star most men would like to kiss at Christmas, with 26% of the vote. Leading the equivalent male poll was Robbie Williams, who took his stage-name from his mother Teresa Jeannette Williams, with 28%

'*Tri anhyborth serchog - nos fer lawiog, drws gwichiedig, a gwraig anhunog ymgeinar*' - old Welsh proverb - 'The three restraints of love - a short, rainy night, a squeaking door and a sleepless, bickering woman.'

**On this day...**

.......................................................................................................................

.......................................................................................................................

.......................................................................................................................

## December 20
David Griffiths, missionary in Madagascar, born near Gwynfe in 1792 (see March 21); In 1843 Francis Elizabeth Hoggan (nee Morgan), physician pioneer, was born in Brecon; In 1865, 34 miners died at Upper Gethin Colliery, Mertyr

Tydful; Jim Driscoll lost to Freddie Welsh at the American Roller Rink in 1910, on Cardiff's Westgate Street, and near-riots ensued; The Conservative politician Geoffrey Howe, who rebelled against Mrs Thatcher (as did the Swansea-born Michael Heseltine), was born in Port Talbot in 1926; In 1947, nine Cardiff players, including all 7 backs, were in the Welsh team that beat Australia; In 1955, Cardiff was officially recognised as the Capital of Wales, making it Europe's youngest capital city; Tony Lewis of Glamorgan became the first Welshman to captain England in a cricket test match in India in 1972; In 2001 a letter in the Western Mail from Conrad Bryant noted *'which other nation would allow a man such as Owain Glyndŵr to disappear into oblivion, unmarked and unremembered for his achievements? Answer: only another conquered and still occupied country; only a country prevented from having the right to rule itself. Fine words are spoken in London about giving freedom to countries all over the world but our Wales is never included.'*

*'Britain – Europe's success story according to its politicians.... The most successful nation in terms of proportion of the population in prison, highest divorce rate, most violent crime, highest number of thefts and burglaries, among the lowest wealth per head, the most expensive shopping items, the highest density of freemasons in high places, most teenage pregnancies, most drug-taking, the fewest church-goers, the worst quality of life, the highest death rates from heart disease and cancer, the greatest amount of dog excrement on pavements and playing fields, the worst litter, the worst and most expensive railway services, the most unmarried mothers, the worst balance of payments deficits, the highest proportion of its industry owned by foreign companies, the highest taxed population who work the longest hours and have the least rights in Europe, and the country with the highest proportionate spend on the armed forces and the war industries – is a septic isle, where all of the people are fooled all of the time'* - from the forthcoming book 'Forget the Future - the Ovinification of the Masses'

*On this day...*

.......................................................................................................................................
.......................................................................................................................................
.......................................................................................................................................

# December 21

FEAST DAY OF SAINTS THOMAS 1st century; and GWYNIN (see December 31); IN THE CELTIC CALENDAR, THE LONGEST NIGHT. The great Welsh warrior and dynasty-maker of the Wars of the Roses, Jasper Tudor, died in 1495; Birth in 1834 at Trecynon of Griffith Rhys Jones (Caradog), the conductor of the massed male voice choir 'Cor Caradog'; Michael D. Jones died in 1899; Birth in 1921 at Llanafan Fawr of Henry Thomas (Harri) Jones, lecturer and poet (see January 30); Wales beat New Zealand in 1935; Richey Edwards' last appearance for The Manic Street Preachers, at the London Astoria in 1994 (see December 22)

Unpublished letter sent this day to The Western Mail by the author: *'Dear Sir, In the remote expectation that one of our Assembly Members in the Cardiff Bay Parish*

Council may be interested, I am deeply, deeply concerned about the impact of more wind farms on the Welsh landscape, as recounted in recent letters to you. I write and publish books on Wales, and am appalled at the lack of industrial and cultural direction that the Assembly gives our land. Wales has 4% of the UK population, 8% of its area, and 46% of its windfarms and rising. We have been despoiled for our coal and iron - all have just about been stripped out, leaving us with a legacy of the worst housing in the UK. We have the poorest wealth per person in the British Isles, still dropping like a stone, with no prospects for our children here, and no native industry except tourism. Forget the Western Mail Top 100 Welsh Companies - Welsh people own none of them. Our health statistics are among the worst in Europe, and we are in the bottom tenth on all social indicators.

Our country has been taken over statutorily by English water authorities, whose customers pay less than the Welsh people for water, and by the Pine Forestry Commission, which owns and blights over 6% of the Welsh countryside. Our farmers, the custodians of the remaining landscape, cannot survive, and their farms are being sold as holiday homes. Our language is under threat from richer retirees from England and from social dumping of problem families, in our most beautiful areas. If any person dares to speak about the decline of culture or language on these grounds, he is hounded by the English-owned media and their politician-allies, who depend on the media for favourable reviews. I am not a Welsh-speaker, nor allied to any political party.

However, the real reason for this letter is the final straw in Welsh 'planning'. I returned to Wales to live five years ago, back to an area which Stan Awbery MP wished designated as a National Park. Now the Vale of Glamorgan has Llandow Airport (a sprawling ugly mass of a factory estate, causing major traffic problems); Rhoose Airport, which started off as an RAF Fighter Station, and which has the ugliest building in Europe on its perimeter, the BA Repair Building, visible for miles and miles instead of being built in a dip; and RAF St Tathan. Houses were wrongly purchased at Nurston for expansion of DARA St Tathan, but land and houses are now being purchased all around St Tathan for a huge new runway, despite residents' fears. A massive new hangar is to be built, to take AWACS planes. The MOD already owns about 54000 acres of Welsh land.

Of even greater concern is that the politicians are bringing a regiment of infantry to the base. Let us consider the cost-effectiveness of this proposal. 700 soldiers = 2500 people including wives and families = at least 700 cars extra in our leafy lanes. The lanes are already used as rat-runs by the workers at DARA, the Aberthaw cement works and of one of Britain's greatest polluters, Aberthaw Power Station, itself built on an area of outstanding natural beauty that I remember as a child. Will these soldiers pay £2.10 a pint for Guinness locally, or 75 pence in the NAAFI? Will there be social infrastructural problems? Llanilltud Fawr has already been altered from perhaps the oldest university town in the world to a sprawling mass of boxes. Where will these people live? The RAF box-houses were sold of to the Japanese firm Nomura Securities, who sold them privately through its Annington Homes subsidiary, back to the British people who had paid for them in the first place. Eglwys Brewys and Sain Tathan are surrounded by ex-RAF houses, and the medieval church of Eglwys Brewys is totally within the secure RAF compound.

So then, Rhodri Morgan, is this your bright future for Wales? A dumping ground for the military? A place where the best and brightest are forced to leave? A pine forestry commission plantation with reservoirs and windfarms and army and airforce bases? Have you read about Trywerin, Clywedog, Epynt, Penyberth, Brecon and Pembrokeshire? Do you want to be associated with the military despoliation of the Vale of Glamorgan - Cardiff's lung, where we have otters, kingfishers, peregrine falcons and herons hanging on? Do you have any powers except to say 'yes' to a scheme which will save the English Army £40 million a year? What does Wales get out of it? A new target for terrorist attacks? Income or job prospects? Please use Eire as a template for what Wales can achieve, not Northern Ireland.

Incidentally, it seems that AM's and MP's have no interest outside Cardiff. As a Barri boy, why has its Town Hall lain empty for 18 years? Why was the fabulous Carnegie Library, responsible for my going to university, allowed to rot? Why were the files shredded, relating to the gift by the Earl of Plymouth in perpetuity to the people of Barri, of Nell's Point? On Nell's Point Butlins built over St Baruc's 6th century holy well; the 'Roman Well' at Barri Island has been built upon; the monastery site will be built upon, and the new housing development on Nell's Point is the only promontory private development in Britain. Look outside Cardiff at what goes on in Wales. There is more to Wales than the glittering streets of the capital - the rest of it is rotting, not gently but quickly, and it is not being helped by its politicians. The increasing apathy of the electorate towards voting is because in Wales we see no difference between the parties. We see either inaction, or action that we disagree with, with no-one to represent the Welsh people's interest.' - (December 21, 2001).

**On this day...**

# December 22

Execution of William Davis of Wrexham in 1690, 'the Golden Farmer', highwayman, hung in chains at Bagshot Heath; Dai'r Cantŵr sentenced to 20 years transportation to Tasmania in 1843 for demolishing Spudder's Bridge turnpike gate near Cydweli; George Eliot (Mary Ann Evans) died in 1880; The Vale of Rheidol Railway opened in 1902; Richard James Edwards (Richey) of the Manic Street Preachers was born in 1967 (see February 1, December 21)

George Borrow, in his 1862 'Wild Wales', wrote before arriving at Wrexham, after talking to a Cheshire man: "A genuine Saxon," said I; "I dare say just like many of those who, under Hengist, subdued the plains of Lloegr (England) and Britain. Taliesin called the Saxon race the Coiling Serpent. He had better have called it the Big Bull. He was a noble poet, however; what wonderful lines, upon the whole, are those in his prophect, in which he speaks of the Saxons and of the results of their struggle; A serpent which coils,

And with fury boils,
From Germany coming with armed wings spread,
Shall subdue and shall enthrall
The broad Britain all,
From the Lochlin Ocean to the Severn's bed.
And British men
Shall be captives then
To strangers from Saxonia's strand;
They shall praise their God, and hold
Their language as of old,
But except wild Wales they shall lose their land. (See December 2)

**On this day...**

## December 23
FEAST DAY OF SAINT JUTHWARA 5th - 6th century (also July 1, 3, 17 and 18), January 6 and November 28, at Lanteglos, Guizeny, Halstock; In 1885, an explosion at Maerdy killed 81 miners

"And Urien, Lord of Erechwydd, shouted,
"If they would meet us now for a treaty,
High on the hilltop let's raise our ramparts,
Carry our faces over the shield rims,
Raise up our spears, men, over our heads
And set upon Fflamddwyn in the midst of his hosts
And slaughter him, ay, and all that go with him!"
There was many a corpse beside Argoed Llwyfain;
From warriors ravens grew red
And with their leader a host attacked.
For a whole year I shall sing to their triumph.'
- From Taliesin's 'Gwaith Argoed Llwyfain' (The Battle of Argoed Llwyfain) of around 580, when Urien and his sons met Deodric of Bernicia (Fflamddwyn, the 'Flamebearer') and defeated his armies.

**On this day...**

# December 24

CHRISTMAS EVE. In 1659, Walter Cradock, the Puritan theologian, died in Trefela, Llangwm, Monmouth; Birth in 1891 at Treherbert of Percy Jones, World Flywight Champion boxer (see January 26 and December 25); Carole Vorderman, TV personality, born in Denbigh in 1960, and brought up in Prestatyn; Death at Aberystwyth in 1968 of Gwenallt* (David James Jones), the superb poet

*'The earth was once so near
As near as a neighbour, and it spoke the dialects of Welsh...
In the inaccesible fastness of the mountains,
We built a lodging place for angels between two worlds.
The earth has been turned into a giant laboratory...
No longer does it speak the homely tongue of man.
Pylons now where angels were,
And concrete damming up the stream.'
- lines from Gwenallt's 'Y Ddaear' (The Earth) from 'Y Coed' (The Wood), 1969

*On this day...*

.....................................................................................................................................
.....................................................................................................................................
.....................................................................................................................................

# December 25

CHRISTMAS QUARTERDAY, NADOLIG *(Nedelic in Breton, and Nadelic in Cornish)* Christmas Evans, the famous Baptist preacher, was born near Llandysul in 1766 (see July 19); Richard 'Berwyn' Jones (born Glyndyfrdwy 1863), Patagonian pioneer and publisher of the colony's first book, died in 1917; Death in 1922 of the great boxer Percy Jones, badly injured and crippled in the Great War (see December 14)

'Very hard frost last night. At Presteigne the thermometer fell to 2 degrees, showing 30 degrees of frost. At Monnington it fell to 4. Last night is said to have been the coldest night for 100 years. The windows of the house and Church were so thick with frost rime that we could not see out. We could not look through the church windows all day. Snow lay on the ground and the day was dark and gloomy with a murky sky.... Immediately after dinner I had to go back to the church, for the funeral of little Davie of the Old Weston who died on Monday, was fixed for 2.30. The weather was dreadful, the snow driving in blinding clouds and the walking tiresome... The snow fell thickly all through the funeral service... The poor father, David Davies the shepherd, was crying bitterly for the loss of his little lamb. Owing to the funeral, it was rather late before we began the afternoon service. There were very few people in the church besides the mourners. The afternoon was very dark. I was obliged to move close to the great south window to read the lessons and could hardly see even then. I preached from Luke ii.7, "There was no room for them at the inn", and connected the little bed in the churchyard in which we *had laid Davie with the manger cradle at Bethlehem.'* - Kilvert's Diary, Christmas Day 1878

**On this day...**

..............................................................................................................................
...... ... ..............................................................................................................
..............................................................................................................................

### December 26

*FEAST DAY OF SAINTS* MAETHLU 6th century at Llandyfalle; TATHAN (See 30); GWYNNO (see October 26); and TYBIE (see January 30); *BOXING DAY, ST STEPHEN'S DAY* - Traditionally when church alms boxes were opened and distributed to the local poor. In 1800 Mary Darby Robinson (Perdita) died; Birth at Buttington near Welshpool of the antiquary and geologist Sir William Boyd Dawkins (see January 15); In 1838 Julia Ann Hatton (Ann of Swansea) died; Sir Owen Morgan Edwards, man of letters and MP, was born at Llanuwchllyn in 1858 (see May 15); In 1863, 14 miners died at the Gin Pit Colliery, Maesteg; The Gwyn Nicholls Memorial Gates were placed at the Arms Park in 1948; In 1953 Lyn Harding, the great Welsh film actor died aged 85 (see October 12); Death in 1963 of the tenor William John Parry Jones (see February 14);

'*A friend in power is a friend lost*' – Henry Adams 1838-1918

**On this day...**

..............................................................................................................................
..............................................................................................................................
..............................................................................................................................

### December 27

*ST JOHN THE EVANGELIST 1st century.* Dolly of Pentreath, the last Cornish speaker, was buried in Paul, Cornwall in 1777; The Gregynog Press begain printing in 1922; John Charles, '*il gigante buono*', football star, born in 1931at Swansea. He is still remembered as one of Juventus' finest ever players, and was Italy's first footballer of the year to come from outside the country; The wonderful cave systems at Dan-yr-Ogof were rediscovered in 1953; The death in 1987 of Anna Williams, at Swansea, aged 114 - Wales' longest-living woman

'*Having satisfied himself with the architectural treasures which had been available to him, he returned to admire the landscape. From Llanthony Abbey he crossed the Black Mountains and went to Pont Nedd Fechan and visited the Porth yr Ogof Caverns. He found, however, that there were several small farmers extorting money from travellers to pass over their land. He wrote: "One of them had the conscience to demand 2s. 6d.*

*from Sir John Guest for the passage of himself and Lady Charlotte. I gave 1penny 1 halfpenny objecting to give more than I might have to pay for one horse at a common turnpike." Having paid, however, a further demand was made upon him when he came to a locked gate. This demand was also for a silver coin but he objected and only gave a penny - which did allow him access. Parker, like all travellers to the area was intrigued by the Fall of the Hepste. His servant Evan rode his horse through the river near the falls while he walked underneath with his guide. He found himself on the other side "with hardly a trace of spray upon my clothes or shoes, or any sign that I had been under water". His fascination was such that he sent the guide back so that Evan could share the same experience.'* - from Edgar Parry's editied version of John Parker's 'Tour of Wales and its Churches', first published in 1862

**On this day...**

## December 28

*THE FEAST DAY OF ST AUSTELL in Cornwall, when it was unlucky to wash clothes. CHILDERMAS DAY, HOLY INNOCENTS DAY* - When Herod killed the children of Bethlehem. This was known in Wales as *GWYL Y FIL FEIBION, the Festival of 1000 Sons.* Aberystwyth was granted its charter in 1277; William Latham Bevan, who held the living of Hay-on-Wye for 56 years, was born in 1821; Birth in 1846 at Llangynwyd of Thomas Christopher Evans (Cadrawd), antiquary and folklorist (see July 24); In 1900, 32 drowned when the Primrose Hill sank off Holyhead; In 1908, Cardiff beat the first Australian rugby touring team (Cardiff have played Australia six times, and have a 100% winning record); 'The Fed', the South Wales Miners' Federation, met for the last time in 1944; The Archdruid John Dyfnallt Owen died in Newport in 1956 (see April 7)

*"The Welsh are very sharp and intelligent. When they apply their minds to anything, they are quick to make progress, for they have great natural ability. They are quicker-witted and more shrewd than any other Western people. When they play their instruments they charm and delight the ear with the sweetness of their music. They play quickly and in subtle harmony. Their fingertips are so rapid that they produce this harmony out of discord... they play three instruments, the harp, the pipe and the crwth (fiddle).'* - Giraldus Cambrensis, 'The Description of Wales', 1193/1194

**On this day...**

# December 29

Cardigan Castle was captured by Rowland Laugharne's Parliamentarians in 1646; Birth in 1782 of Sir William Lloyd, soldier in India and Himalaya climbing pioneer (see May 16); Death of Robert Davies, eccentric and recluse, who gave away over £500,000, at Bodlondeb in 1905 (see April 1); The writer Eluned Morgan died in Patagonia in 1938; Merched y Wawr, the Welsh-speaking womens' movement was founded in 1968

*'The concept of a tax shift is that Western governments tacitly collude with the multinationals which control their economies, in order to move the tax burden off companies and transpose it to employees, while simultaneously reducing employee rights and company welfare provisions - on the state side, the lack of means to tax multinationals means that a decent standard of social welfare, education, pensions and health provision has to now be paid for by the individual. No European politician will say that people are being taxed instead of companies, and that this situation is irreversible.'* - T.D. Breverton, conference papers in Charleston 1995 and Seattle 1996

*On this day...*

...................................................................................................................

...................................................................................................................

...................................................................................................................

# December 30

*FEAST DAY OF SAINT TATHAN* 5th-6th century (also December 26) at Caerwent, St. Tathan and Advent. Evan Herber Evans died in 1896 (see July 5); John George Boots of Aberbeeg (born July 2, 1874), Newport and Wales rugby forward, died in 1928. Known as 'the Peter Pan of Rugby Football', he played first-class rugby for 30 seasons, 27 with Newport; Death in 1989 of Madoline Thomas aged 99 - she had last acted aged 97 (see January 2); The Welsh rugby wing and athletics champion, Ken Jones, was born in Blaenavon in 1921

*'Three things which must wait long before they are attained:*
*Honesty from covetousness,*
*Wisdom from pride, and*
*Wealth from sloth.'* - from the Welsh Triads of Virtues

*On this day...*

...................................................................................................................

...................................................................................................................

...................................................................................................................

## December 31

FEAST DAY OF SAINTS GWYNIN 7th century (also January 21, 31) at Llangwynin, Dwygyfylchi; and MAELOG (see November 13): THE CELTIC FEAST OF OIMELC - The 'Winter Hag', the goddess Cailleach, sends a dragon to kill the lamb of Ffraid of Spring. The lamb always wins. The true origin of the New Year's Eve festivities; THE MARI LLWYD is seen at Llangynwyd, Glamorgan. The 'Grey Mare' is the horse's skull taken round by a party of singers, the Welsh form of 'Wassail'. Death in 1714 of the lead industry industralist John Wynne of Copa'rleni (Trelawnyd, Newmarket); Birth in 1881 of George Henry Hall, 1st Viscount Hall of Cynon Valley at Penrhiwceiber, miner and MP (see November 8); Death in New York of Francis Lewis in 1802 (see March 21); Anthony Hopkins, actor, born in 1937 at Port Talbot; The first Nos Galan races began at Mountain Ash in 1958

| | |
|---|---|
| Y deryn pur ar adain las | The pure bird on a black-blue wing |
| Bydd I'mi'n was di brydar | Be my servant, free from care |
| O brysur brysia at y ferch | Oh hurry to the maiden |
| Lle rhois I'm serch yn gynnar. | That I loved so early; |
| Dos di ati, dywedd wrthi | Go and tell her |
| 'Mod I'n wylo dwr yr heli | That I weep salt water; |
| 'Mod I'n irad am ei gwelad | That I long so to see her, |
| Ac o'l chariad yn ffaelu a cherddad | And because of love for her, cannot walk |
| O Duw faddeuo'r hardd ei llun | Oh God forgive the beautiful |
| Am boeni dyn mor galad | For giving man such pain |

- the first verse of the beautiful traditional air, 'Y Deryn Pur', with words by the 18th century poet Dafydd Nicholas

**On this day...**

..................................................................................................

..................................................................................................

..................................................................................................

*City Hall, Cardiff - Martin S. Green*

*Cardiff Castle from Bute Park  - Wales Tourist Board Photo Library*

*Cardiff Castle - Cardiff Marketing*

*Cardiff Castle - Cardiff Marketing*

*Caerphilly Castle - Martin S. Green*

*Caerphilly Castle - Martin S. Green*

*Llancaiach Fawr, Gelligaer - Wales Tourist Board Photo Library*

*Castell Coch - Martin S. Green*

*Celtic Cross, Carew - Wales Tourist Board Photo Library*

*Dylan Thomas' Boathouse, Laugharne - Wales Tourist Board Photo Library*

*Plas Mawr, Conwy - Wales Tourist Board Photo Library*

*St. David's Cathedral - Wales Tourist Board Photo Library*

*Caernarfon Castle - Wales Tourist Board Photo Library*

*Llanthony Priory - Cathy Crompton*

*Llynnau Mymbyr, Snowdon in background - Cathy Crompton*

*St. Athan Church - Cathy Crompton*

*Gileston Church - Cathy Crompton*

*Trefflemin*

*'Winter Floods' (Flemingston Moors)*

*Llangeinor Church - Cathy Crompton*

*Roath Park Lake - Martin S. Green*

*Llanthony Priory - Cathy Crompton*

*Eisteddfod Ynys Môn - Martin S. Green*

*Eisteddfod Ynys Môn - Martin S. Green*

# AFTERWORD

The following excerpts are from 'A Country of Memorable Honour', published in 1953, by the Canadian Thomas Firbank, who wrote the classic 'I Bought a Mountain' (1940). Firbank bought a sheep farm in Snowdonia in 1931, and came to know the Welsh psyche as an outsider who came to love Wales. After distinguished war service, written as 'I Bought a Star', he intended 'A Country of Memorable Honour' to be a guide *'towards an understanding of the Welsh people, whose generic name of "British" has become the title of a world-wide Commonwealth ... Wales is a small country moated on three sides by sea, and walled on the fourth by mountains. Within its boundaries survive the Cymry, the Compatriots, the British Brotherhood. These British, named Welsh, or Foreigners, in the Anglo-Saxon tongue, are the most remarkable of the many monuments to history which remain in that small but storied land. They have preserved their race through two millenniums against the destructive power of alien storms.'*

Firbank's concluding paragraphs should be read by all who settle in Wales, and by those who represent its people in councils, the Assembly at Cardiff Bay and in the Houses of Parliament.

*'On my personal business in the country the estate agent took me to the top of a low hill to see a view of a district pertaining to our private dealings. Behind, over my right shoulder, was the moat of the Bristol Channel; in front was open, rolling country; but to the left, and stretching northward into a haze, was the mountain rampart of Wales. The agent must have thought me dense and uncommunicative. My mind was not on his discussions, but dwelt beyond that austere wall of hills over which the British had lived through the tens of centuries, and lived still.*

*The wall was a barrier to understanding, as well as to physical mingling. It was a mental barrier of the same nature as a ha-ha ditch and wall, formed to be invisible from the English side, but an obstacle from the Welsh. For the English do not realise that, to the Welsh, a barrier exists between the two races. Until they do realise it their treatment of the Welsh may continue often to be gauche and unacceptable.*

*It is their long race-memory which reminds the Welsh of ancient suspicions even after most of them have forgotten the causes. The causes are rooted fifteen hundred years ago, when the Angles swarmed into what is now England on the heels of the departing Roman legions. It is a pity that the newcomers were members of the Teuton tribes which had remained beyond the farthest fringe of the Roman Empire, and had never known the Roman system of government, their laws, nor the Christianity they had embraced. They came as aliens, and as aliens in thought, to the Romanized Britons of England, and they annihilated the British in England as far as it is possible for one race to annihilate another. In England there was within a short time no trace left of religion, custom, laws or language. There are today in England but a handful of place-names which are not Teuton or Danish.*

*It is not likely that many Britons fled from England to their brothers in the western hills. Forest, swamp, river-crossings, wild beasts, and warlocks would have rendered such a journey almost impossible for families burdened with their household goods. They stayed where they were, and hoped and prayed; and community by community they died.*

*The extrovert modern Englishman, with the practical Danish and Norman blood mixed with the Teuton in his veins, does not see the mental ha-ha between himself and the Britons who survive yet in those Western hills. Or, if he does see, he is impatient. But, right or wrong, the Welsh see the barrier, and it cannot, in their eyes, be removed by ignoring it. Yet implicitly the English do not recognise the barrier. They still call the only surviving Britons "Welshmen", a word of Teutonic origin which means "foreigners".*

As late as 1682 an English traveller expressed the hope and belief that "the British lingua may be quite extinct, and may be English'd out of Wales, as Latin was barbarously Goth'd out of Italy." His analogy was unflattering to his countrymen, and his belief was mistaken for such time ahead as he could foresee. Yet, at last, there are signs that modernity is doing what the English failed to do. Native Wales survived many battles any of which might have ended in her death, but today she is losing the last battle against a modernity cast largely in the English-speaking mould: commerce, radio, television, films, theatre, newspapers, and books. The Welsh, in all their struggles from Anglo-Norman days to Bosworth Field, were consistently outnumbered by about fifteen to one, yet the most their conquerors could ever impose was physical subjugation; they failed always to destroy or absorb. The spirit of the country sustained the wounded flesh. Wales still dare not lose her racial identity, for, more than most nations, she would disintegrate without the unifying love of land and breed.

As Gwilym Lloyd has said at Dolgellau, a Welshman without his roots at home was lost. Perhaps that is why so many Welsh today are fiercely possessive of what is left to them. History has often taken the wrong turn for the Welsh. It was the son of their own first Tudor king who so nearly destroyed Welsh Wales by the instrument of his Act of Union.

The people remember it still. Emrys Humphreys speaks for them:

Spirits grow tired of waiting -
Four hundred years upon a rock
Of disappearing Hope -
Freedom will you not come back?
Our souls are hungry!

But many Welsh realise that the practical English are not to be much moved by the nostalgic heartburning of a small romantic nation. The Welsh point to the words in the preamble of the Act of Union which describe their land as the "dominion, principality, and country of Wales." They say that Wales is the oldest and only British-speaking dominion in the British Commonwealth. They ask why it may not rule itself, and by so doing retain the spiritual possessions which remain to it.

Henry Treece has written a poem about the Red Dragon, who has survived for so very long against all the guile of many hunters,

Ho, Draig Goch! They tell me you are dead;
They say they heard you weeping in the hill
For all your children gone to London Town.
They say your tears set Tawe in a flood.

I'm older now, but still I like to think
Of your great glass-green eyes fixed on the Fferm,
Guarding the children, keeping them from harm.

Don't die, old Dragon, wait a few years more,
I shall come back, and bring you boys to love.

The Welsh do not wish to preserve the Red Dragon in a shrine of memory. They wish him to pass his old age among the youth of a living country.'

# SOURCES

There is no particular order in the following books and references - they are all in the author's possession, and have been supplemented with newspaper cuttings, general reading and internet research. Dozens of different sources are referred to in the above text.

'*The Dictionary of National Biography down to 1940*' , under the auspices of The Honourable Society of Cymmrodorion (1959) is a marvellous reference work, heavily weighted towards those wishing to direct us upwards in death. A Martian reading this would believe that Wales was a world of '*Methodist exhorters*', and other assorted preachers of Calvinism and Wesleyanism. The recently published '*The Dictionary of Welsh Biography 1941-1970*' again is weighted towards religious worthies, but again an outstanding reference work.

'*The Dragon Entertains - 100 Welsh Stars*' by Alan Roderick of Newport (Wales Books - Glyndŵr Publishing, 2000) is a book which the author had the pleasure of commissioning, and is readable and punchy, detailing Wales' immense value to the entertainment sector over the last 100 years.

'*The Book of Welsh Saints*' by Terry Breverton (Wales Books - Glyndŵr Publishing, 2000), is an immense 600-page hardback crying out for the restoration of 900 Welsh saints' feast-weeks across Wales, to help enhance year-round tourism and economic regeneration.

'*The Enlarged Devil's Dictionary*' (Penguin 1989, edited E.J. Hopkins) is by a Welsh-American, Ambrose Bierce, a wonderful collection from his journalism - in 1867, he decided to toss a coin whether to stay in the army or become a journalist, and became a journalist, before vanishing in the Mexican Revolution, aged 71 in 1913.

'*100 Great Welshmen*' and '*100 Great Welsh Women*', by T. Breverton, (Glyndŵr Publishing, 2000 and 2001), the first two volumes of '*Eminent Britons*'.

'*A Country of Memorable Honour*', by Thomas Firbank (George G. Harrap, 1953)
'*I Bought a Mountain*', by Thomas Firbank (George C. Harrap, 1940)

'*The Journey Through Wales/ The Description of Wales*' , by Gerald of Wales, (Penguin Classics 1988)

# Addresses & Contacts......

**A**

# Addresses & Contacts......

**B**

# Addresses & Contacts......

# Addresses & Contacts......

**D**

# *Addresses & Contacts......*

E

# Addresses & Contacts......

**F**

# Addresses & Contacts......

**G**

# Addresses & Contacts......

# Addresses & Contacts......

# Addresses & Contacts......

# Addresses & Contacts......

**K**

# Addresses & Contacts......

**L**

# Addresses & Contacts......

**M**

# Addresses & Contacts......

# Addresses & Contacts......

**O**

*Addresses & Contacts......*

P

*Addresses & Contacts......*

Q

# Addresses & Contacts......

**R**

# Addresses & Contacts......

# Addresses & Contacts......

# Addresses & Contacts......

**U**

# Addresses & Contacts......

**V**

# Addresses & Contacts......

*Addresses & Contacts......*   **X**

*Addresses & Contacts......*   **Y**

*Addresses & Contacts......*   **Z**

# REVIEWS OF OTHER PUBLICATIONS FROM WALES BOOKS (GLYNDŴR PUBLISHING)

**100 GREAT WELSHMEN** - T.D. Breverton ISBN 1-903529-034 £18.99, 376 pages, illustrated, edition limited to 900 copies (Glyndŵr Publishing, 2001)
**Review from The Western Mail, May 11th 2001:**
'New Book springs some surprises on history's greatest Welshmen:
POETS, PRESIDENTS AND A PIRATE TO BOOT
The lives of some of Wales' most famous figures are set out in a new book published today. Terry Breverton's new book *100 Great Welshmen* celebrates the achievements of 100 men of Welsh blood who have left their mark on history. It contains the names of four American presidents, Hollywood superstars, Christian saints and some of the political and cultural minds who have shaped the modern world. Some, like Dylan Thomas and Owain Glyndŵr, immediately spring to mind, but others to make the list include great architects Frank Lloyd Wright and John Nash, and Confederate president Jefferson Davis. Below are just some of the famous names to make the list. The list is in alphabetical order.....
**Part of a double-page Review from the Western Mail Magazine, June 1st 2001**
'... *100 Great Welshmen is a revealing volume illustrating the great and the good with Welsh connection, either by birth or family ancestry. Admittedly all the usual suspects are included - Richard Burton, Tom Jones, Sir Geraint Evans, Gareth Edwards, Gwynfor Evans, Idris Davies, Aneurin Bevan, Jimmy Wilde and Saunders Lewis. But probably the most fascinating are the ones we either tend to forget are Welsh, or had no prior knowledge of their Celtic connection in the first place. John Adams, the first occupant of the White House; father of the American Revolution Samuel Adams; revolutionary Oliver Cromwell; cinematic pioneer D.W. Griffith; comedian Tommy Cooper, the list goes on and on. From heroes of Waterloo and computer engineers to lethal pirates and gold champions, Breverton has attempted to include them all, and that's no mean feat given our colourful heritage. Hats off to him for the painstaking research involved in every single one, a trademark which is typical of his previous work in "An A-Z of Wales and the Welsh", followed by "The Book of Welsh Saints" and "The Secret Vale of Glamorgan", all printed in Wales....*'
**Review from Ninnau (US) by Dr Peter Williams**
'*Now and again a book comes along that answers most, if not all your questions about your Welsh heritage. Who are the Welsh, who are their military heroes, political leaders, writers, poets, kings, princes, saints, historians, explorers, men of industry, famous actors, athletes, and religious leaders? T.D. Breverton, who gave us The Book of Welsh Saints and An A-Z of Wales and the Welsh, has provided the answers in his latest body of knowledge: a single volume with the informative title l00 Great Welshmen. The author includes not only those who have contributed so much to the making of Wales, but also many personalities who made their mark on American history. The single volume reference book gives biographical information on those persons of Welsh descent whom became influential in the political and industrial life of the United States, such as Presidents John Adams, John Quincy Adams, James Monroe, and Thomas Jefferson; the father of the American Revolution Samuel Adams; business tycoon J.P. Morgan; film pioneer D.W.Griffith, explorers John Evans and Meriwether Lewis and so on. The author even includes those terrors of the high seas, Black Bart, the infamous pirate, and Captain Henry Morgan. The amount of research that went into the making of this book is astounding; it seems that the author left no stone unturned in order to ferret out information concerning his subjects. He has produced a veritable gold mine of a book that you can dip into again and again. 100 Great Welshmen will make you proud of your Welsh heritage by reminding you that the little country of Wales has contributed so much to the modern world in so many different areas...*'

# THE BOOK OF WELSH SAINTS - T.D. Breverton ISBN 1-903529-018 £24.99

hardback, 606 pages, illustrated, edition limited to 900 copies (Glyndŵr Publishing 2000)

**Review from 'Cambria', January 2001:**

'*Another work from the prolific pen of Terry Breverton who is blazing a trail in producing bodies of knowledge about Welsh heritage and history. The Book of Welsh Saints is* **an enormous work of research and will provide a welcome and ready book of reference** *to the men and women who in Tad Deiniol's words "created Wales". The much bandied term "The Dark Ages" may well have meant just that east of the Severn, but to us this period is the Age of Saints. And there are hundreds of them - over 900 in fact - monks, scholars, warriors, missionaries. Breverton places Arthur firmly in the context of Welsh history and shows how the seminal folk legends of European romance and literature originate in Wales. We see Wales at the very heart and very root of western Christian civilisation, a pre-eminent position...*

**e-mail from Dr Rowan Williams, Archbishop of Wales:**

*...the book is a really extraordinary achievement: a compilation of tradition, topography and literary detective work that can have few rivals. I have enjoyed browsing in enormously, and have picked up all sorts of new lines to follow up...'*

**Meic Stephens, in 'The Western Mail Magazine', April 7th, 2001**

*An even more impressive work is Terry Breverton's Book of Welsh Saints, which lists over 900 saints - those holy men who lived as ascetics and hermits in the first centuries after Christ and to whom, so often, miracles were attributed. These men were the first representatives of Rome in Celtic Britain and their names and places of worship still reverberate throughout our history and dot the landscape, reminding ourselves of a civilisation which went into the making of the Welsh landscape. There are informative notes on Saint Cewydd (the Welsh equivalent of St Swithin), Patrick (who became the patron saint of Ireland), and many another saint remembered only because there is a village called Llan, followed by his name. (I am reminded that the awful, corrupted name Llantwit seems to be named after a saint called Twit - surely its time the people of that splendid village rose up and demanded the correct form Illtud). The book was written with one eye on the potential tourist market, because it argues in favour of celebrating the saints' days in villages the length of Wales....'*

**Review from Ninnau (US) by Dr Peter Williams**

'*Did you know that Wales had a St Elvis?...According to local tradition, St David was baptised by his cousin St Elvis at a church near Solva, in Pembrokeshire, where St Elvis Parish is now the smallest in Britain. Within the parish is also St Elvis farm, St Elvis Holy Well, St Elvis Cromlech (prehistoric tomb). Off the coast at Solva are St Elvis Rocks. St Elvis is only one of the hundred of Welsh saints of the 5th and 6th century, a time when the light of Christianity shone brightly in Wales when it had been extinguished over all of Europe, a time when England was still pagan. It was a time when Christianity itself was in danger of disappearing, the survival of the Church in Wales creating a bastion from which Ireland was first converted, and from the Irish missionaries, the rest of Britain and Europe. Over 100 Welsh saints are associated with the leader Arthur, long before the legends had taken hold in France. It was a time when the stories of Arthur and Guinevere, of the Holy Grail, Tristan and Isolde, The Fisher King, the Black Knight, the Green Knight and all of the great and famous knights associated with Camelot and Avalon came into being, and all originated in Wales. Wales certainly seems to have not only the oldest surviving language in Europe, but also the oldest Christian heritage; for the first millennium, it was accepted by Rome as "the cradle of the Western Church". The unique historical importance of Wales has for too long been neglected until now...the book lists over 900 saints, gives not only their history but the historical background of each saint, their feast-days and feast Weeks, and the religious events associated with them. The book is a veritable goldmine of information. Its appendices give the derivation of Welsh place-names, the location of Roman sites in Wales, a discussion of the language problem, and even an essay on the state of parliamentary representation in Wales. The* book is a must for anyone interested in the history of the Church in Wales, indeed for anyone interested in learning the glorious heritage bequeathed to them from the time when Wales was the only Christian country in the world.'

## THE DRAGON ENTERTAINS - 100 Welsh Stars - Alan Roderick ISBN 1-903529-026 £12.99 paperback, illustrated 230 pages, edition limited to 900 copies (Glyndŵr Publishing 2001)

The Dragon Entertains is a reference book with a difference - a highly readable, informative account of the lives of One Hundred Welsh Stars. Within its pages the reader will find 100 concise mini-biographies, word pictures detailing all the relevant, basic facts of the entertainer's career. For a small country, on the western fringe of Europe, a nation of only 3,000,000 people, Wales' contribution to the world of entertainment is immense. Actors and actresses, playwrights and directors, singers and musicians, composers and comedians - Wales has produced them all. And what other nation of comparable size can boast four Oscar winners? The first Welsh film star, the Welsh influence on the *James Bond* movies, *Monty Python*, *Dr Who*, *The Goon Show*, the Beatles films and the original Angry Young man can all be found in the pages of Alan Roderick's new book. Stars of Broadway and the West End stage, the Silver Screen, television, radio, the worlds of opera and contemporary rock music - *The Dragon Entertains* has them all. Welsh-speaking and non-Welsh-speaking, North Wales and South Wales - Welsh showbiz life in all its many facets can be found here.

### Review by Meic Stephens, The Western Mail Magazine, January 2001

*Lastly, another book published by Wales books, The Dragon Entertains (£12.99) by Alan Roderick, a highly-readable reference work listing 100 of the most famous Welsh stars of stage, screen and radio, from The Alarm to the TV comedian, Ronnie Williams.The list is a roll-call of the theatrical talent that Wales has produced over the last century: Ivor Novello, Tommy Cooper, Donald Houston, Donald Peers, Emlyn Williams from among the dead.And Tom Jones, Anthony Hopkins, Bryn Terfel, the Super Furry Animals, Harry Secombe, Kenneth Griffiths, Victor Spinetti and Max Boyce among the gloriously alive and still performing. It also includes fascinating information about the Welsh connections of stars like Glen Ford, Bob Hope, Rolf Harris, Griff Rhys Jones and Petula Clarki.*

*This is the book to reach for the next time someone tells you that Wales has not nurtured any great talent in the world of entertainment and showbiz.*

## THE SECRET VALE OF GLAMORGAN - T.D. Breverton ISBN 1-903529-00X £13.99 paperback, illustrated 230 pages, edition limited to 400 copies (Glyndŵr Publishing 2001)

In between what may be the oldest university in Europe, and a cradle of early Christianity, Llanilltud Fawr (Llantwit Major), and another shining monastic light from the Dark Ages, the Welsh *Age of Saints*, lies the village of Sain Tathan. From the introduction of this millennium history, we read: '*We tend to think of where we live as unremarkable, compared to the strangeness of the new. However, the village of St Tathan and the hamlets of Flemingstone, Gileston, Eglwys Brewys and West and East Aberthaw are not only attractive, and set in wonderful countryside, but have a history almost unique in such a small area. We have buzzards, kingfishers and partridge, the Heritage Coast, two deserted villages, four mediaeval churches, three conservation areas, traces of rebellion by the great Welsh heroes Llywelyn Bren and Owain Glyndŵr, Roman remains, the great antiquary Iolo Morganwg who reintroduced the Eisteddfod to Wales, mediaeval wells, four sixth century saints, an astronomer consulted by Sir Isaac Newton, a Rebecca Rioter, the remains of a thriving port, wreckers, ghosts, smugglers, West Indies slave-ships, hymn-writers, a thatched 14th century pub and no less than four castles. In the 1980's even a Humpback Whale visited...*

**Review by Meic Stephens, in 'The Western Mail Magazine', April 7th, 2001**

*Terry Breverton belongs t that rare breed of Welshmen who stake their livelihood on trying to publish books in which they passionately believe. His imprint Glyndŵr Publishing/Wales Books has already made its mark on the Welsh publishing scene by bringing out substantial and handsomely produced books on Welsh subjects, particularly local history. He was born in the Vale of Glamorgan, to which he has returned after many years as a management consultant in Britain and overseas. He is the author of several useful books such as An A-Z of Wales and the Welsh and One Hundred Great Welshmen. What drives him as a publisher is the belief that the Welsh people have been deprived of their own history. He aims to provide the information that will make them proud of their country. If that means he has to lose some money, he thinks it's well worth it. Among his most recent books is The Secret Vale of Glamorgan (Glyndŵr Publishing, £13.99) which shows a local man's pride in the history and culture of his native patch, combined with a historian's delight in tracing the past and relating it to the present. For anyone born or living in the Vale, this book should be essential reading. There are chapters on Cowbridge, St Athan, Gileston, Aberthaw, Flemingston, and all the places in between, together with a wealth of information about the area's most famous son, the wayward genius Iolo Morganwg.*

**'100 GREAT WELSH WOMEN'** - T.D. Breverton ISBN 1 903529 042 £16.99 paperback, illustrated 394pp (1000 copies - Glyndŵr Publishing 2001)
**Meic Stephens, The Western Mail Magazine, March 16th, 2002**
(Reviewing both '100 Great Welshmen' and '100 Great Welsh Women')
*'These are not necessarily books that you wan to read from cover to cover, but to browse in, following your nose, as one section leads to another in a serendipitous sequence that throws up some pleasant surprises. Both are really extraordinary achievements by a single author whose industry and enterprise seem to show no bounds … Terry Breverton is to be congratulated.'*
**Dr Peter N. Williams, Ninnau (The North American Welsh Newspaper) January 1, 2002**
*'Perhaps the most prolific Welsh author today is T.D. Breverton, of Glyndŵr Publishing, in the Vale of Glamorgan, South Wales. This astonishing worker has recently produced such practical reference books as 'An A-Z of Wales and the Welsh', 'The Secret Vale of Glamorgan', 'The Book of Welsh Saints' and '100 Great Welshmen' (Volume I of Eminent Britons), as well as published important books by other Welsh authors. Now Terry has done it again. His latest book has finally arrive to fulfil the enormous gap in our knowledge of the enormously important, but sadly unheralded contribution of women, not only to Welsh society and Welsh history, but to Western civilisation itself. Titled '100 Great Welsh Women' (Part II of Eminent Britons), it gives short biographies to those of the fairer sex who deserve to be added to out pantheon of Welsh heroes. Acknowledging that women have so often played subordinate roles in our male-dominant society (and Wales is no exception), Breverton's list of suitable candidates is purely a personal one, but all those included are those who have connections with Wales and who have been an inspiration for all women, everywhere. Included are queens, princesses, writers, mothers of famous men, poets, civil rights activists, politicians, and so on to include women of every imaginable activity and social status.*
*This most invaluable addition to every bookshelf and library begins with the little-known Saint Almedha (5th-6th century) and ends with Jane Williams (19th century). In between, you can read of such modern notable Welsh women as singers Charlotte Church, Shirley Bassey, and Petula Clark; of world-class athletes such as Tanni Grey-Thompson; of such historical characters as Nell Gwynn, mistress of Charles II, or Saint Helena, the mother of Constantine the Great; of Catherine Zeta Jones, whose recent wedding to Michael Douglas caused such a stir; and so on. The book is an absolute must for all those who value their Welsh heritage, and for all those who wish to see Welsh women accorded their rightful place in history…'*

**THE PATH TO INEXPERIENCE** - T.D. Breverton ISBN 1-935209 £11.99, illustrations by Kris Jones, 158pp (500 copies - Glyndŵr Publishing 2002)
'*Terry Breverton is well-known as a tireless recorder of Welsh achievements in many fields. In this poetry collection, he allows us a glimpse of the tumultuous feelings that drive him. A tortured energy rushes through this book. There is bitter anger, a keen sense of injustice, national pride, compassion, fear of loss. The images whirl. He jokes and parodies, he gets drunk on words; and there are quieter moments too. Sometimes he gives us a long 'found poem' like his 'inventory' of statistics about the sufferings of the miners of South Wales, where the plainly stated facts are the agonised poem; or his final 'partial list of endangered species' with their evocative and often musical names. It is good to know that out of this turmoil have come - and are still coming - books so positive in their celebration of Wales, its people, history, religion and arts.*' - Ruth Bidgood

**FROM WALES TO PENNSYLVANIA: THE DAVID THOMAS STORY** - Dr Peter N. Williams ISBN 1-903529-085 £8.99/$15 paperback, illustrated 112pp (Glyndŵr Publishing 2002 - 500 copies printed, 250 for sale in the USA and 250 in Wales)
The story of the man who emigrated from Ystradgynlais, to transfrom the American iron industry and make America an economic superpower

**AN A-Z OF WALES AND THE WELSH** - T.D. Breverton ISBN 0- 715407-341 £14.99 paperback 296 pages (2000, available from Christopher Davies Publishing and the Welsh Books Council)
**Review from 'Ninnau' (US)**
'*This A-Z has many surprising as well as predictable entries and is clearly the result of a passionate interest in post-devolution Wales combined with impeccable research... an important addition to the Welsh reference bookshelf*'
**Review from 'Cambria', January 2001**
'*Hwyl and Hiraeth, heritage and history, people and places, myths and imagination all come together in Terry Breverton's comprehensive anthology and compendium of Welshness. He starts by asking the question "What is Wales?" and then goes on to show us. The book is, as Breverton says, a sort of "Hitchhiker's Guide to the Galaxy" that is Wales and declares modestly that his background is more modest than academic. We have just what's needed in this unashamedly proud-to-be-Welsh work. Everythin from "Assassination" (Owain Llawgoch) to "Zulu Wars" (Rorke's Drift) is covered with few stones unturned (sadly Tom Ellis, one of the greatest of our political heroes, fails to get a mention).* **A massive treasure chest of facts and figures covering thousands of years of history, which no collector of books on Wales can overlook.**'*
**Review from the 'South Wales Echo'**
'*The author wants the world to know what Wales has to offer... alongside the Cool Cymru actors and pop stars, there is a wealth of information on more traditional Welsh culture, history, legend, art, literature and so on...*'
**Review from New Welsh Review**
'*This book is great fun....*'

# FORTHCOMING TITLES

**WALES BOOKS AND GLYNDŴR PUBLISHING ARE NON-PROFIT-MAKING ENTERPRISES DEDICATED TO PUBLISHING BOOKS UPON WALES, ITS HERITAGE, CULTURE AND HISTORY.** Our (non-subsidised) books are all produced in Wales, and are available via the Welsh Books Council, direct from the publisher, from walesbooks.com or from 'good' book shops. Our publications all have a two-fold purpose - to tell the world about Wales and encourage tourism, and to tell the Welsh people what they have never been taught in schools, colleges and universities. The Welsh legacy has been deliberately suppressed for hundreds of years, and publication policy is to open up the truth about their past to the Welsh people. Without culture, a nation cannot exist. Without a knowledge of its culture, a nation will quickly die - there is nothing to hold it together.

Printed in Wales for Wales Books (Glyndŵr Publishing), Porth Glyndŵr, Sain Tathan, Bro Morgannwg, CF62 4LW  01446-751693 (tel/fax) by J&P Davison, 3 James Place, Trefforest. The walesbooks.com website was created and is maintained by wit-systems.net, Trefforest.